Rob,

Come t[...]

Michael & Alex.

Sept '96

Complete
Amateur Boat Building

Complete
Amateur Boat Building

Michael Verney

NAUTICAL

Fourth edition 1990
Published by Nautical Books
an imprint of
A & C Black (Publishers) Ltd
35 Bedford Row, London WC1R 4JH

First edition 1959
Second edition 1967
Third edition 1979

ISBN 0 7136 5731 6

A CIP catalogue record for this book is available from the British Library.

Printed in Great Britain at
The Bath Press

By the same author:

The Compleat Book of Yacht Care published by Adlard Coles.

Boat Repairs and Conversions – new edition in preparation.

Acknowledgements

The author wishes to thank the following friends, firms and organizations for providing the illustrations listed.

David Jerram, Photo 1
The GP14 Class International Association, Photo 19
Jack Coote, FRPS, FIIP, Photos 18, 28, 43, 45, 47, 50, 67, 68, 69, 70
Airex AG, Photos 51, 55, 58
Alan Newton, C.Eng, MRINA, Photo 49
Derek Kelsall, Photos 52 and 53, and Fig 148
SP Systems Ltd, Photo 54
Alan Buchanan, C.Eng, FRINA, AMRAeS, Fig 17
Eventide Owners Association, Fig 81

Plans for the Lilliput pram in Photo 21, the fishing cruiser in Photos 5 and 28, and the Ortac class racing cruiser in Fig 17 are available from Alan Buchanan, La Ville au Bas, St Lawrence, Jersey, Channel Islands, U.K.

Plans for the Waterwitch (Photos 1 and 2) and the YM 3-tonner (Photo 29 and Fig 81) are available from the Eventide Owners Association, 24 Wortley Road, Croydon, Surrey, CR0 3EA, U.K.

Preface

Happiness is elusive. Enthusiasts are happy people. So are those who create what they desire with their own hands. The vast majority of modern boats have been factory-built to standardized designs in similar fashion to automobiles. Good they may be, but cheap they are not.

From a range of several hundred designs of all types and in all materials, the amateur boatbuilder can take his pick and start a fascinating hobby. For the impatient and less impecunious, bare hull shells for many current production boats are available. Even then, a lot of enjoyable building work remains before completion. Spreading the cost over a long period is one advantage of the boatbuilding hobby. That cannot so easily be done when the hull (or a kit of parts) is bought.

Here is the fourth edition of this book since 1959. In spite of constant updating, the original concept is still inherent – to dispel the mystique which surrounds boat building, to instil confidence, and to present to the amateur full details of all the methods and materials available to him, from lapstrake planking to fibreglass and ferrocement.

Now, with the two companion books, the sailor has a trilogy covering every aspect of practical boatwork. No previous experience is necessary before getting on with it. Although you may come across some unfamiliar terms in this text, most of them are explained in the glossary on page 168.

Wood is still used somewhere in most modern boats. Because its uses are so varied and its nature so fickle, it has had to be treated comprehensively here. The technique of epoxy saturation, by removing nearly all its former defects, has given wood a new lease of life for hull construction. The careful amateur will find wood a friendly material which is neither malodorous, sticky, nor noisy to work with.

MICHAEL VERNEY

Contents

Chapter 1
How to Start

People of all ages can become boat building enthusiasts. Most of us get the bug by reading the practical boating magazines, exploring boatyards, or as an extension of home carpentry. The layman considers boat building to be a complicated pursuit with a baffling language of its own. We will now proceed to unravel such mysteries and provide the average handy person with all the confidence needed to create a dreamship.

Few amateur building projects fail. Once a start is made, you will find that each operation falls into place and the anticipated problems solve themselves.

Timber and plywood are still the most convenient materials for the amateur to work with: they are certainly more enjoyable to handle than cold metal or malodorous resins. In this age when most new boats are stereotyped mouldings, the amateur boatbuilder is able to own a craft with character and individuality that few could afford to have built professionally.

What to Build

Racing dinghies of wood are still competitive with their plastic counterparts, and many yachting folk prefer cruising boats built of wood. Few plans are available to the amateur for fibreglass dinghies, but for bigger boats he or she is well catered for in plastics, metal, ferrocement and wood.

The type of craft one chooses may depend on the classes raced at a local club, the size of one's family, or the type of moorings available. For example, a bilge-keeler may be best for a harbour which dries out.

A few seasons' crewing with friendly owners helps to formulate the beginner's ideas. However, it should be mentioned that boat building is a hobby in itself and some prefer it to sailing or other forms of boating. Enthusiasts of modest means can start by building a dinghy or canoe, then sell this in order to buy the materials for a bigger boat. The process can be repeated, resulting in much enjoyment, satisfaction, increasing skill and profit.

Helpers As most projects are of fairly long duration, the cost of materials can be spread to match one's income. With the exception of a few tasks, almost any boat can be built singlehanded, but one or two helpers can speed up work and make it more pleasant still. Mistakes are less likely to occur if each stage of the work is discussed beforehand—but try to avoid having too many helpers! You will find that enthusiasm increases as the hull takes shape, and your main difficulty could well be learning to ignore the advice of onlookers who never achieve anything creative themselves.

Hull Shapes

Before discussing further how to choose a design, we must consider the merits of the many different hull shapes. Nearly all craft nowadays fall into three main categories: chine construction, round-bilge construction, and some combination of the two.

Sections Typical outlines of the more popular configurations are shown in Fig 1. View **h** shows a section towards the bow, but all the other views are amidships. Each type will now be described.

a. Flattie or Punt. These simple boats usually have a more or less pointed bow and a transom (flat) stern, but some have swim-ends, sloped upwards, like the front of a sleigh. They can be made to sail. Big cruising versions are often called *barge yachts*.

b. Hard-chine or Vee-bottom. The one illustrated has bilge keels, popular for many cruising classes. Widely used for racing dinghies, canoes, catamarans and motor cruisers. High-speed powerboats have a deep Vee carried right through to the transom. Sailing dinghies of this form are known as *sharpies*.

c. Soft-chine. A more attractive variation of b as the rounded chine becomes almost invisible. Construction can be complicated and expensive. On any hull, the angle amidships upward from the keel to the chine or turn of bilge is called the *deadrise*.

d. Double-chine. Best suited to frameless plywood hulls. Planking is easier to fit than for single chine. With three or more chines the shape is called *multi-chine*.

e. Round-bilge with clinker (lapstrake) planking. Has remained popular since the Viking era. Increasingly revered by amateur boatbuilders, especially for dinghies and fishing boats. The shape is often simulated in plastics.

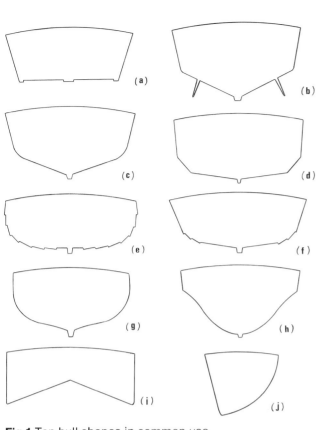

Fig 1 Ten hull shapes in common use

Photo 1 Designed for amateur boatbuilders: the 30 ft (9 m) Waterwitch

f. Clinker bilge. Generally used for medium sized cruising boats, with similarities to types *c* and *d*. Chiefly found in kit boats using glued plywood planking.

g. Round-bilge carvel. Although carvel strictly consists of solid planks laid fore-and-aft with flush seams, the same smooth appearance is achieved today with cold-moulding or strip-planking, and also in plastics, metal and ferrocement.

h. Round-bilge with knuckle. A product of the plastics era, used for both sailboats and powerboats. Curtails spray while avoiding the extra weight of wide decks forward.

i. Sea sled or cathedral hull. Another product of designing for plastics. Makes a beamy, shoal-draft and stable hull, readily driven at high speed in choppy water.

j. Asymmetrical hull. Used mostly for racing catamarans. Cruising *multihulls* (both catamarans and trimarans) generally adopt the *b*, *g*, or *h* shape.

Some useful information on choosing a suitable style of boat for one's individual requirements is given in *The Compleat Book of Yacht Care.*

Wooden Construction

Well designed chine hulls have proved their seaworthiness, but a round-bilge shape is generally superior in extreme weather conditions. Chine boats are not necessarily lighter or easier to build. However, chine construction resembles simple carpentry and may thus be considered ideal for the beginner who is working alone and lacks confidence.

A lot of waste timber results when cutting out traditional clinker or carvel planks, and only a little of this can be utilized for other parts of the boat. Although there is wastage when planking with plywood, the offcuts can be useful for making such parts as laminated knees, locker doors, packing pieces, hatch covers and templates.

Although amateurs can build boats with any of the modern materials, timber and plywood still prove most suitable for the majority. Traditional methods have often become too expensive for professionals, but they are feasible for the amateur, with the added advantage of an almost limitless range of stock designs. Wooden boats are quieter, warmer in winter and cooler in summer, than most other types.

Working with Epoxy

The most remarkable improvement to wooden boat construction since the advent of reliable resin glues has been the use of the Wood Epoxy Saturation Technique, widely referred to as WEST®.

Every piece of very dry wood is soaked with a special epoxy catalyzed resin, which is allowed to set hard before fitting. Complete saturation rarely occurs; just sufficient penetration to make the wood impermeable to moisture. At the same time this increases the strength dramatically and inhibits decay. With the addition of special fillers, some types of joints can be glued and reinforced with resin fillets to provide the same security as old-style tenons, notches and dovetails.

The process can be adapted wholly or partially to nearly all designs in wood. Although epoxy resin saturation adds weight, reductions in wood thickness are possible, while lighter softwoods may be used in place of the traditional heavy boatbuilding hardwoods. All epoxy resins are costly, but so are good hardwoods, while the elimination of rot and wood-boring insects is a fine bonus.

Snags For the amateur working in a cold climate epoxy saturation does have problems. All the wood needs to be extremely well dried before doping, and the ambient temperature needs to be kept fairly high for good results. Kiln drying instead of natural seasoning is adequate, but you do have to ensure that the dryness is maintained after the delivery of new stock.

Stockists The originators of WEST SYSTEM, Gougeon Bros Inc. of Bay City, Michigan, have worldwide stockists, and any good chandler can obtain their products for you. In the UK they are produced by Wessex Resins & Adhesives Ltd of Southampton. As with all revolutionary ideas, similar resins and fillers are now produced by rival firms, such as SP Systems Ltd, Isle of Wight, England. This has made such products more readily available in small as well as large quantities, and the manufacturers are helpful on technical questions.

Versatility of Wood

Wooden boats are normally constructed with one of the following three systems:
1. fully framed,
2. frameless (stressed-skin or space-frame construction),
3. with steam-bent ribs.

The *fully framed* method is widely used for hard-chine boats of all sizes and for the biggest round-bilge craft. The shape is provided by widely spaced permanent sawn frames (Fig 2 and Photo 2) to which the planking is fastened. In *composite* construction, galvanized steel frames are used.

Frameless construction is suitable for small chine and round-bilge hulls, producing shells of light weight. The shape is obtained by means of a jig, bulkheads, or temporary moulds (formers) of rough timber, as seen in Fig 3.

Photo 2 Typical chine framing

Permanent or temporary fore-and-aft battens may be fitted to the moulds, the planking is added, then the moulds are discarded.

To produce a rigid shell, such planking is usually plywood for a chine shape and multi-skin for round bilge. Nowadays, the latter is nearly always *cold-moulded*, several layers of narrow strips of veneer or thin plywood being laminated together, the strips in adjacent layers laid at a different angle for maximum strength.

Canoes and other simple Vee-bottom boats (Photo 10) can be built without jigs if the plywood panels are cut to

Photo 3 Building a glued plywood clinker dinghy

precise shape, then pulled together and fastened along chines and keel with wire ties, later covered with resin and fibreglass tape (see Chapter 5).

Frameless construction is also achieved in *glued clinker* plywood planking. Full length fore-and-aft planks of plywood are laid as for traditional lapstrake work (Photo 3) but the overlapping seams are permanently bonded with resin glue or epoxy: on dinghies no internal ribs are necessary. The method can be used for bigger craft where sufficient bulkheads and furniture are built in to provide stiffness.

In the third system, temporary moulds are again used to establish the hull shape and when planked up (generally with either clinker, carvel or strip-planking), closely spaced steamed timbers, or ribs, are bent and fastened inside the hull. In big craft, methods *1* and *3* can be combined, two or three steam-bent ribs being fitted between each sawn frame.

Major parts Most wooden craft have a 'backbone' assembly composed of the parts labelled in Fig 4. The major parts of an open boat are indicated in Figs 5 and 6. Similarly, the midship section in Fig 7 shows some of the additional components in a wooden decked yacht, while Fig 8 gives further details of a typical deck structure (see also Chapter 13).

Fig 2 Sawn frames extended to the floor

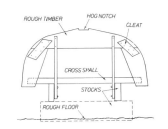

Fig 3 Mould set up on stocks

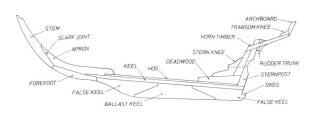

Fig 4 Backbone assembly for traditional cruising sailboat

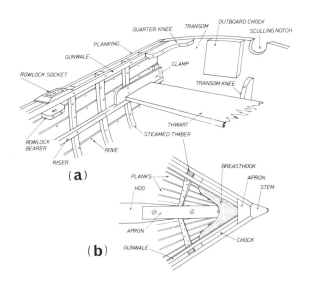

Fig 5 Parts of an open rowing boat

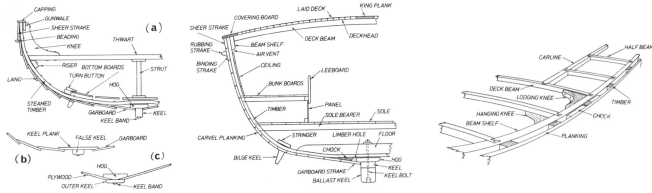

Fig 6 Wooden dinghy details   **Fig 7** Midship section of a traditional wooden yacht   **Fig 8** Deck framing with wood

Plastics

With hulls now often reinforced with materials other than glass, the term FRP (fibre reinforced plastics) is universally used to describe them.

The most common system of building, in fibreglass, was intended for factory production. It would prove tedious and costly for the amateur to copy this, when more suitable alternatives are available (Chapter 14). Factory produced solid fibreglass shells (Fig 9a) emerge from their costly moulds (Photo 50) with a superb glossy external finish, though the inside is usually more uneven and a matt surface.

Many fibreglass dinghies adopt thwarts, gunwales and bottom boards of hardwood. Alternatively, thwarts, side benches, buoyancy tanks and a false bottom can be achieved by fixing a separate internal moulding (shown dotted in Fig 9b) with a mixture of anti-slip and glossy exposed surfaces. Sometimes just a double bottom is used, or the thwarts are formed on separate buoyancy boxes.

Reinforcement Big boats of solid fibreglass often have ribs or stringers moulded inside when insufficient strengthening is possible by means of bulkheads, tanks, bunks and other permanent features. Hollow or cored ribs are formed with tubular metal or foam plastic top-hat formers or D-section paper rope (Fig 10), glassed over before the final internal fibreglass is laid up. Simulated clinker planking is a novel method for stiffening a thin solid skin, especially on flat areas.

Foam sandwich Eminently suitable for amateur FRP work, sandwich construction (see Chapter 14) has a cen-

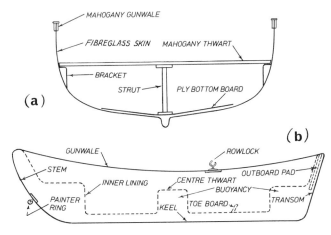

Fig 9 Two types of fibreglass dinghy

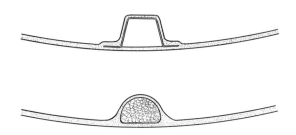

Fig 10 Metal and paper cores for fibreglass stiffeners

tral core of rigid PVC or PU foamed sheet (or end-grain balsa wood) with a skin of solid fibreglass bonded to both sides. Its great rigidity without the need for stringers or frames, and its freedom from internal condensation, make it superior in almost every respect to solid fibreglass for

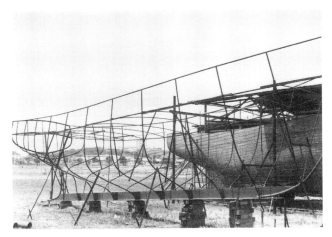

Photo 4 Pipe frames for a ferrocement yacht

Photo 5 Moulds set up for a 36 ft (11 m) fishing cruiser

cruising boats, but except for decks, factories find it unsuitable for mass-production work.

The core material is tacked to a light inverted jig (Photo 50). After bonding on the outer laminate, the jig is discarded and the inside lamination laid up. The resulting stiff structure has considerable buoyancy.

Making the battened former seen in Photo 50 is no mean task, so various systems have appeared which permit a core to bend in true curves across simple, widely-spaced moulds or bulkheads. First in the field was the American C-Flex method. Narrow planks of woven glass reinforced with longitudinal fibreglass rods are used to clad the moulds. These are impregnated with resin, then conventional laminations are laid up on either side— the inner one after stripping out all temporary moulds.

More recent ideas include the Hultec system in England and the RFK system from Germany. With Hultec, H-section fibreglass pultrusions of 10 mm or 15 mm thickness are secured to the moulds, while at the same time semi-rigid foam panels with rabbeted edges are set between these miniature girders. The panels are thick enough to allow them to be faired off by coarse sanding before fibreglassing, as for C-Flex. With RFK, the moulds are strip-planked with hollow square-section plastic tubes to form the core, then glassed over.

All the fibreglass methods are particularly suitable for round-bilged hulls. For equivalent rigidity the flat surfaces of chine and some other hulls require great thicknesses, coring, or some other type of reinforcement. Most designs sold for fibreglass construction by amateurs are round-sectioned.

Ferrocement

Building with ferrocement is fully described in Chapter 16. Again, the method is best suited to the strong curves of a round-sectioned shape. Its fireproof property gives it a big advantage over plastics.

Two systems of construction are in common use. In the first, permanent steel frames are formed to the shape of the hull (Photo 4) and braced by welding on thin steel rods the length of the boat. Having covered this structure on both sides with numerous layers of fine wire mesh, the whole skin is impregnated with rich cement mortar, as described in Chapter 16.

In the second case, a fully planked, inverted, wooden male former is made. The bars and mesh are stapled to this, then the mortar is forced through and trowelled to a fine external finish. After it has set and cured the hull is turned right-way-up, the jig dismantled and the inside made good.

The bigger ferro hulls are not excessively heavy for their size and prove cheaper to build than those of any other material. However, although the lone amateur can do most of the work solo, a team of expert plasterers must be hired to apply the mortar, backed up by a host of other helpers who can be amateurs as long as they are led by someone experienced.

Using Steel

It can safely be said that correctly built metal boats are superior in almost every respect to all the other materials so far mentioned. Their lack of popularity for commercial construction in countries other than Holland is due largely to their unsuitability for the sort of production with semi-skilled workers on the lines evolved for fibreglass.

One warning. All welding must be perfect. The enthusiastic amateur metalworker who is not an experienced welder should team up with a partner who is.

With chines A perfect exterior finish is sometimes difficult to achieve in metal, and internal condensation can be a problem for cruising boats in damp climates. However, metal is hard to beat for toughness, watertightness, resistance to damage and ease of repair. Apart from the above welding warning, the keen amateur need have no qualms about starting a chine design in metal. The skin plating is similar to plywood with one exception—thin plate does not always bend to a fair curve, but tends to kink across the frames. Permanent or temporary stringers help to prevent this.

Metal chine boats may be fully framed, or else stressed-skin and frameless, built on a jig (or on bulkheads or temporary frames) in similar fashion to many plywood craft. For either type, keel and chine members may be formed from tube or bar (see Fig 11a) to give great strength and protection just where required. Sometimes angle bar is used to strengthen chines (11b), improving spray deflection and particularly useful in high-speed powerboats.

Steel keel Shoal-draft barge yachts with leeboards or drop keels can be built on a thick baseplate (Fig 12a) whereas some chine sailing cruisers are built on a strong box keel (12b) wide enough to house the auxiliary engine as well as tanks and ballast. Similar round-bilge craft usually have keel plates rolled to conventional shape as seen in Fig 13. At the stem and where the keel narrows, a flat bar on edge is often fitted to provide strength and a foundation for the bow plating.

A fin keel may be cut from solid plate, passing right through the hull (Fig 14), perhaps with a torpedo-shaped ballast keel at the bottom, formed by bolting to each side an iron or lead casting. The method is also ideal for a rudder skeg, and it may be adopted for the entire backbone of a shoal-draft sailing yacht or motor launch, with a flat strip or round bar welded to the lower edge to form a shoe.

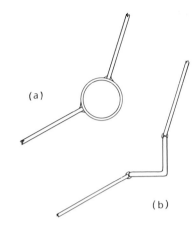

Fig 11 Simple chine knuckles for metal hulls

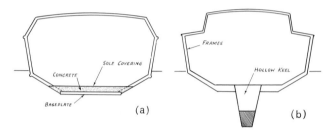

Fig 12 Shoal and deep draft in steel

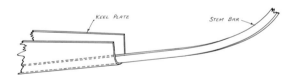

Fig 13 Steel stem bar and keel trough

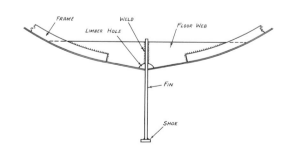

Fig 14 Unballasted fin keel

Upside down Welded multi-chine keelboats under about 40 ft (12 m) in length are simple to fabricate over an inverted wooden jig, all frames, stringers and bulkheads being fitted when the shell is removed from the jig. The idea is similar to stitched-and-glued plywood.

1. An accurate wooden open-battened jig or mockup is made representing one half of the hull, port or starboard. This jig is then clad with butt-jointed panels of hardboard, cut to the size of the available sheets of steel plate.

2. These lightly pinned templates are then numbered, stripped off and a pair of plates shaped to match for the port and starboard sides.

3. To facilitate bending, individual sheets are welded end to end, making panels the full length of the boat.

4. A few rough inverted timber moulds are then erected on the ground or shed floor and well braced. Just enough support to avoid kinking enables the long plates to be brought together and welded along chines, keel, stem and transom.

5. The assembly is turned over and further supports added to receive the deck and superstructure in similar fashion.

6. The temporary framework is removed, seal welds are run along all seams inside the hull, then simple steel bar and plates on edge are welded where required to form frames, stringers, floors and brackets for the attachment of plywood bulkheads and joinerwork (see Chapter 17).

Designs and Drawings

Certain firms specialize in plans for amateur building and may be found in the advertisement pages of the practical boating magazines. Some also supply materials and advice. Other advertisements appear for kits of parts. The advent of the American magazine *WoodenBoat* and later *Classic Boat* in England gave a surprising fillip to boat building in wood, and this is continuing.

To have a cruising boat design specially prepared will cost at least £2500 in Britain or $5500 in America, but some designers are willing to supply drawings of their older designs for about one-eighth of this cost.

Copyright Few amateurs are capable of designing a boat, but if one does this the plans should be vetted by a professional designer before any materials are ordered. Never try to work from the small-scale plans sometimes published in yachting magazines, or from photocopies: they may be distorted in one or both dimensions. All plans are the copyright of the designer or sponsor, and a royalty fee must be paid on all boats built to a certain design. The copyright laws can also be infringed by taking templates from an existing hull or by making a female fibreglass mould in similar manner. However, no copyright may exist for certain traditional craft of great age.

A royalty is normally paid when a set of plans is ordered. In the case of a class racing dinghy the designer or class secretary will issue a sail number for each new boat. Remember to tell them beforehand if you prefer to have the sail number issued after the boat is built: you will then possess the most up-to-date number in the class!

Templates All the details for building a small dinghy may be given on one sheet of drawings. As the size increases, more sheets become necessary to include every part. Many designs for amateurs include full-size templates for the frames or moulds. These are not always accurate, due to distortion of the paper, but measurements are always included for checking purposes. For bigger craft some designers will supply templates on stiff waterproof paper and these may include a whole keel assembly. Few round-bilge clinker or carvel plans contain full-size templates.

Basic drawings A complicated design might include 20 or 30 sheets of drawings, but more commonly there are not more than six or eight. Below is a description of the main drawings and documents likely to be found in a typical set of plans for a small cabin sailboat.

1. Preliminary drawing. When a naval architect starts on a new design he normally submits a preliminary drawing for his client's approval before commencing details. Sometimes to a small scale, this sheet gives outlines of the hull and sailplan, perhaps with dotted lines showing main bulkheads and other cabin features. Sometimes the preliminary drawing for a stock design is reduced in size still further for mailing to potential amateur boatbuilders who are trying to choose a design.

2. G.A. (General Arrangement) of Construction (see Fig 81). It gives details of the boat's backbone, framing, deck and superstructure, and is often well covered with notes, instructions and dimensions. Some of the detail sketches in Fig 81 would normally be on a separate sheet. Sometimes each individual part is given a number and a

separate list is supplied giving full details of each item. This is common practice for a boat in kit form.

3. Lines Drawing. Simplified examples are shown in Figs 15 and 16. An explanation of how this drawing is used is given in Chapter 2. For assembling a kit of parts, or when full-size templates are provided, this drawing loses most of its importance.

4. Table of offsets. This eliminates the need to scale any measurements from the lines drawing. Blueprints and all paper are notorious for changing shape according to the weather!

5. Sailplan. As well as providing all the data needed by a sailmaker, this may include details of standing and running rigging, mast fittings and spars. Part of a typical sailplan is seen in Fig 17, from a design by Alan Buchanan.

6. Deck plan. This may show deck framing for the port half of the boat, while to starboard is shown the deck surface, superstructure, sheet leads, ventilators and other fittings.

7. Accommodation plan. The whereabouts and dimensions of all joinerwork below deck and in the cockpit are indicated. There may be views looking to port and to starboard, from above, and at sections near main bulkheads.

8. Engine installation. For a small craft the G.A. drawing could include all engine and sterngear information, but for big ones (especially powerboats) many different views are necessary to show particulars of the engine bearers, exhaust system, fuel pipes and tanks, batteries, generating set, pumps, propeller shafts and brackets, perhaps also including the rudder and steering gear.

9. Detail drawings. Professional boatbuilders need few detail drawings, except when the designer wants to introduce innovations. On plans intended for amateur use, separate detail drawings may be supplied to show important joints, cabin top construction, coamings, hatches, skylights, cabin fitments, special fittings, tiller, gooseneck, drop keel arrangements, mainsheet horse and rudder bearings.

10. Building stocks. Often a perspective view showing how the stem, frames or moulds, keel and transom are set up. Frameless boats, particularly those with cold-moulded planking, are built on a battened jig which may be detailed on this sheet.

11. Specification. A most useful document listing the fastenings and materials to be used for each part with dimensions and other advice. It may include information on anchors, furnishings, safety equipment, navigation lights, trimming ballast, etc. The sizes of wooden framing parts are known as the *scantlings.* Most parts have a constant thickness (the *sided* measurement) while the width, or *moulded* dimension, is tapered or shaped in some way.

12. Schedule of materials. This greatly simplifies ordering or requests for quotations. Sometimes all items are numbered, the same reference appearing on the drawings wherever a certain part is visible. For fibreglass and ferrocement hulls approximate quantities may be quoted for ordering bulk materials. Very few small clinker boat plans include a schedule of materials.

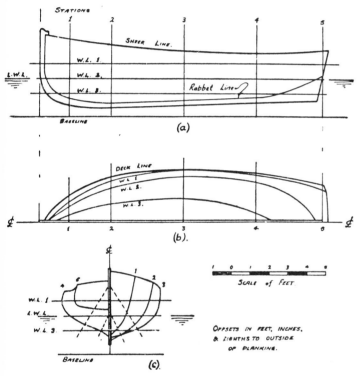

STATION	FROM BASELINE TO					FROM CENTRELINE TO			
	SHEER	WL 1	WL 2	WL 3	KEEL	SHEER	WL 1	WL 2	WL 3
1	3-11-1	2-8-1	1-11-2	1-2-1	0-11-4	1-3-7	1-0-6	0-9-5	0-3-3
2	3-7-3	2-8-1	1-11-2	1-2-1	0-11-3	2-3-0	2-0-6	1-8-1	0-10-6
3	3-3-7	2-8-1	1-11-2	1-2-1	0-9-7	2-7-3	2-7-3	2-3-6	1-2-4
4	3-2-3	2-8-1	1-11-2	1-2-1	0-11-6	2-4-6	2-6-1	2-0-7	0-6-4
5	3-4-3	2-8-1	1-11-2	1-2-1	—	1-8-4	1-10-1	—	—

(d)

Fig 15 A simple lines drawing

Building Site

A good building site helps considerably towards success and speed of construction. A dinghy smaller than about 14 ft (4.3 m) can be built in a home garage, if necessary adding a temporary extension at the doorway. Before building a boat indoors, check whether any major demolition will be involved when getting her out!

Work is speeded up considerably when a boat is built under a roof, though cruisers are quite often built in the open air, perhaps with a winter covering of translucent polythene sheeting over a light framework. Try to avoid a site some miles from home, for this will mean missing many short spells of work which can add up to hundreds of manhours in a whole year.

A level floor is not essential. As small to medium sized wooden boats are usually built upside-down, either on bearers known as stocks (Fig 3) or with the frames extended in the form of legs (Fig 2), appropriate allowances can be made for undulations in the floor. Most ferrocement hulls (and large wooden ones) are built right way up and need support from above (see Photo 5) so that no struts will get in the way. Although this is easy to arrange in a shed with a strong roof, it can also be done outdoors by erecting a stout tripod at each end of the boat supporting an overhead beam or *strongback* in line with the keel, or as in Photo 59.

Launching

For those fortunate enough to have a building site close to the water, launching a big craft presents few difficulties. A temporary slipway is simple to construct. Greased planks called *standing ways* (Fig 18) are laid down on soft ground for the short corresponding *sliding ways* attached to the cradle to run on. How to shift heavy boats and step masts is covered in *The Compleat Book of Yacht Care*.

Most cradles are founded on athwartships balks, well braced diagonally, sometimes having raised blocks called *poppets* placed centrally to support a rockered or raked keel. Vertical *soldiers* at each side, or *squats* under the bilges, prevent the vessel from falling over.

With standing ways sloping more than 1 in 8, craft of considerable size can be made to slide entirely by means

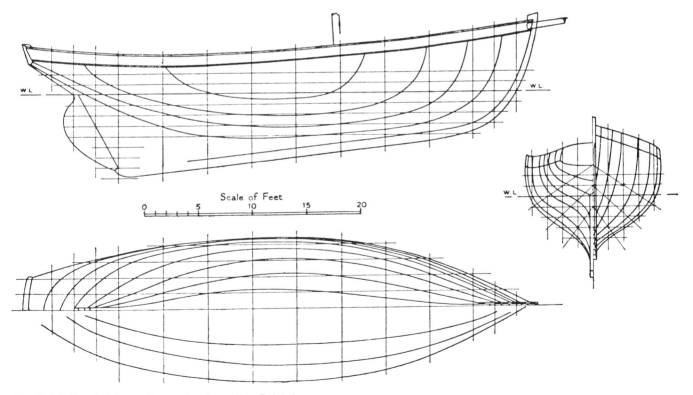

Fig 16 A full set of lines. The author's replica Bristol Channel pilot cutter *Alhena*.

21

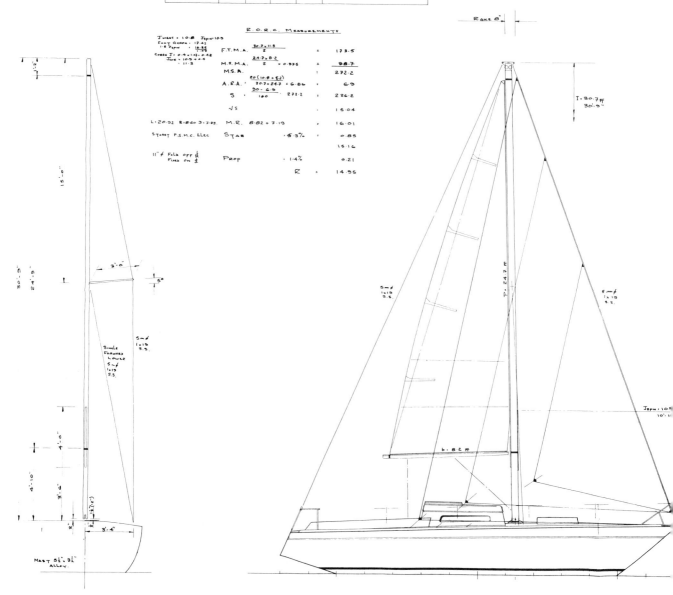

Sail	Luff	Leach	Foot	Area	Remarks
Mainsail	24'-3"	26'-2"	8'-3"	117.7	R.O.R.C. "Short" Battens "6" Slides :- Sliding Gooseneck
N°1 Genoa	31'-3"	30'-4"	17'-5"	239.6	Stretch Luff "Droop" Foot L.P. = 16.95 Luff is Max Length!
N°2 "	25'-0"	24'-0"	14'-0"	161.5	
Staysail	17'-6"	15'-0"	8'-6"	70.5	
Spinnaker	30'-11"	30'-11"			Max Width : 1.8 J' : 19.62 ft 0.95 √ I²+J² : 30.95

R.O.R.C. Measurements

$J_{meas} = 10.8 \quad J_{spin} = 10.5$
$Foot\ Genoa = 17.42$
$1.5\ J_{spin} = \dfrac{15.75}{1.29}$

$Cordb\ J : 0.4 \times 17.42 = 6.97$
$J_{num} = 10.8 + 0.4 = 11.3$

F.T.M.A. $\dfrac{30.3 \times 11.5}{2}$ = 173.5

M.S.M.A. $\dfrac{24.7 \times 8.2}{2} \times 0.875$ = 88.7

M.S.A. = 272.2

A.R.A. $\dfrac{30(10.8 + 8.2)}{30.7 + 24.7} = 6.86$ = 6.9

S $\dfrac{30 - 6.9}{100}$ 272.2 = 226.2

√S = 15.04

$L : 20.92 \quad B : 8.60 \quad D : 7.83$ M.R. $8.82 + 7.19$ = 16.01

Stores P.S.M.C. Elec. S_{TAB} · 5.3% = 0.85

= 15.16

11" ∅ Fold off ⅌ Prop · 1.4% = 0.21
Fixed on ⅌

R = 14.95

Rake 8"

I = 30.7 ft 30'-9"

P = 24.7 ft

5 m∅ 1×19 S.S.

5 m∅ 1×19 S.S.

$J_{spin} = 10.5$ 10'-6"

b : 8.2 ft

Single Forward Lower
5 m∅ 1×19 S.S.

5 m∅ 1×19 S.S.

3'-0"

5°

15'-0"

30'-9"

24'-9"

4'-0"

4'-0"

3'-6"

3'-4"

Mast 3½" × 3½" Alloy.

Principal Dimensions

L.O.A. 27'-1¼"   L.W.L. 19'-2¾"
Beam 8'-10"   Draft 4'-1"
Displacement 2⅝ tons approx.

Fig 17 Part of a sailplan: Alan Buchanan's cold-moulded Ortac 27.

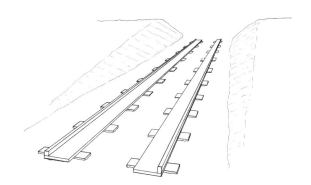

Fig 18 Standing ways for launching

of manpower and levers. Failing this, a hand winch and wire rope is generally utilized, often leading through a snatch block anchored offshore.

A cradle is designed for assembly beneath the boat while first one end and then the other is jacked up temporarily. Once on the cradle, winching around corners and over any distance is possible by shifting the standing ways in sections.

When building a big boat far from the water, launching is usually accomplished by hiring a mobile crane to lift her on to a transporter or trailer, perhaps using a dockside crane at the end of the journey. A boat smaller than about 25 ft (8 m) may have her own trailer towed by a car, to facilitate laying up at home each year. Storage on the trailer eliminates jacking up. If the wheel systems are not harmed by submersion, launching and recovery can be effected on a ramp or beach.

Detail Data

This book is intended to provide all the information needed to tackle almost any type and size of boat. However, it does not attempt to confuse the reader with data on every tiny part of complicated craft for the following reasons. First, components such as coamings, cabin trunks, side benches, windows, berths, lockers, galley, tabernacle, chainplates, mast fittings, rubrails, etc. are normally well detailed on the plans.

Examining other boats also reveals much useful detail—and there are few more entertaining pastimes! It pays to have a sketch pad or notebook handy. Useful items to study on dinghies include rowlock sockets and cheeks (or perhaps thole pins), bottom boards, foot stretchers, toe or hiking straps, sculling notches, outboard motor mountings and attachments for rigging. On larger craft, attention might be given to tillers, tabernacles, chainplates, guardrails, deck fittings, joinery, grabrails, hatches, upholstery and gadgets, and running rigging leads.

Complete technical data sheets and installation hints are almost always available from the makers of complicated equipment such as steering gear, trim planes, engine controls, automatic pilot and electronic instruments.

The author's two companion volumes contain a lot of useful detail information for boatbuilders, or those who prefer to complete a ready-made bare hull. *Boat Repairs and Conversions* deals with bulkheads, deckhouse, coamings, ventilation, joinery, cabin layouts, anchor gear, electrical wiring, cabin sole, drop keel, leeboards, mast and spar making, ballast, fabricating fittings, pattern making, engines, hatches and skylights, windows and portlights. *The Compleat Book of Yacht Care* includes such items as canvaswork, ropework, pumps and toilets, painting and varnishing, waterlines and boottops, deck coverings, hull sheathing, caulking, stoves, tanks, sterngear, plumbing, mast stepping, hauling out and launching, rigging, propellers and cathodic protection.

The two brief chapters which follow this one describe the chief phases of boat building that sometimes baffle the beginner. These tasks have little to show for themselves in a finished boat, and are not required at all for either kit boats, those built on a borrowed jig, or simple plywood craft with no internal frames. The newcomer who has not yet decided to build a boat from scratch, but who wishes first of all to gain a mental picture of how the bits are fitted together, could well skip Chapters 2 and 3 until a later stage.

Surveyor

It may not matter much for boats under about 18 ft (5.5 m) in length, but for most bigger ones it pays to engage a qualified yacht surveyor to issue a certificate at several stages during construction. This is not expensive if the surveyor lives locally and it could well mean an increase of 50% in the boat's value should the amateur builder ever wish to sell.

Chapter 2
Laying Down the Lines

If the designer has not provided full-size patterns for the backbone and framing, the first task in building a boat of almost any size, in any sort of material, is to enlarge the lines drawing to full size. This process is traditionally called *lofting* as some boatyards have a special attic room for it known as the *mould loft*, in which the moulds and patterns are made.

On the mould loft floor, the loftsman reproduces the lines drawing to full size, then makes patterns in thin wood or hardboard of all the curved members, and many straight ones also. He may have to rub out all the lines long before the boat is erected, to lay down the lines for some other boat. The amateur is often similarly placed: his boat may have to be built on top of his lofting floor! This difficulty can sometimes be overcome by laying sheets of hardboard on the floor, as in Photo 6. After lofting and making the various patterns and moulds, these sheets can perhaps be nailed to the wall of the shed for future reference. Sheets of $\frac{3}{8}$ in (9 mm) plywood serve even better. You can nail into them, and later use them for joinerwork.

Working in the open air, it may be possible to borrow some scaffold boards to lay underneath the hardboard or plywood. At a pinch, the stiff waterproof kraft paper used by builders will do instead and is easy to store in a roll. On an earth floor, a thin temporary screed of concrete can be laid, then broken up on completion.

Small chine boats may not need complete lofting. Good results are often obtained by merely plotting the shapes of the frames, transom and stem. If full-size paper templates come with the plans do check their accuracy before starting to cut.

The Lines Drawing

An explanation of the somewhat complicated lines drawing shown in Fig 15 is now indicated. View **a** is called the *profile plan* and gives an outline of the stem and stern, keel and sheer. View **b** is called the *half-breadth plan*. The outermost line is the sheer, seen as though looking down on the boat from above. The horizontal line at the bottom represents the boat's centreline, indicated by the symbol combining letters C and L. View **c**, the *body plan*, has a vertical centreline with the boat's curved cross-sections on either side, as seen end-on. The sections to the right are those from the stem back to the point of widest beam. Those on the left show the stern half.

Plotting The Table of Offsets labelled **d** lists all the measurements necessary to enable the three views to be drawn out full size without having to scale any dimensions off the drawings. It can be likened to a list of map references, the drawings bearing lines in two directions like the grid on a map. Some modern designs give each dimension in millimetres, but on most British and American plans you will find them in feet, inches, and eighths of an inch, with a hyphen between each number as in Fig 15.

The grid lines have names and their functions are easy to understand. The *baseline* seen in views **a** and **c** always comes well below the lowest part of the keel. *Waterlines* are drawn parallel to this (usually at equal spacings) nearly up to the lowest point of the sheer. Only one of these lines is the true load waterline of the finished boat. In **b** all waterlines appear as bold curves.

The vertical lines on views **a** and **b** are called *station lines*. They are normally spaced at the same intervals as the moulds or frames, in which case the shape of each one appears as a curve on the body plan. Once lofting is com-

Photo 6 Full-size lines being plotted on hardboard

plete, any number of additional station lines can be struck in across view **b** and the offsets from the centreline to each waterline transferred to **c**, enabling a new section to be drawn in. This can even be done for cant frames (see Fig 24), which radiate at strange angles. Alternatively, temporary moulds may be erected in this vicinity and exact cant frame patterns made while strips of bendy wood are tacked around the hull.

Full-size Enlargement

The dimensions between station lines and between waterlines should be detailed on the lines drawing. If not, they can be scaled off, as they are always round numbers to the nearest inch or centimetre. One station line spacing may be different from all the others if the boat's length is an odd amount, so all intervals should be totalled to check this before lofting.

Accuracy Full-size lofting of the profile plan is obviously necessary before the backbone (see Photo 7) can be made, and an accurate body plan is also essential to enable moulds or frames to be cut. If the body plan is not accurate much time-consuming work will be entailed later, shaving off wood or gluing on packing pieces. Such corrections are even less convenient with a metal or ferrocement hull. With widely spaced moulds or frames small inaccuracies may not matter. With closely-spaced frames, or for a racing hull which must have very smooth planking, it pays to take great care at the lofting stage.

Designers prepare the table of offsets by scaling from the original lines drawing and a surprising number of inaccuracies may creep in. If the designer checks his offsets when the first boat is built and amends the table accordingly, one can usually plot a perfect set of body plan sections without having to lay down the whole of the lines drawing full size.

As checks to ensure accuracy, two further sets of grid lines are normally included (see Fig 16) and the table of offsets is then much longer to include these references. The *buttock lines* appear as curves on the profile plan and as straight lines parallel to the centreline on the other two views. The *diagonals* are those radiating lines on the body plan (also shown dotted in Fig 15) which intersect the curved station lines approximately at right angles. On the half-breadth plan, the diagonals are shown in similar fashion to the waterlines but on the opposite side of the centreline.

Photo 7 Assembling an oak backbone structure

Fairing In

The art of lofting is to get all the curved lines fair, i.e. without kinks or flat places. First, the straight grid lines must be drawn on the floor just as they appear on the lines drawing, then marks are made on these corresponding to each offset, measured outwards from the centreline or upwards from the baseline. Each curve is drawn by springing a thin wooden batten through all the points on that curve and drawing a pencil line along it. It may be found that to obtain a fair curve the batten has to miss several of the offset points. It takes a bit of juggling to discover which points to miss and by how far.

Having produced a fair set of waterlines (including the chine if there is one) on the half-breadth plan, any deviations from the original offsets must be transferred to the body plan, to ensure that those curves can still be drawn fairly. This might entail amending a further offset or two on the body plan, but on transferring these back to the waterlines a bulge may be created which is impossible to iron out. This is where the additional buttock lines and diagonals prove of value. If both these sets of lines stay fair with a certain questionable offset point on the body plan left in its original position, there is little doubt that this one is correct and one or more points adjacent to it need shifting instead. With any luck, when those adjustments are transferred to the waterlines, it will be possible to strike in a perfectly good curve which is slightly different from its predecessor.

To save floor space, the half-breadth plan can be superimposed over the profile plan by making centreline coincide with baseline, while the body plan can be superimposed over the other two by making its centreline correspond to a station line near amidships. Bright crayons are useful to differentiate between the sets of lines, but this is rarely necessary in practice. Once a perfect body plan has been completed and the backbone drawn in, all other lines can be ignored.

Chalk Lines and Lofting Tools

The straight grid lines are most readily marked on the floor by *snapping* a chalk line. Use a piece of thin string the length of the boat, and before marking each line drag a stick of blackboard chalk all along the string (chalk powder or talc is more messy). Now secure one end of the string (under a heavy weight or tied to a nail) and fix the other end similarly after tensioning. Holding the middle of the string between thumb and forefinger, raise it a few inches above the floor and then release it smartly. This will leave a thin, straight, chalk line on the floor surface. More durable intermittent marks can then be made along it with crayon. On a whitish surface use artist's charcoal instead of chalk.

Splines Few tools are required for lofting, but some good quality splines of springy wood are essential; also some thin but wide battens to make straightedges. Some boatyards and sawmills keep a stock of thin planking off-cuts which can be planed up to make splines. Silver spruce and Agba are ideal woods, but they must be straight-grained and free from knots and shakes. For a 12 ft (3.7 m) hull, a couple of $\frac{5}{8}$ in (16 mm) square splines about 14 ft (4.3 m) long will be necessary, plus a few $\frac{3}{8}$ in (9 mm) square ones 5 ft (1.5 m) long to bend around the body plan curves and the stem. Plastic curtain rail might serve for these. For a 20 ft (6.1 m) hull, the sizes would be about $\frac{7}{8}$ in (22 mm) square and 23 ft (7 m) long, and $\frac{1}{2}$ in (12 mm) by 8 ft (2.4 m). Lightly chamfer all corners by sanding, to inhibit breakage.

For straightedges, mahogany or good pine will do. A 12 ft (3.7 m) straightedge would be made from wood about 3 in (75 mm) wide by $\frac{1}{4}$ in (6 mm) thick, while a 20 ft (6.1 m) strip is best made about 4 in (100 m) by $\frac{3}{8}$ in (9 mm). If they warp, it may be necessary to plane down one edge, then make a series of paint marks to indicate which edge is the true one.

Loftsmen use heavy weights called *ducks* which are placed on either side of a spline prior to marking out the curves with a pencil. Old weighing machine weights will

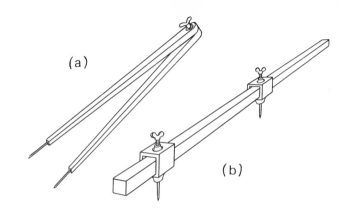

Fig 19 Tools for transferring offsets

do, preferably with thin cork glued underneath them. With square weights place one corner against the spline. Thin nails can be used instead on a wooden floor and a combination of ducks and nails may prove best. Lead ducks are quite small but weigh 20 lb (9 kg).

An accurate tape measure the length of the boat is useful when setting out the grid lines. A shorter tape is best for measuring offsets, though much kneeling can be avoided by making up a pair of long dividers for this operation (Fig 19a). With the long tape stretched near the baseline, the dividers can be set from this, preferably with a helper to call out each measurement. Trammel heads (19b) sliding on a wooden batten can be used similarly, but this entails kneeling. A big try-square is essential, easily made by cutting a triangle from the corner of a sheet of thin plywood.

Backbone Shape

Offsets are not normally included in the table for plotting the curve of the stem. More often, actual measurements are shown against it on the profile plan. To get the full shape of all backbone members needed when making patterns, the positions of the inboard surfaces must be scaled from the construction drawing, when such dimensions are otherwise lacking. Remember that all lines drawings show the outside surface of the hull. Unless you want your finished boat to be bigger than intended, you must deduct a little from each of the lofted body plan curves to represent the *inside* of planking. This will then be the exact shape of all moulds or frames.

Plank Thickness Allowance

Near to amidships and along the keel the planking meets the frames approximately at a right angle, so the amount to be deducted from the body plan is, near enough, the thickness of the planking. Everywhere else the planking touches the frames at an angle known as the *bevel*, shown in exaggerated form in Fig 20.

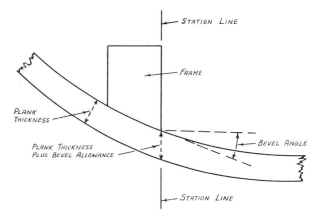

Fig 20 Sawn frame bevel

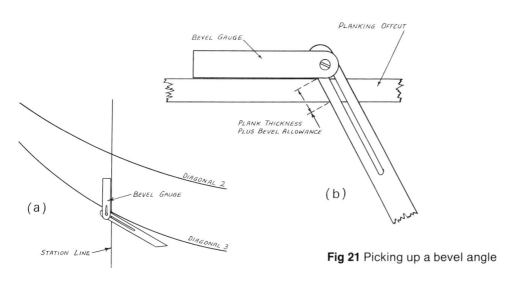

Fig 21 Picking up a bevel angle

Varying bevel To find out what deduction to make at various points around each body plan curve, refer to the half-breadth plan. The diagonals show the most accurate bevel angle on the underwater regions of the hull. The waterlines must suffice where no diagonals exist, and the waterlines are as close as you need for topsides. Pick up each angle with a carpenter's bevel gauge, as in Fig 21a, then hold this across the edge of a strip of wood the same thickness as the boat's planking and scribe a pencil line (21b). The length of this line is the distance we are seeking at that particular spot, so measure it (with rule or dividers) and transfer it to the body plan. Repeat the process for the next diagonal or waterline.

Having swept a new curve through all the marks on one station line, remember to lower the sheer mark also (to represent the underside of the deck) by deducting the deck thickness. Add a small allowance if the sheer in profile has an appreciable upward sweep from the horizontal towards stem and stern. The allowance is readily checked at the severest slope by using an offcut of deck thickness and scribing a vertical line across it, just as described for planking above.

Skins thick and thin The necessity for lofting is not restricted to wooden hulls. The same process is required for a fibreglass plug and for nearly all ferrocement and metal hulls. Due allowance for skin thickness is needed, though this is a very small dimension in the case of metal plating.

Chapter 3
Patterns and Bevels

With the few lofted lines that are finally needed marked indelibly, all other grid lines may be erased. However, delay this as much as possible in case a pattern gets lost, the position of a frame needs to be shifted, or an extra bulkhead fitted. The exact shape of any additional section may be obtained readily by striking in a new station line across the half-breadth plan, then transferring all the waterline and diagonal offsets along that line to form a new curve on the body plan.

To preserve important lines they may be painted in using a fine brush. A quicker way is to paint a series of small dots all along each line. If the floor is to be walked across frequently, arrange for a covering of polythene sheeting or kraft paper.

Picking up Patterns

Making patterns from the body plan or backbone lofting is quite simple on a softwood floor. If the heads of tacks are tapped lightly into the flooring, as shown in Fig 22a, corresponding marks can be transferred to the pattern wood by laying this carefully on top and then pressing downwards. Although hardboard makes excellent patterns it has a tough surface, so light hammering may be necessary to provide good imprints of the tacks. On a concrete floor, the same principle can be adopted by grinding or filing a flat on one side of each tack head (22b). Great care is still required to prevent the tacks from shifting as the imprint is made, but it can be done.

Particularly for small boats, the outline required can be drawn on tracing paper, then, slipping the pattern board underneath this, a sharp spike can be used to prick along the line. Having cut out the pattern or template, always check its accuracy by holding it on the lofted line, then shaving bits off as necessary. In the case of moulds or sawn frames only one template is needed to make the two identical halves, but do not forget to measure carefully the total top width after joining the two parts together.

Stiff patterns As the moulds for frameless boats are normally made from rough-sawn boards, somewhat as in Fig 3, one can save a bit of time by marking them out direct from the loft floor. However, $\frac{1}{8}$ in (3 mm) hard-

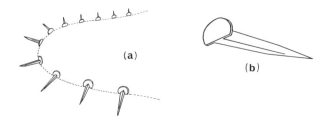

Fig 22 Utilizing tack heads to mark patterns

board, or rough sawn pine about $\frac{1}{4}$ in (6 mm) thick, is not too expensive and makes excellent patterns from which heavy moulds may be shaped. Hardboard offcuts can be utilized for making patterns as they are readily joined together with scraps of the same material. Fixing is easy using small nails with their points bent over and buried on the far side. Such thin straps enable a pattern to be used either way up when marking the final wood—a great advantage when making moulds and frames, one side of which is a mirror image of the other. Although rough moulds can be made without patterns, this is difficult to do for sawn or laminated frames.

A full set of patterns has a considerable value and it may be possible to sell them on completion, especially if the plans are complete and still legible. The buyer or seller should ensure that the design fee for the next boat is duly paid, however. The same applies to moulds and jigs for frameless boats and to the plug or female moulds for a fibreglass hull. To save smudging a delicate body plan with constant use, reproduce it on a sheet of plywood called a *scrieve* (pronounced 'skrive') *board*, which you can shift about. This might also have a resale value. Beware of using or selling photocopied plans.

Popular designs Later in this book you will find details concerning the building of the round-bilge carvel planked YM 3-tonner and the chine Waterwitch sailing cruiser. Owners and builders of these boats usually belong to the Eventide Owners Association in England, which also supplies all plans and advice; the address is given under the Acknowledgements. Advertisements for the buying and selling of patterns appear in the EOA quarterly Bulletin.

Sloping Transoms

The majority of small craft today have flat or curved transom sterns, and when viewed on the profile plan nearly all are sloped to obviate a boxy appearance. Here lies a snare for the amateur loftsman: the outline of the transom on the body plan is projected into a dwarfed vertical view, as though parallel to all the other stations. The distorted view appears as in Fig 23a and we wish to stretch the height to obtain the true outline (23b) viewed at a right angle to the transom surface.

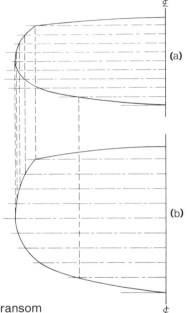

Fig 23 Lofting a raked transom

True height To draw this on the floor, scale the full depth of the transom (along its outside surface) from the profile plan or from the G.A. of Construction drawing and mark this off on a centreline, as in 23b. Divide this distance into any number of equal spaces, and from each mark draw a line at right angles to the centreline and long enough to extend beyond both sides of the transom. Now divide the centreline of the body plan view (23a) into the same number of spaces. Each space will be smaller than those in the true depth view. Again draw lines at right angles to this centreline, just long enough to reach the outline.

Full width Transfer each width to the corresponding line on the expanded drawing, repeating this on the opposite side of the centreline to produce a full-width transom.

Using a thin spline, draw a curve through the sets of points at each side. Strike in the deck camber curve and you will then have an accurate outline from which the transom can be made.

Watch bevel Remember that the lofted outline represents the after face of the transom. Although the size must be reduced by an amount equal to the plank and deck thickness (as described in Chapter 2), do not cut the final wood to this shape without making an outward allowance for the planking bevel, as the boat's beam is lessening towards the stern, somewhat similar to one end of a barrel. Therefore the inboard surface of the transom (or its framing) will be bigger than the outboard surface as lofted. Due allowance must be made as described later.

Radiused transom Some lines drawings show a separate developed view of the transom of the sheer (profile) plan. Extra views and full dimensions are often provided when a transom is Vee-shaped or curved like a bow window. The former type requires a development of the one half, viewed square on, while the latter may need a series of offsets at various waterlines. Any bulge in a transom will fall into place automatically as the framing is constructed, provided that the outline where the planking and decking meets it has been correctly lofted.

Frame Bevels

The fact has already been mentioned that a boat is somewhat barrel-shaped, so the outer edges of most frames must be bevelled to form a snug fit to the planking. These bevels are normally most severe towards the bow and to lessen this many beamy craft with heavy sawn ribs incorporate *cant frames* as shown in Fig 24.

Light craft normally have such narrow framing that bevels can, if preferred, be cut after the frames are erected

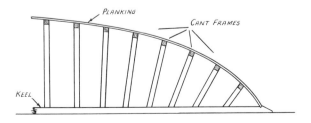

Fig 24 Cant frames

on the keel. However, if lofting has been properly done, all bevelling can be applied at the bench, leaving only a few small adjustments to be made when the boat is in frame.

Although temporary moulds (Fig 3) are similar to sawn frames, they do not normally require any bevels at all. When steam bent ribs are inserted between each mould, most of them will draw up tightly to the planking surface without need to bevel them either.

Ceiling Note that certain craft have planking on the inside of the frames. This is called a *ceiling* and may be used in yachts as well as to line the hold of a fishing vessel. To receive this, sawn frames would be bevelled on the inside as well as outside. This looks better even when there is no ceiling. The ceiling on most yachts is in the form of thin panelling or battening, perhaps with gaps between for ventilation. Panelling up under the deck is called *headlining*.

Frame edge There is little difference between picking up bevels for the planking thickness allowance (see Fig 21a) and applying these to obtain the correct angle for the frame edges. All you need do is use the bevel gauge in the manner shown in Fig 25.

Surmarks In order to know the exact location of each reference point (waterline or diagonal) these positions should all be transferred to the pattern or directly onto the frames. Such symbols are called *surmarks* and they include the sheer mark and centreline at keel, which are essential at later stages of construction. When making surmarks for waterlines or diagonals, scribe lines the full width of the pattern or frame which follow the general direction of these grid lines as they appear on the body plan. By aligning the bevel gauge along each of these lines in turn, you will obtain more precise bevels than by using the gauge at right angles to the planking surface at all points.

Bevel Boards

It would take a long time to keep taking bevel angles from the loft floor to the bench, so it pays to make a *bevel board* from an offcut of hardboard for each pattern, across which are scribed all the required angles (Fig 26). Until the sawn frames are made, each bevel board can be attached to its respective pattern with a piece of cord.

Provided that all frames are spaced at equal intervals, a *universal bevel board* can be made. This has a range of angles drawn across it sufficiently comprehensive to

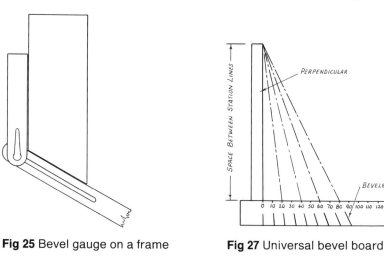

Fig 25 Bevel gauge on a frame   **Fig 27** Universal bevel board

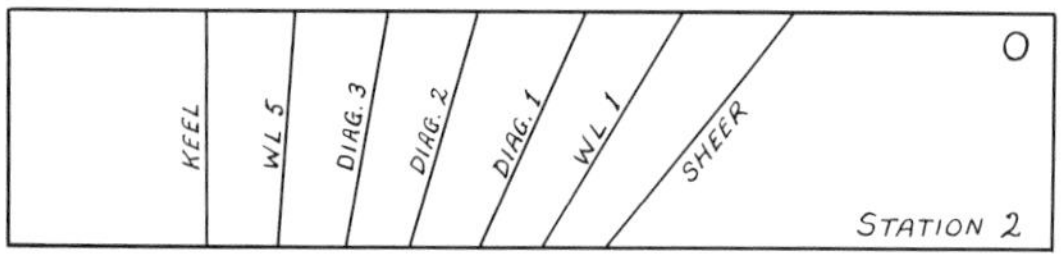

Fig 26 A bevel board for one frame

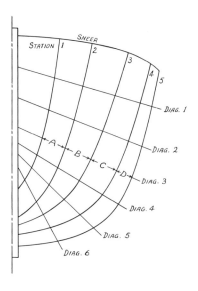

Fig 28 Finding the right bevel

include every bevel on the boat. To set these out, all you do is erect a temporary perpendicular at one end, as sketched in Fig 27, using a piece of batten the same thickness as the bevel board or simply a pencil line drawn on the floor. The upper edge of the bevel board is marked out like a rule at $\frac{1}{2}$ in or 10 mm spacings, and a mark is made on the perpendicular at a distance above the bevel board edge equal to the distance between each station line. The bevel angles are drawn by following the direction of the radiating lines shown in Fig 27.

All you need to know is which bevel angle to choose at each of the various surmarks. Where great accuracy is called for, such as for a large vessel with closely spaced frames, additional diagonals can be struck in, each cutting the body plan lines almost at right angles (see Fig 28).

To find the bevel where Station 4 meets Diagonal 3, for example, get the average of measurements **C** and **D** by adding them and dividing by 2. If this is 4 in (100 mm), set your adjustable bevel gauge to the line radiating from the 4 in or 100 mm mark on the universal bevel board and you then have the correct bevel to apply to the edge of the sawn frame at that particular point. All such values can be written close to each surmark on the patterns, eliminating the need for any reference to the loft floor once patterns have been made.

Under cut In cases where the spaces each side of a station (such as **C** and **D**) are almost equal, there may be no point in calculating the average value. Instead, adopt the smaller of the two, which will leave a small amount of bevel to be shaved off the frame edge later. If the higher value is adopted too much bevel may be cut; a troublesome fault to correct.

The same procedure can be used for obtaining bevels from waterlines instead of diagonals, but there may be a loss of accuracy, particularly at the stations nearest to bow and stern. These are the regions where a high degree of accuracy is most desirable.

Jigs and plugs Most jigs for cold-moulding, foam sandwich, FRP and ferrocement hulls do not involve bevels to any great extent. However, when making a planked plug for a fibreglass female mould, it usually pays to lay the planking on bevelled frames for perfect rigidity when planing and sanding the surface to a fine finish. In welded metal boats no frame bevelling is needed as the plate frames present such a narrow edge to the plating.

Chapter 4
Timber Talk

Having learned in the last two chapters how the shape of a boat is developed, the next step concerns the materials for her construction and the methods of fixing the various parts together. Much information on the special materials used only in the construction of boats in fibreglass, ferrocement and metal are to be found in the later chapters on those subjects. Wood is still used extensively in nearly all yachts, irrespective of the hull material, so newcomers to boat building need to know all about it.

Marine Plywood

Plywood in furniture has been a familiar feature for over sixty years. Genuine marine plywood is a superior material having all laminations composed of high quality hardwoods bonded with a resin glue which will not fail after prolonged submersion in boiling water.

Few materials are perfect and plywood is no exception. Its advantages over solid wood include freedom from shrinking, warping and cracking, rigidity and uniform strength; but its main disadvantages are:
1. It cannot easily be bent in both directions at the same time, hence plywood boats tend to have a boxy appearance.
2. Its resistance to chafe is poor. A plywood hull can chafe right through during a rough night if not tended properly.

Plywood can be so much thinner than solid wood for a given strength that protection from chafe, particularly on edges, is most important. However, much the same thing applies to fibreglass shells, which also do not have very good resistance to abrasion. Therefore, the average lightweight plywood boat is ideally suited to launching from a storage place on shore, or for trailing on the road.

Although generally more costly than solid wood, marine ply can be used to make almost every part of a boat. Its screw-holding properties are not very good, but by using resin glue in addition for all joints, success is assured, while epoxy saturation is often better still.

The birch, fir, and gaboon exterior grade plywood used by house builders is cheaper than marine ply and is sometimes used for cabin joinery on cruising boats. Such material can advantageously be impregnated with a fire-retarder and a rot-proofer before installation.

Most true marine plywood is produced in Britain or Holland. Make sure all sheets bear either the British quality marks BS 1088 and WBP 1203, Lloyds Register marks YSC/QA 116, or European mark DIN 68705. Just in case dirty work is afoot, ensure that all laminations consist of dark brown hardwood without voids, and carry out the above mentioned boil test on a sample.

Sheets of plywood are available with a variety of decorative finishes, including fine veneers for joinerwork, simulated teak deck planking, and hard, patterned plastics. Standard sheets measure 8 × 4 ft (2400 × 1200 mm). Even in America thicknesses are often given in millimetres, the most common being 3, 3.5, 4, 6, 9, 12 and 18. Some works will fabricate sheets up to 8 m long to eliminate the need for jointing, but the cost is high unless ordered in large quantities. A few stockists keep 10 × 4 ft (3000 × 1200 mm) sheets.

Ply up to 4 mm thick is usually composed of three laminations, all of about the same thickness in the best quality sheets. Cheaper versions with a thick core and thin outer veneers give little scope for planing or sanding at joints to produce a fine finish, but this type has to be used for severe bending, as in the Unicorn class racing catamarans. Most 6 mm sheets contain four laminations of nearly equal thickness; while 9 mm is usually 5-ply and 12 mm is 7-ply.

Butt Straps

The simplest joints between sheets of plywood are made as in Fig 29 by butting the edges together and backing this with a *butt strap*, the width of which is about 12 times the plywood thickness. Butt straps must be made with the outside grain running in the same direction as that of the sheets being joined. The butted edges must be thoroughly glued as well as the strap face. Under 12 mm, turned copper nails (see Chapter 5) staggered in two rows

Fig 29 Plywood joint with butt strap

each side are generally preferred to screws or ring nails. A glued butt joint without fastenings is not easy to clamp properly.

To eliminate leakage, butt straps are best recessed into the boat's framing at each end. If butted against the framing, a close fit with ample glue is essential. In general, all plywood edges should be concealed by glued joints. Quarter-round moulding may be glued to the sides of butt straps.

Plywood Scarfs

When the appearance of butt straps inside a boat is objectionable or where weight is critical, all joints must be scarfed—an established way of joining all types of solid wood as well as plywood almost invisibly and with little loss of strength. Details are given later in this chapter.

The method of planing scarf tapers is indicated in Fig 30. Planing both sheets back-to-back in one operation helps accuracy and is also quicker. The temporary backing piece is essential to prevent damaging the feather edge. Always check that the tapers are dead flat by holding a try-square (or the bottom corner of a tilted steel plane) across them while viewing against the light.

When ready to glue, one sheet is turned over and the tapered faces brought together. When lubricated with glue and clamped, all scarfs tend to slide apart. To prevent this, drive a few temporary nails remote from the scarf, or fit stops at the ends of the sheets. A backing piece of straight plank covered with clingfilm or cellophane enables the scarf to be clamped by means of temporary wire nails driven through both parts and with film-covered ply offcuts under their heads to distribute the pressure and facilitate withdrawal. Another method of clamping is shown in Fig 31. The two slightly curved battens exert even pressure on the joint when clamped right down. Strips tacked across each end of the joint make an alternative method to stop sliding.

To utilize wedges for scarf clamping, fix a stiff beam above the joint and drive closely-spaced folding wedges between beam and scarf. How to scarf plywood panels together as they are fitted onto the boat is described in Chapter 12.

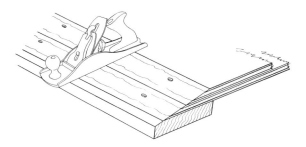

Fig 30 Planing a plywood scarf

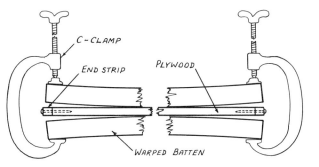

C-CLAMP

END STRIP   PLYWOOD

WARPED BATTEN

Fig 31 Clamping a scarf joint

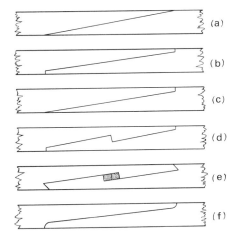

(a)

(b)

(c)

(d)

(e)

(f)

Fig 32 Six types of scarf

Scarfing Wood

Softwood generally becomes excessively expensive when longer than about 25 ft (7.5 m). The same applies to oak above 16 ft (5 m) and most imported hardwoods above 20 ft (6 m). Correctly made scarf joints (Fig 32) enable the economical shorter pieces to be lengthened without appreciable loss of strength.

The diagonal angle adopted depends on the method of fastening, whether glue is used and the likely stress. For joining solid masts and spars, relying on glue with no fastenings, a length/width taper ratio of 12 : 1 is necessary. Glued plywood scarfs (previously described) are normally made 8 : 1. Bolted hardwood backbone members (see Chapters 8 and 12) require about 6 : 1, while glued and screwed plank scarfs (Chapter 12) can be satisfactory at 4 : 1. More is better.

Simple straight scarfs (32a) are the strongest and look best on varnished parts, such as spars. They are ideal for plywood and for strip-planking (Chapter 12), where each scarf is bordered by other strips.

Elsewhere, *lipped scarfs* (32b) are best, avoiding delicate feather edges. The depth of such lips usually varies from about one-tenth plank thickness for massive parts to about one-sixth plank thickness for thin pieces. Sometimes, a lip at one end only is used, as in (32c).

The *hooked scarf* (32d) is common for heavily stressed joints in thick wood. The step in the middle prevents the parts from sliding and relieves the bolts from shearing loads. A *wedged scarf* (32e) becomes self-locking when the opposing wedges are driven. The parts do not need such precise fitting at the lips as for some other types.

Scarfs cut by router or spindle machine may have rounded lips (32f) which are less likely to crack under load. The type of scarf in Fig 32b is used for joining clinker and carvel planks (see Chapter 11) while that in 32c is better for rounded members such as sheer beadings, fendering and rubrails.

Traditionally, on the external parts of a boat (including decks) *trailing scarfs* are preferred. These have the aftermost tips on the outside. Thus in a collision, usually when forging ahead, exposed scarfs are discouraged from tearing asunder.

Jigs like carpenters' mitre boxes are useful for cutting numerous identical scarfs, such as in strip-planking. Most other scarfs need careful marking out on both sides of both parts, followed by careful sawing. It often pays to hollow the *faying surfaces* (where one puts the glue) slightly with a sharp wood chisel or disk sander to ensure that the visible joint lines are tight. If the mating parts fail to fit snugly, whittling with plane and chisel will soon put matters right, but at the expense of some wood length.

As with plywood, preventing the parts sliding is essential. If the ends cannot be chocked or clamped to stop this, the pilot holes for the fastenings must be set over slightly as described in Chapter 6.

Ordering Timber

Although stockists are prolific in most countries, few of them carry materials such as prime (knot-free) pine or exotic hardwoods. However, when using WEST SYSTEM epoxy one need not deplete the tropical forests for high quality stock. Most good stockists are able to order the unusual. Many boatyards are helpful in this respect, and suppliers of traditional woods advertise in the practical boating magazines.

It pays to get fine quality stock for spars, clinker dinghies and lightweight racing hulls. In some places, one can still find rural sawmills equipped to supply oak, elm, larch or cedar suitable for heavy traditional construction. An enthusiastic yard manager is a treasure when seeking the best pieces for each job!

Many unusual species are comparatively cheap and can look attractive in joinerwork. Holly is revered for light coloured cabin soles and trim, while ash, sycamore, popular and common elm make attractive panelling, drawer fronts, grabrails and cappings. Balsa wood is used for sandwich decks and cabin soles. Many unusual woods are available as veneer. Some fine clear hardwoods such as ramin and obeche are widely used for commercial mouldings nowadays.

Appendix I gives the properties of many species used for boat building in Europe and America. Other excellent woods are available in such countries as Japan and New Zealand.

Trade terms Wood which has been planed all over is often listed by sawmills as PAR or prepared. Although quite an additional expense, it pays to get all important stock machine planed, making it more comfortable to handle, easier to mark out, and revealing any flaws. Going a stage further, certain pieces are best machine sanded also, particularly for dinghy thwarts or cabin joinery.

Timber merchants always work in nominal measurements (the sizes when rough sawn), and PAR stock can measure from $\frac{1}{8}$ in (3 mm) to $\frac{1}{2}$ in (12 mm) under the nominal figure. All the dimensions on boat plans (and all those referred to later in this book) are the finished sizes. One needs to stress this point most carefully when ordering. Badly undersized pieces should be rejected unless of use for other purposes.

Pressure treatment Wooden dinghies and other craft which are frequently hauled out of the water should rarely get damaged by rot (unless from rainwater) or fire. Softwood for bigger craft can be pressure-treated against these hazards, or against marine borers and woodworm. However, no stock which is to be epoxy glued or impregnated should be treated before assembly. Fire retardants are most often used on decks, superstructures and joinery. They do not inhibit the burning of paint or varnish coatings, and eventually the wood will burn too. Teak has quite good natural fire retardant properties.

When your supplier is unable to arrange for pressure treatment, application by brush is well worth while. This should also be done in addition to pressure treatment after fabrication to ensure that freshly cut surfaces are well soaked. There are several types of anti-rot solutions and it is worth consulting the manufacturers to obtain the one that is compatible with whatever paints and adhesives you will use.

The Timber Schedule

Not all plans include a complete list of materials suitable for presentation to a stockist. Those for traditional craft mostly have no list at all. Such a list is not difficult for the amateur to make and in fact it helps one to become conversant with the drawings. The best procedure is to imagine the boat being built stage by stage, jotting down each part in the correct order, at the same time making a separate list of all the bolts and other fastenings likely to be needed. Some parts can be listed to exact size—with notes alongside stating whether sawn or planed, plus the best species of wood to use—while for other parts allowances must be made for wastage. Included in this latter category would be about 15% extra pieces for steamed timbers, which are liable to crack while being bent, and about 25% extra board width for certain clinker and carvel planks which must be cut to gentle curves.

Keep as near as possible to the designer's specification regarding the various types of wood, but remember that there may be plenty of alternatives, as you will see by studying Appendix 1. Cost is often all-important and it pays to discuss matters with your supplier in some detail.

Having expended numerous manhours in constructing a first-class hull, it might be sensible to insist on teak for the varnished parts above deck. Although expensive, no wood has ever been found to match its appearance and immunity to ageing. When in doubt about the properties of unusual species, obtain advice from the forest products research associations found in most countries.

Planking Boards

When ordering clinker or carvel planking which is thicker than about $\frac{3}{4}$ in (18 mm) it usually pays to get this cut *through-and-through*, that is in boards the full width of a log as shown in Fig 33a. For a big boat, buy a whole log and have this sawn into a variety of thicknesses to suit other parts of the boat as well as the planking.

Although relatively cheap, additional wastage is likely with this method. The *sapwood* (with lighter coloration next to the bark) is useless, and unexpected flaws may reveal themselves, particularly up the middle of the log. However, several boat planks can be cut from one wide board and the majority of defects can be avoided without too much wastage.

Looking at grain Inspecting Fig 33a, you will note that boards through the middle of the log have end-grain running vertically, like comb teeth, while the layers of the outer boards run almost horizontally, especially near the middle. Acting like a leaf spring, a board of the latter type bends readily in the direction required for planking a boat. Furthermore, such planks tend to warp after drying out, the surfaces remote from the middle of the log becoming concave. Such warping comes in useful when planking a round-sectioned hull as the concavity (if not too severe) can be turned to meet the curvature of the frames. For a plank which must be dead flat, minor warping can often be removed by moistening the concave face, perhaps by laying it on a lawn. Once firmly fastened it is unlikely to warp again.

Converting Boards with end-grain of this latter type are said to be *slash* or *plain sawn*. When a log must be converted into a maximum number of slash sawn planks, the saw-cuts may be arranged somewhat as indicated in Fig 33b. Boards with end-grain like comb teeth are said to be *rift* or *quarter sawn* (33c). Such boards are stiff and stable, much favoured for decking because the surface wears evenly, splinters are less likely to form, and shrinkage at seams is minimal (see final paragraph of this chapter). In the average consignment, the grain in most boards will come somewhere between the two extremes. Many boards combine a slash sawn central portion with outer parts close to the rift sawn condition. Choosing the right grain for the job is not normally as important with hardwoods like mahogany, oak and teak as with the softwoods such as cedar, larch and spruce.

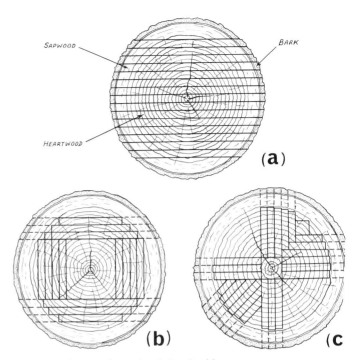

Fig 33 Converting a log into planking

Cracks and Defects

No cracks should be visible on the surface of correctly seasoned good quality stock. Except for joinery, there is no need to reject most of those pieces which have the familiar longitudinal hair cracks. These are not necessarily a sign of weakness and are easy to fill at the painting stage. The deep cracks that form at the very ends of a board are often called *checks*: steer clear of these completely. Paint or hot-wax the ends of boards in stock or being seasoned to minimize this type of splitting.

Cracks which were present in the log before sawing are called *shakes*. They may be a growing fault, but can also be caused by damage to the trunk during felling. *Thunder shakes* are often difficult to detect until the surface of a plank has been planed. They occur mostly in mahogany and appear as hair cracks at right angles to the grain, sometimes with a whitish discoloration. Although not necessarily disastrous in wide boards, thunder shakes in narrow stock can cause the wood to break under its own weight! They mean that the fibres are severed – one of the risks attached to buying a whole log.

Sawn material with no big knots or other defects is referred to as *prime* or *clear*. Being costly, its use is generally limited to joinery and parts which are varnished.

Prime boards are easy to obtain in some species such as silver spruce, cedar, teak and parana pine, whereas little prime stock of any great length is available in fir, oak or larch. Small *live knots* are normally of little consequence, but the larger ones can form serious weaknesses in narrow boards, causing them to bend erratically or break. Knots in softwood exude resin and must be sealed before painting (see *The Compleat Book of Yacht Care*). *Dead knots* sometimes fall out to leave clean holes through a plank. In any case, dead knots must be cut out and hidden with a diamond-shaped *graving piece* inlaid into the surface, as described in *Boat Repairs and Conversions*. Softwood of poor quality, known as *carcassing*, finds uses for moulds, stocks, struts and shelter framing.

Tiny cracks will be filled by the paint, but a crack longer than about 3 in (75 mm) needs special treatment. To prevent it spreading, bore a hole at each end of the crack (Fig 34). Hole diameters of $\frac{1}{8}$ in (3 mm) will suffice for the smaller cracks and about $\frac{1}{4}$ in (6 mm) for the bigger ones. To ascertain the angle of a crack to the surface, jab a knife or feeler gauge into the crack and align the drill to this. Bore right through, or well beyond the depth of the crack. Lastly, cut slivers of matching wood to fit freely into the crack and glue them in. With wooden pegs glued into the holes, the surface should be made good with epoxy filler. For small cracks the filler may be used alone.

Seasoning

Steamed ribs bend most readily when the wood used is *green*, that is, moist and straight from the sawmill. All other wood used in a boat should be seasoned first for as long as possible. Although seasoning continues after fabricating in any case, the process often involves shrinkage and twisting, leading to gaping joints and strained fastenings. The moisture content of boatbuilding woods should be kept at about 12%, certainly not above 18%. When using epoxy saturation and gluing a value of 8% is ideal. However, one should remember that the lower values are almost impossible to retain in many climates unless a humidity-controlled workshop is used. Wood readily takes in moisture from its surroundings, so dry timber needs to be epoxy-sealed immediately.

Electronic instruments are made for measuring the moisture content direct, but it can also be determined by taking a small offcut of wood well away from the ends of a plank, weighing it on an accurate balance, heating it in the domestic oven at around 220°F (105°C) for several hours,

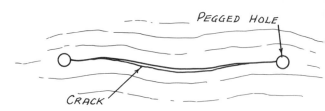

Fig 34 Preventing a crack from spreading

weighing it again and then applying the following calculation:

$$\text{Moisture content} = \frac{\text{initial weight} - \text{dry weight}}{\text{dry weight}} \times 100$$

To check complete dryness, return the sample to the oven for a further hour and weigh it again.

Most suppliers can arrange for stock to be kiln dried, but this is expensive. Amateurs take a long time to build boats, so air drying at home is usually practicable. Good air circulation is advantageous, but stacking indoors is preferable to an exposed site with inadequate protection from rain and sunlight. Raise the bottom board at least 12 in (300 mm) above ground on *bunks* of scrap wood about 3 ft apart, as in Photo 8. Use $\frac{1}{2}$ in (12 mm) thick *stickers*, all in line vertically, to space the stacked boards. Knot-free pine makes the best stickers, causing minimal discoloration.

The seasoning time depends greatly on the humidity and temperature. In cool climates softwoods take about three months per $\frac{1}{2}$ in (12 mm) of plank thickness. Imported hardwoods such as mahogany and iroko take about five months, while home grown oak takes about nine months.

Various methods have been tried to prevent surface cracking during the drying process. Urea crystals spread between closely packed boards have been used for forty years. Even better is submersion in an aqueous solution of PEG (polyethylene glycol) for three weeks before air drying. Such curing is obviously most suitable for small parts like natural crooks for knees, nameplates, trailboards and the mounting chocks for deck fittings.

The making of *knees* (the wooden brackets used in traditional construction that hold two parts together at right angles) is a fascinating subject mentioned further in Chapters 6 and 9. Although oak is the most popular wood for knees, one can use pieces from the crooked limbs of such trees as apple, holly and cherry. Ash and hickory crooks are useful for making bent tillers.

Photo 8 Through-and-through oak seasoning 'in stick'

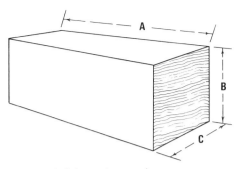

Fig 35 Unequal shrinkage in wood

Shrinkage Wood does not shrink evenly on drying. Referring to Fig 35, shrinkage along the grain (direction **A**) is almost negligible. The greatest movement occurs across direction **C**, while at right angles to this (**B**) it alters about 50% of **C**. The same thing happens in reverse when dry wood takes up moisture.

Chapter 5
Boat Fastenings

Even in the trade, there is some confusion concerning the meaning of the terms *fastenings* and *fasteners*. Among craftsmen, especially in the boatbuilding industry, nails, screws, bolts and rivets are called fastenings. The word fasteners is used to describe clips, hooks and eyes, toggles and press studs.

Steel

Iron, copper and bronze have been used in boats since prehistoric times. True wrought iron is rarely seen today, but was nearly immune from rust. It has now been almost entirely superseded by galvanized mild steel. This has a long life if no dissimilar metals or stray electric currents are allowed to come near it. These can cause *electrolytic* or *galvanic* action, which destroys the zinc. Once this happens the steel starts to rust away. Craft are still said to be iron fastened when the metal used is mild steel. Hot-dip galvanizing deposits a thick layer of zinc on the surface of steel. Most popular bolts and woodscrews are sold with a thinner zinc plated, sheradized or cadmium plated finish which may look like galvanizing but lacks its permanence.

Where galvanizing or zinc spraying is not possible, the ancient practice of *hot-tarring* or Swedish galvanizing is a passable alternative for steel bolts and fittings. To do this,

the part is heated evenly to redness, then plunged into warm coal tar or thin bitumen and hung up to dry.

Suspect stainless When constantly exposed to the air, the correct grade of stainless steel is an almost perfect metal on boats. But for underwater use it has proved untrustworthy due mainly to *crevice corrosion*. This occurs where a stainless steel bolt passes tightly through moist wood, fibreglass or ferrocement. It can even happen where a stainless steel propeller shaft stays motionless for long periods in babbit metal or cutless rubber bearings. Flaws, threads and cracks are also vulnerable.

Yellow Metal

Wooden hulls which avoid the use of steel are said to be copper fastened. Although copper is the best material for riveted fastenings (due to its excellent malleability when annealed), various bronze alloys are better for bolts. Alloys of copper (except Monel) are broadly referred to as *yellow metal*, contracted by many boatyard workers to just 'metal'. Common brass is to be avoided in seagoing vessels, for the action of salt water causes *dezincification* to occur. The zinc content of the alloy is eaten away leaving a porous copper which is brittle.

Bronzes Naval brass is only slightly superior to common brass. Woodscrews for hull construction should be of either silicon bronze (Everdur), cupro-nickel (Monel) or stainless steel. Aluminium bronze and manganese bronze are ideal for bolts. Common brass woodscrews are sometimes used in yacht joinery.

Castings Yellow metal castings for rudder fittings and floor knees are usually of gunmetal or phosphor bronze. Propellers may be of manganese bronze, aluminium bronze, stainless steel (for hulls of light alloy), or aluminium alloy for outboard motors.

Light Alloy

Although most types of fastenings are available in aluminium alloy, one needs to ensure that a genuine marine grade has been used. Pure aluminium woodscrews are available, but are best avoided for boatwork.

The above caution applies to the purchase of any sort of metal. When fabricating your own bolts, make sure that the bar is of marine grade, suitable for hand threading, and for brazing or welding as the case may be. Preferably buy your materials through a supplier conversant with such uses. In some cases there is no perfect metal: advantages are accompanied by disadvantages.

Corrosion is a highly complex subject, and affects every part of a boat—from mast to engine. It has been comprehensively covered in laymans' language in *Metal Corrosion in Boats* by Nigel Warren (Adlard Coles Ltd).

Nails

Bronze barbed *ring nails* (Fig 36a and Photo 9) have been proven during the past forty years and are used in place of screws and plain nails for many purposes in boat building. The fact that withdrawal is almost impossible and will cause damage, could be deemed their only disadvantage! They come with either pan heads (as on common steel wire nails) or countersunk heads like woodscrews.

Copper All other types of boat nails have been in use for well over a century. The most widely used for traditional construction are square (sometimes round) copper boat nails (Fig 36b). They are intended to pass right through a

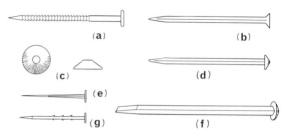

Fig 36 Boatbuilding nails

joint, with the pointed ends riveted over special cup-shaped copper washers (36c) called *roves* (*rooves*) or *burrs*, as described later in this chapter. This enables parts to be pulled tightly together, and is the secret behind the success of clinker (or lapstrake) planking over such a long period of time. No other through-fastenings are of lighter weight. Copper nails as thin as darning needles were used in the early days of aviation for making fuselages and seaplane floats.

Copper boat nails usually have countersunk heads. Rose heads (Fig 36d) were popular once for working craft, requiring no stopping over them. Cut copper tacks (36e) have pan heads and are stocked by good hardware stores in lengths from $\frac{3}{8}$ in (9 mm) to $1\frac{1}{2}$ in (38 mm).

Spikes Galvanized steel square boat nails are still used for cheap iron-fastened boats, particularly with strip planking. Roves are made for them, but as riveting destroys the zinc a good coating of paint or varnish is expedient to stop rust. Such nails in the range 4–9 in (100–230 mm) are called *deck spikes* (36f). They usually have rose heads, but they can be let in flush.

Photo 9 Driving bronze ring nails

Dumps Big bronze nails called *dumps* were once widely used in heavy copper-fastened hulls, but they have now been almost entirely superseded by ring nails, such as Gripfast or Anchorfast.

Pins One other type of bronze nail is the serrated pan head sheathing nail (see end of chapter and Fig 36g). Hardware stores keep galvanized and aluminium wire nails for roofing and fencing which can sometimes prove useful in boat building. Also easy to obtain are brass panel pins, brads and escutcheon pins, useful for joinery and plywood dinghy construction.

Woodscrews

Every handyman knows something about screws (Fig 37a) and there are few differences between their uses ashore and afloat. However, the boatbuilder is advised not to put them in with a hammer, then finish off with just a couple of turns of the screwdriver!

Screws are expensive in comparison with nails, but they are essential for some joints. Readily removable, they enable parts to be held in place temporarily prior to final fitting or gluing. They enable a joint to be pulled up tightly, and big screws enable a plywood panel under stress to be drawn up in stages when the use of clamps is impracticable.

Bronze or stainless steel screws are fine for most hulls, but galvanized screws (not just zinc plated) are compatible with other iron fastenings. If the heads of aluminium screws are kept painted or varnished, this will prevent the white oxide forming. Stainless steel self-tapping screws work fine into wood, fibreglass and thin metal.

Thick countersunk washers called *screw cups* are made to fit under screw heads. The heavy brass type are intended to be recessed flush; the thin stainless steel or brass ones sit on the surface. Brass may be either natural finish or plated with nickel or chromium. Similar white plastic washers are made to hold clip-on ornamental covering domes.

Lag Bolts

Heavy duty screws from about 3 in (75 mm) to 10 in (250 mm) in length often have square heads for turning with a wrench and are called *coach screws* or *lag bolts* (Fig 37b). A washer is inserted under each head, and all may be countersunk flush when the wood is thick enough. Galvanized coach screws are not always easy to get, but

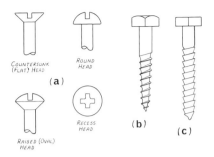

Fig 37 Woodscrews and lag bolts

ordinary black ones can be sent away to be hot-dip galvanized or zinc sprayed. In heavy work, where bolts cannot be fitted, coach screws are handy and secure, especially for knees, chocks and brackets. Black ones are useful on temporary work such as moulds, stocks and struts.

The makers of sterngear sometimes supply bronze lag bolts for securing propeller shaft glands and rudder bearings. More often, *hanger bolts* are used. These wind in like lag bolts, but have threads and nuts at the exposed ends.

Coach screws for boat work should have Nettlefold threads (Fig 37b), but they are also made with buttress threads (Fig 37c). This type is intended for driving most of the way with a hammer.

Nuts and Bolts

The most common bolts in all materials are known as HRH (hexagon-round-hexagon) in the trade (see Fig 39a). They have hexagonal heads and nuts, and are generally threaded over a length equal to about four diameters. When threaded for the entire length, they are known as hexagon *set screws*. These are not always supplied with nuts. Set screws with countersunk flat slotted heads are often referred to as *machine screws*.

Nuts In Navy fashion, a thin locknut is put underneath the full nut to prevent loosening. Boatyard fitters often put the thin nut on top, to avoid the need for a special thin open-ended wrench. Self-locking nuts work well in places of high vibration. Other types you may need are castle nuts or capstan nuts which take split cotter pins for security, also certain butterfly (wing) nuts and plated cap nuts. When you go shopping for the latter, take a small magnet: many so-called brass ones are actually brass-plated steel!

For big steel bolts which may need to be removed or tightened after many years, such as ballast keel bolts, huge square heads and square nuts (SRS) are still revered.

Fabricating Bolts

Bolts up to about $\frac{1}{2}$ in (12 mm) diameter are easy to make at home from round bar of any desired metal. Some handymen possess dies for cutting the threads, but you may prefer to borrow these or pay a fitter to cut them for you. Split dies are best to enable the head nut to be fitted very tightly. If the bolt is to be galvanized or zinc sprayed, the running nut should be made a very slack fit. Taps (which cut female threads) are not adjustable, so the only way to ream a nut oversize is in a screw-cutting lathe.

Studding Without access to dies, bolts can be made from threaded rod or *studding*—usually made in 24 in (600 mm) lengths—stocked by most big chandlery stores and boatyards, especially in brass and stainless steel.

Head fixing To prevent the nut which forms a bolthead from loosening, leave the shank proud and rivet it over with a ball-pein hammer. Preferably, countersink the nut a bit to receive this. Brazing or welding will suffice equally well. Such a head can be filed into a dome shape or turned in a lathe to make a countersunk head. For this sort of treatment a plain collar is better than a nut. With bronze, such a head may be fixed with silver solder instead of threading. Use Easyflo No. 2 and apply the flux all through before heating. Brazing is not so reliable as it rarely runs into the joint.

Head forming Copper bolts or nails with countersunk heads in any length or diameter can be made by beating the top while held in a split jig of the appropriate shape (Fig 38). To make the jig, clamp two chunks of bright mild steel together in a machine vice under a drill press and bore a hole the same size as the bolt centrally through the joint. Countersink the top of the hole to the requisite depth for the shape of bolthead. Take the chunks apart and draw-file the mating surfaces slightly so that the bolt is gripped firmly when the assembly is tightened in the jaws of the bench vice. Two pegs across the joint make a superior tool. If you have numerous heads to form, the jig may get damaged by hammering. In that case, drill several holes through it, or make it from gauge plate or oil-hardening tool steel, duly tempered.

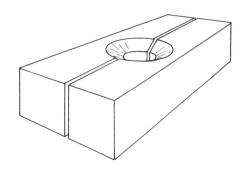

Fig 38 Jig for making bolt heads

Anneal it Have a trial run to discover how much bar to leave protruding above the top of the jig before peening starts. Support the bottom of the bar to stop it slipping downwards. Anneal the tip first, by heating to bright red and quenching in water. After about twenty blows with a ball-pein hammer, the copper will work-harden, necessitating removal from the jig for re-annealing.

Keel Bolts

As well as the HRH and SRS bolts already mentioned, one other type is sometimes made by boatyards, the *upset head* bolt. The tip of the bar is heated in a forge and bumped to form a bulge, then hammered into the shape shown in Fig 39b, either on an anvil or in a specially shaped cast steel swage. Such bolts are used to secure cast iron or lead external ballast keels having holes cast in them of correct shape to fit the upset heads. The taper ensures that the

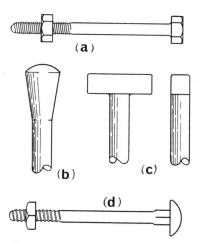

Fig 39 Manufactured and custom made bolts

bolt will not rotate when the nut needs tightening or removing, perhaps thirty years later.

Narrow *tee-head* bolts (Fig 39c) can be home made by brazing or welding. They are particularly useful for bolting through a boat's stem, also along the narrow keel of a small launch, all heads being recessed in slots running parallel to the grain of the wood. The leading edge of a stem is normally streamlined into a tapered *cutwater*. The large counterbore needed for a normal bolthead would burst through when shaping the cutwater, and the bolthead itself might become exposed if not recessed far enough.

Other Bolts

Cup head (css) or carriage bolts (Fig 39d) have certain uses in boatwork. As with all bolts, a washer is necessary under the nut when directly on wood, but no washer is needed under the head: on tightening, the short, square shank beneath the head pulls into the wood and prevents rotation. Galvanized css bolts must be obtained through chandlers or boatyards. Hardware stores often keep black or zinc plated versions which are fine for stocks and cradles. They also keep zinced gutter and roofing bolts—$\frac{1}{4}$ or $\frac{5}{16}$ in (6 or 8 mm) set screws with domed slotted heads.

Oval head (raised head) stainless steel bolts are neat for fixing external rigging chainplates, but they should be checked for crevice corrosion every three years. Protruding hexagonal heads can cause damage in this position, so css bolts are sometimes used on iron-fastened craft. In this case the chainplate holes are filed square prior to galvanizing.

Using Copper Boat Nails as Rivets

In general, unless a correctly sized pilot hole is bored first (see Chapter 6) a square copper boat nail will buckle on driving. Being smooth, they will not hold securely when driven *dead* into thick wood: they are intended to pass right through and be riveted. If you must drive copper nails dead, twist each one beforehand to improve their grip. Use two pairs of pliers, give about half a turn for a $1\frac{1}{4}$ in (32 mm) nail and about one full turn for a $2\frac{1}{2}$ in (64 mm) nail. Grip is improved even more by forming barbs on all the corners. Do this with a sharp $\frac{3}{8}$ in (9 mm) cold chisel and make a little hardwood jig to lay each nail in.

Even with a good pilot hole, a long copper nail can buckle during driving. To obviate this, boatbuilders each

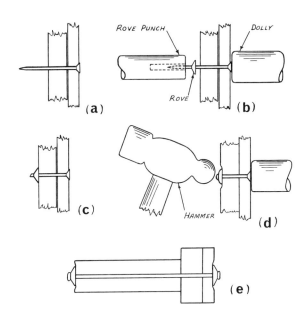

Fig 40 Copper nail riveting procedure

have their own pet remedy, from squirting thin oil or soft soap into the hole with a hypodermic syringe to smearing Vaseline, grease or candle wax onto the nail. Any lubricant helps and a candle is the most convenient.

The procedure when fitting a riveted copper nail is illustrated in Fig 40. This is really a job for four hands, although with a certain amount of ingenuity it can sometimes be done singlehanded.

Having driven the nail flush with a hammer, a heavy chunk of bar known as a *dolly* is held on the head while the rove is forced over the pointed end with a hollow punch and hammer. Surplus nail is then clipped off to leave about $\frac{1}{16}$ in (1.5 mm) beyond the rove for thin nails and about $\frac{1}{8}$ in (3 mm) for medium thickness nails. This part is then riveted over while the dolly is pressed on to the head. Riveting is best accomplished with a light ball-pein hammer, starting with light, rapid blows and finishing with a few heavier ones.

When correctly done, the roves should not be completely flattened and there should be no sharp edges. A rove punch is easy to make by cutting off an old bolt about 3 in (75 mm) below the head, then drilling a long hole into the middle of the freshly cut end. A nail should fit just snugly into the hole. The bolt diameter should be a little larger than the rove.

A short piece of round steel bar with the edges well chamfered makes an ideal dolly: 1 in (25 mm) diameter for the smallest nails, $1\frac{1}{2}$ in (38 mm) for medium, and 2 in (50 mm) for the thickest. Where heads are countersunk below the surface, a short stub the same diameter as the nail head should be screwed into the end of the dolly. For riveting just a few nails, a heavy hammer will serve as a makeshift dolly, while a pin punch of appropriate diameter placed on the nail head and backed up with the hammer will deal with the occasional countersunk head.

Turning the Point

Another traditional though somewhat rough-and-ready way of securing copper nails is *turning*. There is no rove. The protruding nail point is dressed back into the wood, becoming almost invisible when painted. Nowadays, turning is often called *clenching*, though this term really means riveting. Clinker work was originally called *clencher*, derived from the clenched copper fastenings which had to have roves due to the frailness of the steam-bent timbers.

The procedure for turning is shown in Fig 41. The nail is hammered through a prepared hole and the tip is clipped off obliquely to leave a crude point, with $\frac{3}{8}$ in (9 mm) showing for thin nails, $\frac{1}{2}$ in (12 mm) for medium gauges, and $\frac{5}{8}$ in (16 mm) for thick ones. The point is then dressed over with light hammer blows, rolling it back into the wood and forming a small eye. With a dolly on the head, this eye is hammered further in. Then, transferring the dolly to the turned end, tightening is completed by using a punch and hammer on the head.

To prevent the wood from splitting, the eye should be formed at an angle to the grain of the wood, as shown in Fig 41e. This represents a view looking towards a sawn rib from inside the boat.

Ordering In Appendix 2 you will find tables listing the standard sizes of square copper boat nails normally available, also the numbers of nails and roves for ordering by weight. Try to avoid using needlessly thick nails, leading to wastage, excess weight and cost, and weakened timbers. Drawings usually indicate the gauge of nail for each purpose, but nail lengths may not be mentioned. At one time it was customary to use nails at least an inch longer than necessary. That was because they did not have a powerful vacuum cleaner!

Clenches

Long enough copper nails cannot always be obtained for

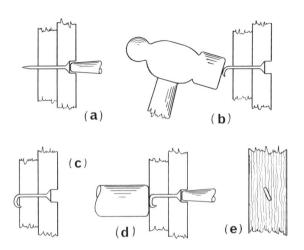

Fig 41 Turning a nail point

certain riveted fastenings. The knee at each end of a thwart may be more than 4 in (100 mm) thick at the throat. Lengths of copper rod are used instead, riveted over roves at each end (Fig 40e). The most popular thicknesses of rod are $\frac{1}{8}$ in (3 mm) and $\frac{3}{16}$ in (5 mm). In big boats, *clenches* up to $\frac{1}{2}$ in (12 mm) may need to be used. Naval brass rod is sometimes used for very long clenches, but copper rivets much better. Soft iron clenches were used in old wooden ships, being cheaper and neater than bolts. In modern heavy construction bolts are used almost exclusively.

The small hole found through a rove may have to be enlarged with a twist drill to allow a push fit over the bar. For clenches of $\frac{1}{4}$ in (6 mm) diameter and up, standard thick, flat, copper washers are used instead of roves. For neatness they may be countersunk below the surface and filled over on completion. However, exposed riveting is wiser for wood shrinkage may necessitate further riveting after a time.

Rivet up A clench should be a snug tap fit in its prepared hole. If working singlehanded, cut each bar to length, anneal the ends and start riveting one end, much as described above but using a flat jig without the countersink. Slip a washer under the head and drive the clench through its hole. With a dolly on the pre-formed end, fit the other washer and start riveting that end. Alternate dolly and hammer occasionally until both ends are neatly closed and the joint is pulled up tight. Minimize the hammering to avoid work-hardening: you cannot withdraw a clench for re-annealing!

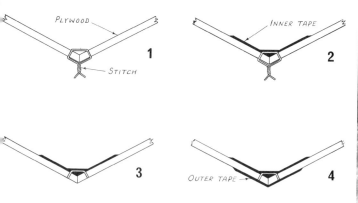

Fig 42 Wiring and glassing a plywood joint

Unusual Fastenings

Drift bolts have few uses on small yachts, but they come in useful for fixing heavy backbone members together, and for big wooden rudders. The idea is to hammer a long bar so tightly into its prepared hole that it cannot be withdrawn. With copper, place a washer over it, drive to completion, cut off the surplus, then rivet the end over as for a clench. On steel and bronze drift bolts the outer end is threaded to receive a nut. A temporary steel cap is made to screw onto the thread while driving; the same cap may be used to drive several drifts. Always make a slight taper on the leading end, not a point.

Stitch-and-glue Sheets of plywood can be stitched together with copper wire and the joint sealed inside and out with strips of fibreglass (see also Chapter 12). This method is used for many popular canoe and sailboat designs, including the Mirror dinghy and the Unicorn catamaran. With 3 mm or 4 mm plywood, use 18-gauge wire ties at 3 in (75 mm) intervals (Fig 42). For 6 mm plywood use 16-gauge spaced 4 in (100 mm) apart. Pairs of holes are bored well back from the ply edges. Short lengths of wire are bent to form stirrups and the legs are pushed through the holes from the inside. On the outside, the protruding wires are twisted together to tighten the joint.

Once the joint is securely taped inside, the ugly bits of wire outside are clipped off, then further polyester resin and glass tape (see Photo 10) is applied to that side. One big hint: always run a fillet of resin putty along the inside of the chine angle before laying up any tape, also fill any gap between the two parts on the outside.

Trenails One ancient type of fastening is made entirely of wood, usually oak. The round pegs used are called *trenails* or *treenails*, usually pronounced 'trennels' or 'trunnels'. They are shaped with a special hand tool or turned on a lathe from rough-hewn stock, gauged to drive snugly into holes bored with a standard sized auger or bit. Trenails through $1\frac{1}{4}$ in (32 mm) planking into heavy sawn frames should be about $\frac{5}{8}$ in (16 mm) diameter. For 2 in (50 mm) planking, use $\frac{7}{8}$ in (22 mm). A tapered reamer is used to bellmouth all hole ends slightly, as in Fig 43a. Wedges are driven into saw-cuts across the grain (43b). Alternatively, two wedges crossed as in Fig 43c may be used. Sink trenails enough to hold a skim of filler, or a matching glued plug on varnish work.

To avoid weakening the frames trenails may be set in blind holes, as in Fig 43d. The wedge is fitted lightly into the saw-cut and inserts itself on hitting the base of the hole. Setting in epoxy resin is a superior modification for this type. Without resin, all trenails should be pickled in rot preservative before insertion.

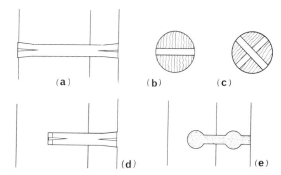

Fig 43 Trenail details and a resin button

Trenails are incapable of tightening a joint, so effective clamping is essential. The same applies to the epoxy button illustrated in Fig 43e, a clever idea to eliminate the use of metal fastenings and reduce weight. While the joint is clamped, a pilot drill is inserted, equipped with a depth gauge to stop it passing right through. The bulges are then formed by means of a *burr*, a thin shank with a toothed ball on the end. Miniature burrs are used by dentists; bigger ones can be obtained from tool stockists.

The pilot drill must be the same size as the ball of the burr. Manipulation of the burr at the base of the pilot hole and again just beneath the outer surface produces the bulbous shapes required in a few seconds. It then remains to press epoxy putty into the hole with the aid of a stick of dowel wood. The putty forms its own surface stopping.

No fastenings When using an epoxy saturation technique most fastenings can be eliminated except where essential to clamp a joint. Where extra strength or security proves necessary, standard carpentry dowels make cheap and corrosion-free fastenings reminiscent of the ancient trenail.

Underwater Sheathing

Details and costs for six hull sheathing systems are given in *The Compleat Book of Yacht Care*, together with application procedures for fibreglass and nylon (Cascover) sheathing. Hulls shorter than about 40 ft (12 m) do not normally need underwater sheathing, as slipping, beaching or careening for scrubbing and painting is fairly simple. Zinc sheathing can be used for iron-fastened boats, but copper is compatible with most wooden hulls and suits the abilities of amateur boatbuilders well.

Copper has almost permanent antifouling properties, saving its cost in paint over a period of about five years. As copper does corrode away gradually, especially near the waterline, the temptation to use sheet thinner than 24-gauge must be avoided. Most sheet copper comes in the hard state, so be careful to order it annealed or soft. Standard sheets usually measure 4×2 ft (1200 mm × 600 mm)—an ideal size for wrapping most keels—while halving sheets lengthwise generally makes them ideal for most other hull surfaces.

Joints should overlap by at least 1 in (25 mm), fastened by means of serrated bronze sheathing nails, normally available in lengths of 1 and $1\frac{1}{4}$ in (25 and 32 mm). For $\frac{3}{4}$ in (18 mm) planking you have to use $\frac{5}{8}$ in (16 mm) bronze ring nails. Space the nails about 1 in (25 mm) apart, $\frac{3}{8}$ in (9 mm) back from the sheet edges. Also drive three rows of nails at about 6 in (150 mm) intervals across each sheet, to maintain the copper in close contact with the hull. Traditionally, hulls were given two coats of black varnish (coal tar and naphtha) followed by a layer of common brown paper doped with more black varnish. Nowadays, use black bitumastic paint and builders' waterproof kraft paper. Lay the paper just ahead of sheathing, with overlaps of about 1 in (25 mm).

Sheathing should start from the boottop downwards and from the keel upwards, finishing with shaped panels midway. Each row should proceed from stern to stem, producing trailing joints with the overlap on the downstream ends. A set of panel-beater's rubber-faced mallets is ideal for dressing the copper around keel, stem, rudder and other tricky places before the straightforward sheathing starts. Further annealing before nailing down may be necessary in awkward places as copper work-hardens when beaten. To permit sheathing to turn up into a drop keel slot without getting chafed, a rabbet about $\frac{1}{8}$ in (3 mm) deep should be cut all around the aperture, to allow for a turn-up of about $1\frac{1}{4}$ in (32 mm).

The most tedious aspect of copper sheathing is punching all the nail holes. This is best done off the hull with a tiny but sharp pin punch while the sheet is backed up with a chunk of scrap lead. This leaves a slight dimple which helps to settle the nail head. On the overlaps use a thin steel spike to pierce through the underlying copper. Naturally, this means that plain panels can only be pre-punched along one side and one end while on the bench.

Unfortunately, only the owners of robust wooden hulls can benefit from copper sheathing. However, fibreglass and ferrocement can be sheathed with the professionally applied Mariner 706 system. This utilizes cupro-nickel foil and possesses antifouling properties nearly as good as copper.

Chapter 6
Boring and Gluing

It has already been mentioned that holes of correct size need to be bored for nearly all fastenings in wood. The same applies for fibreglass and metal when self-tapping screws, rivets and bolts are used. To give lasting satisfaction fastenings should permit no movement. But if they are too tight a drive, materials may split and fastenings may be bent, weakened or broken, or permanently seized.

Pilot Holes

Making trial holes in scrap material is always worth while. In wood, trial fastenings can be retrieved by cleaving apart with a mallet and chisel. Trials are particularly important for copper nails and drift bolts.

For copper nails in softwood, make the pilot hole diameter about one-half the *diagonal* thickness of the square nail. For hardwoods, make it the thickness of the nail measured across the *flats*. For very long nails enlarge the pilot holes slightly and use a lubricant such as Vaseline or wax. Clenches need to be a snug push fit. You may need to grind down the outside of a twist drill (Morse bit) to obtain a hole the exact size. The galvanizing on steel drift bolts often creates the correct fit when using a drill the same diameter as the ungalvanized bar, but you must first file off any nibs and blobs of zinc which stand proud.

Pilot holes for bronze barbed ring nails are generally half the overall diameter of the nail. In some hardwoods trials to full depth are essential.

Screw Holes

Brass and aluminium woodscrews shear off with ease while being driven if the holes are too small, especially in hardwood with screws narrower than 10-gauge. Screws of bronze and stainless steel are much tougher, but they can still shear when driven by a power tool or a screwdriving bit in a carpenter's brace.

Drills The tables in Appendix 3 list the correct drill sizes for all common screw gauges. For big and important fastenings it pays to drive a mild steel screw all the way first, to make sure that the final one will enter faultlessly. Flat combination drills (Fig 44a) work best in power

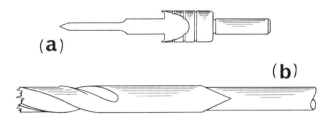

Fig 44 Combination drill and a brazed extension

drills, but at modest speed. In softwoods, a single combination drill will suffice for several screw sizes, but in hardwood they need to be exactly the right length and gauge for the screw. Small bits can break quite easily, so it pays to keep spares. They can overheat when used for more than ten holes in quick time.

Common metalworking carbon steel twist drills bore good pilot holes in wood by hand or power, but try to clear swarf from the flutes every inch of depth to avoid overheating. High speed steel (HSS) twist drills are not necessary for wood or plastics; they also cost more than carbon steel and break more readily. By paying a lot of money you can buy drills that will bore into hardened tool steel! Somewhat cheaper are masonry drills, that you are sure to need if building in ferrocement.

Coming back to wood, brad-point drills are ideal. They look similar to twist drills, but the tip is flat with a spike in the middle. Causing no surface damage, they are ideal for plugs. A brad-point drill bores a blind hole with a flat bottom. Twist drills leave a cone-shaped bottom. This angle is not the same as the countersink angle for a screw head, but the difference is not too serious in softwood when you have no suitable combination drill. A proper countersink bit, or rose bit, is best for screws set flush with the surface.

How deep? For covering with filler, the minimum depth to sink a screw head is about $\frac{1}{16}$ in (1.5 mm). The depth to take a glued plug or dowel is $\frac{3}{16}$ in (4 mm) for head diameters up to $\frac{3}{8}$ in (9 mm) and $\frac{1}{4}$ in (6 mm) for larger screws. To judge accurate counterboring, depth rings are scored into the bodies of combination drills: see Fig 44a.

Veneer plugs For the varnished topsides of some cold-moulded racing yachts, screws may be sunk only $\frac{1}{32}$ in (0.75 mm). With the aid of a sharp wad punch, cut disks of matching veneer for these and glue them with epoxy resin.

Screw cups Ship's name boards and panels which may have to be removed periodically may be attached by flush woodscrews with screw cups under their heads. An ordinary brace with auger bit is the best tool to sink cups flush: remember to use this before boring each screw hole.

Bolt Holes

In most hardwoods bolts need to be a light push fit; in softwoods slightly tighter. When boring edgewise through a board, guide battens clamped on are essential to prevent a disaster. Through fibreglass nothing must be tight. Holes must be lined with thick epoxy resin, for which room has been left. When hard, bolt insertion can start, each one being bedded in mastic all the way through. This is particularly important for keel bolts.

Drills can wander when boring long holes. In severe cases a bolt may refuse to drive through. In wood, one traditional but drastic remedy for this was to heat the tip of a spare bolt to redness and thrust it through!

Even if tight holes are made for bolts passing through a wooden hull (especially under the waterline) the heads and nuts must be caulked to prevent any leakage. To do this, make a grommet (pronounced 'grummit') under each head or washer, formed from a few turns of caulking cotton wound around the bolt stem. Old-style boatbuilders dope the cotton with a mixture of white lead paste and auto grease, but a modern bedding compound is better and not so messy.

Tight scarfs Bolts through scarf joints (see Chapter 4) need fairly tight holes. To ensure that the ends of the joint (Fig 32b) press home securely, the following procedure is often adopted on bolted scarfs, and sometimes also when woodscrews or lag bolts are used. Holes are bored through one member and with the other piece offered up the positions of the holes are marked on it with paint on a long thin art brush or dowel, or by tapping in a fairly slack bolt having a point filed on its tip. With a strip of batten pushed into each hole in turn, direction lines are pencilled right across both pieces to preserve alignment.

On dismantling the parts, the second set of holes are bored. However, instead of centering exactly on the marks shift each hole back about $\frac{1}{64}$ in (0.5 mm) for hardwood or $\frac{1}{32}$ in (1 mm) for softwood. This will ensure tight fits to the scarf ends. All too often such holes have been shifted the wrong way!

Hints on drilling Galvanized bolts are usually too tight if the bit size equals the bolt diameter before galvanizing. You may need to grind down a drill the next size up. Expanding wood bits usually range from $\frac{1}{2}$ in (12 mm) to 3 in (75 mm). They can be adjusted to exact size, and can be lengthened: see below.

You can buy or borrow long-handled augers in common sizes. The business end is either a normal scotch pattern wood bit, or the single-twist ship auger type. The shaft is either made to fit into a brace, or eyed for a tommy bar. Lengths range from 15 in (375 mm) to 30 in (750 mm) according to hole size.

Any drill or bit can be lengthened. The added bar should be at least $\frac{1}{32}$ in (1 mm) smaller than the drill shank to allow for swarf and slight misalignment, but remember to have the tip small enough to fit your drill chuck. For a brace, part the drill shank with a grinder and braze the chuck square back on to the extension bar. To make the joint, grind a male Vee on the drill shank (Fig 44b) and cut a corresponding female Vee into the bar, using hacksaw and file. Miniature or big drills can be home-made from round or square silver steel drill rod, as described in *Boat Repairs and Conversions*.

Except for bullnose or shell augers (see below), most wood bits and augers have a pointed lead screw at the cutting end which can be a nuisance. When such bits are used to sink a bolthead below the surface, bore the bigger hole first so that the drill point has wood to bite into. If you forget this, drive a peg of wood into the smaller hole temporarily. Gouges are useful for correcting such mistakes, also for cutting the curiously shaped countersink necessary where a woodscrew enters at an oblique angle.

Sterntube Boring

Where a propeller shaft or sterntube passes through the hull, a large-diameter hole is required, perhaps over 3 ft (1 m) long (Fig 45). Naturally enough, many amateurs view boring this with trepidation, but provided proper care is taken it cannot fail to turn out successfully.

Although boat plans should indicate the propeller shaft line, this may be accurate for only one model of

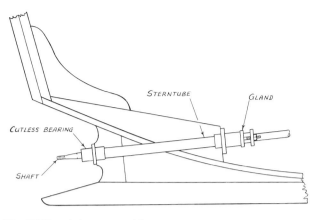

Fig 45 Sterntube assembly

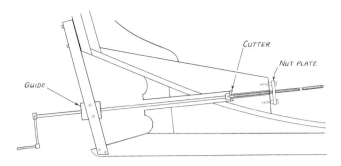

Fig 46 Threaded boring bar

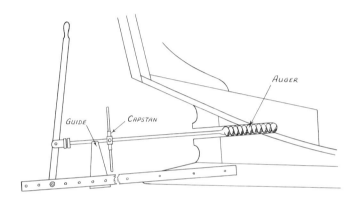

Fig 47 Boring with a bullnose auger

engine. Plans for hulls of fibreglass, ferrocement or metal often show a bronze or light alloy sleeve moulded or welded in to house the sterntube. It pays to defer sleeve installation until all power pack details are finalized. Until then, leave a rough aperture large enough to permit shaft angle adjustment.

Boring through wood is best done before a hull is fully planked. This might not be possible with a twin-screw vessel where the sterntubes pass through chocks called *blisters* bolted outside the planking, with corresponding chocks inside called *shaft logs*. Boatyards often partly bore both chocks while on the bench. Blisters and shaft logs are also to be found on single screw speedboats and fin-and-skeg sailboats.

With wood, scribe a pencil line on one side of the appropriate backbone members. Square from this across the inboard and outboard faces and mark where to start boring. Two popular methods of boring the big hole are illustrated in Figs 46 and 47. In the first, a pilot hole is bored to take a threaded boring bar. In the second, a full-size bullnose or shell auger does the job in one pass. In either case the secret of success is to mount an accurate guide. For a pilot hole, a sharp lengthened twist drill is ideal. It can be used from both ends to meet in the middle, and will not be ruined if it strikes a fastening. Should the holes fail to meet, check the alignment and repeat with a larger drill. If the meeting is inaccurate, bore past it in both directions until the boring bar will fit through dead on line. The bar's cutter will correct any misalignment.

It takes quite a time to make a boring bar, but as boatyards rarely use them nowadays you can most likely borrow one. The cutter is simply one, or preferably two, $\frac{3}{8}$ in (9 mm) square lathe toolbits held in a collar with grub

screws. Make three or four passes, adjusting the cutters each time.

You will definitely have to borrow the shell auger shown in Fig 47. Not only is this type of auger rare, but the shaft needs a groove milled along it so that the turning handle stays roughly in the same place as you bore. It needs a thrust race at the pressure end—plus a helper to apply the pressure. However, with ingenuity one can improvise a big spring adjusted by a rope tackle when singlehanded. Although these augers rarely wander, it pays to keep checking by withdrawing the tool and inserting a long dead-fit dowel or pipe which can be aligned both with the shaft angle and the boat's centreline.

When setting engine bearers, a thin piano wire is aligned through the sterntube boring. A good idea is to use this earlier with the Fig 46 method to check the nut plate and guide positions through the pilot hole before starting the big bore.

Irrespective of hull type, in a metal boat the sleeve to house a sterntube simply needs pushing through a hole, aligning by taut wire, welding in place, then reinforcing with webs or brackets. The flange at one end must, of course, be welded on *in situ*. Glassing a sleeve into a fibreglass hull should be done in stages to avoid overheating. Through ferrocement, a sleeve needs one or more baffle rings welded around the outside, to obviate any possibility of water seeping past the mortar-to-sleeve interface.

Further information about fitting sterntubes and boring for them is given in *Boat Repairs and Conversions*.

Large Apertures

The boring of big round holes in any relatively thin material is called *trepanning*. Tool stockists sell trepan bits and tank cutters in standard sizes up to 3 in (75 mm). It requires a lot of power at low speed to drive them properly, however.

A jigsaw or sabre saw will make short work of big apertures of any shape in suitable materials, provided corner holes are bored to start from. By hand, a hacksaw, padsaw, keyhole saw or coping saw will often do the same job. Quite the best tool for metal under $\frac{1}{8}$ in (3 mm) thick is a power nibbler. Cheaper ones are available as power drill attachments.

In thick wood or metal, bore closely-spaced small holes within the outline. If possible, place the work on a backing block before chiselling between the holes. A router will tackle the job in quite thick wood, and is unbeatable when it comes to forming rabbets around window apertures. Using hand tools you would need to proceed as follows.

Windows Do not saw out the aperture until the rabbet is formed. With a depth gauge on a wood bit, bore closely spaced holes to the rabbet depth (Fig 48a). Cut the clear aperture, or bore further holes as in 48b and break it out. Trim up the rabbet (48c) and remove all roughness with rasp and sandpaper. When boring right through with a wood bit, always avoid an ugly breakout at the far side. Once the point pokes through (48b), complete boring from the other side. At the start, always use the correct trepan drills to form the corners of large radius which all smart windows need (48d).

Exposed edges not covered by bezels or portlight flanges need generous chamfers or roundings. Bevel the bottom edges as in 48e to prevent moisture trapping.

No rabbet is required around apertures for most fixed

or opening portlights, as each one is equipped with a sleeve or spigot to pass right through the boat. Much the same applies with windows of all shapes and sizes that are mounted in frames of brass or light alloy.

Glazing Plexiglass or Perspex scratches easily, toughened glass has to be factory cut and polycarbonate is generally the most suitable. Makrolon 280 Hard Grade is highly resistant to scratching by windshield wipers, and very strong, but its cost is high. It should not be drilled, and the edges must be carefully filed and then sanded smooth.

Laminating

With good gluing, almost any part of a wooden boat can be built up by lamination from shorter pieces, without loss of strength. The most popular parts include stems, frames, beams, planking, knees, floors and tillers. One could also add hollow masts and spars, which are made as described in *Boat Repairs and Conversions*.

Although laminated members are strong and relatively free from warping and cracking, they are heavy, take much time to produce, and use quantities of expensive adhesive. Without epoxy resin, you must use resorcinol (see below) for oak, teak or iroko, though the cheaper resin glues are reliable on most other species. An ideal bending wood, such as agba, can be much thicker for a given curve than many other species, thus saving glue and time. For straight parts almost any species might do, with even thicker strips. With planed wood, all faying surfaces need coarse sanding after they have been made a good fit. Scratching or grooving does more harm than good. Close-sawn strips should glue well without further preparation.

Formers Quite basic jigs suffice for most laminating jobs. A few chocks screwed to the floor or bench may do, provided clearance is available for the clamps. The curved coaming corners seen in Photo 11 were clamped in the portable jig shown in Photo 12. The big former in Photo 13 is typical for long members such as gunwales, beam shelves, keels and stringers. Curvature is readily adjusted by nailing on sundry packing pieces. Jigs for deck beams are sometimes called crown (or camber) moulds. Where possible, laminate parts straight into place in the hull, eliminating the need for jigs. Parts commonly made this way include curved beadings as in

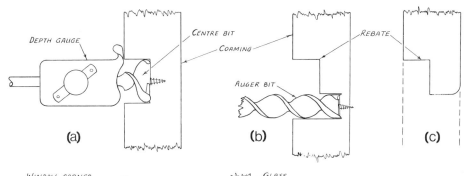

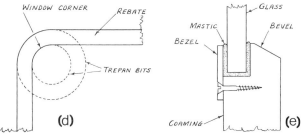

Fig 48 Window rabbets and glazing

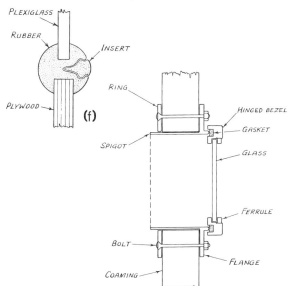

Fig 49 Hinged portlight components

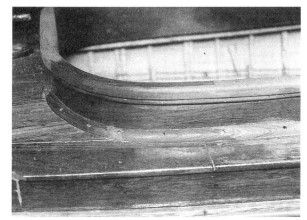

Photo 11 Rounded corner for teak launch coaming

Photo 12 Bending jig for small parts

Photo 13 Jig for big laminations

Photo 11, and the strap floors and cold-moulded work described in Chapter 12.

The assembly of complicated laminations needs efficient preparation to beat the glue setting deadline. Always set clamps at close intervals with stout packing pieces to distribute the pressure evenly. Temporary or permanent fastenings sometimes eliminate the need for clamps, but they might take too long to get into place.

Strips 2 in (50 mm) wide will take a slightly smaller radius of curvature than 6 in (150 mm) strips. When narrow, agba $\frac{1}{16}$ in (1.5 mm) thick should take a 4 in (100 mm) radius. Use $\frac{1}{8}$ in (3 mm) around a 9 in (230 mm) radius, then approximately $\frac{1}{4}$ in (6 mm) for 20 in (500 mm) or more, $\frac{1}{2}$ in (12 mm) for 4 ft (1200 mm) and 1 in (25 mm) for 10 ft (3 m). Strips bend more readily when lubricated with glue. If steaming proves necessary, dry out the wood completely before gluing or use thinner strips.

When thick strips are laminated into keels and other long bulky parts, well shifted scarfs ensure full strength with the economy of short timber.

Epoxy The WEST SYSTEM brand (or its equivalent) is ideal for laminating. Added filler (such as colloidal silica) prevents unsightly gaps, and cheaper woods if fault-free will give much the same strength and durability as more costly species when properly resin saturated. If someone is willing to get the nails out, free demolition rafters are tempting! See also Chapter 4.

Bleaching Galvanized fastenings and fittings can cause a purple stain on oak. The acid hardener used with some two-part resin glues has a similar effect. Planing or sanding may remove such stains (and will certainly clear the brown marks from resorcinol glue, which lies on the surface), but if not try a weak aqueous solution of oxalic acid as a bleach.

Fibreglass too This chapter is not exclusively for the wooden boat enthusiast. Most well-finished fibreglass, steel or ferrocement yachts of any size have some curved woodwork in coamings and below decks. If you fit side windows as in Fig 48f, get the car-type rubber sealing strips before laying-up the fibreglass, as there must be a close fit. Admittedly, the following section is pure wooden boat talk, but after that comes oars: does anybody prefer plastic oars to wooden ones?

Knees

Natural grown crooks (Chapter 4) were the traditional material for knees (Fig 50a) and floors—the bigger ones in oak, but often in apple or cherry for smaller ones. Suppliers often advertise in the traditional-boat magazines. Occasionally straight grain is suitable, as in 50b. Laminated knees (50c) are better, but time-consuming to make and not always of correct appearance when varnished.

Simple jigs (50d) cut from thick plywood (or pieces of thin plywood glued together) suffice for laminating most knees. The large holes allow clamps to be fitted. When using such a jig, three or four strips are glued first. When set, these are freed and used as a jig to clamp the remaining strips. The corner chock of matching wood takes little load and may be glued on later. An extra strip or two allows for edge bevels and for juggling the outline template into the best position.

Wipe surplus glue from all laminated parts after clamping to save blunting tools during finishing. Blobs of glue scrape off easily once gelled but before hardening. A disk sander is handy to rough down before planing.

When concealed or painted, knees built up from plywood offcuts glued face to face as in 50e are fine. One can also build up from two bits of straight-grained hardwood jointed together as in 50f with the grain in each part set at right angles. Forged metal knees have been used for centuries, and fabricated webs are a good alternative. See Chapter 9 for further details of shaping and fixing knees, breasthooks and floors.

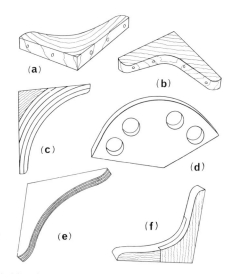

Fig 50 Making knees

Making Oars

Silver spruce is revered for dinghy oars, being so light. Any clear pine will do, and why not make a spare one in case of breakage or loss overboard? Ash or hickory is ideal for the long sweeps and yulohs used by engineless sailboats. Each sweep is normally handled by one person, so the weight is not too critical though the balance and leverage matter.

Spoon-bladed sculls are for smooth water and racing skiffs. For all other purposes, flat-bladed reversible sea oars are better—especially on a dark night. They are also easier to make! Borrow an oar of correct size to serve as a pattern. Typical lengths are 6 ft (180 cm) for 6–8 ft (1.8 m–2.4 m) dinghies; 6 ft 6 in (200 cm) for 10 ft (3 m) boats; 7 ft (215 cm) for 12 ft (3.7 m); 7 ft 6 in (230 cm) for 14 ft (4.3 m) and 8 ft (240 cm) for 16 ft (4.9 m) pulling boats.

Start with square stock for each *loom* or shaft and order this oversize to allow for some warping. Glue a pair of matching blocks at one end to form the blade. With plane, spokeshave and drawknife, shape the blade. Taper the loom, make it octagonal, round it off, and finish with sandpaper over a block of wood hollowed to the correct radius.

Cap the blade tip with 28-gauge sheet copper, held with epoxy glue and a few copper tacks clipped to length. This protects the end against chafe and splitting. Alternatively, use a $\frac{1}{2}$ in (12 mm) wide band of 24-gauge copper right around the blade, set about $\frac{3}{4}$ in (18 mm) back from the tip.

After varnishing, use the oars a little. The rowlocks will make scratches indicating the ideal middle point for the leathers. The procedure for fitting these and their buttons is fully described in *The Compleat Book of Yacht Care*. If you prefer to buy plastic sleeves, make your looms to suit. Leave a slight bulge in way of each sleeve, so that it slips on easily but stays put in the right spot. Tough plastic sleeves and collars from racing blade makers may fit: the plastic 'leathers' are shrunk on with heat.

Using Glues

Waterproof resin glues have proved successful in boats for over 40 years. Research continues, of course, and now we have special epoxies superseding the other resins in many spheres.

The cheapest urea formaldehyde glues perform superbly on most woods. Available as either Cascamite (one-shot) or Aerolite™ (two part) in British hardware stores, they have almost disappeared in America, replaced by epoxies and PVA woodworker's glues. PVA resists moisture but is unreliable for marine use. Resorcinol glue (Aerodux, Weldwood, et al) is dearer, but the best for oily woods such as teak and iroko. Warm water and strong detergent will normally clean the above glues from brushes. For epoxies you need the makers' special solvents, though car-paint thinners containing xylene will do.

The thick epoxies, such as Araldite™ and Polypoxy, have been used in home and factory to bond almost anything, for some 30 years. WEST SYSTEM and related epoxies are intended for well dried wood only, with good penetrating qualities. As well as the amazing gap-filling properties, these resins will bond *to themselves* without loss of strength. No other resin glues can do that. It means that you can dope a piece, let it soak in and harden, then glue it into place, even along the end grain. The thick epoxies are valuable for bonding other materials to fibreglass and ferrocement—teak deck planking for example. Certain epoxy putties will stick in place under water, but they are intended as fillers, not adhesives.

Some resin glues require a syrup to be spread on one piece while a watery hardener goes on the mating piece. This makes for speedy work with mechanical and hand applicators. The syrup may be prepared by mixing a powder with water. Such powder generally has a much longer shelf life than a ready mixed syrup.

After storing for six months or so, some glues can deteriorate, especially when in a partly used container. Glue may look good, but it pays to make a test piece and hammer this to destruction before risking the glue on important joints. For a big epoxy saturation and bonding job one needs the special pumps which dispense the correct quantities of resin and catalyst, at the same time excluding air from the cans. Even then, test when one year or more old. Thorough stirring is essential with all added catalysts.

Jointing

In modern boat building nearly all joints are glued. Most resin glues are sufficiently gap-filling to allow for *slight* humps and hollows in joint faces. Gaps of $\frac{1}{32}$ in (0.8 mm) are easily bridged with filled epoxy, but one should

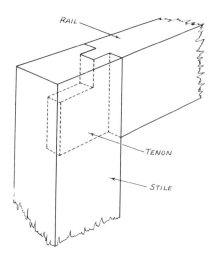

Fig 51 Traditional door joint

remember that glue is expensive and also heavy. Clamping too tightly results in glue starvation at the points of contact, which can lead to weakness. A good fit is always desirable.

The opposing faces of a joint are called *faying* surfaces in boatwork. Without glue, faying surfaces must always be painted. Where wetness could reach, such joints must further be *luted* (smeared) with a good bedding compound or mastic. Information on these substances will be found in this book's two companion volumes.

Strength Although resin glues bond more strongly than the wood itself, narrow joints still need fastenings to prevent splitting alongside the glue line.

To clarify this, consider a panelled door. The joints between stiles and rails (see Fig 51) would fail if resin glued without either dowels or mortises, mainly because such glues are not happy on end grain. When used properly, WEST SYSTEM epoxy bonds perfectly to end grain.

Degrease During manufacture, plywood surfaces are said to become *case hardened* and need conscientious sanding to ensure a good glue bond. If a urea formaldehyde glue must be used on teak, the surfaces must be degreased beforehand as specified by the manufacturer. The process is described for varnishing in *The Compleat Book of Yacht Care*.

Application and Storage

Modern glues are complex chemicals and the maker's instructions need careful study before mixing—especially when an unfamiliar product is to be used. Take care not to contaminate unmixed resin with hardener. A minute amount of the latter can ruin a whole can of resin. A disposable stick or spatula of wood is the best tool for mixing, though a paddle attached to a low-speed electric drill has advantages for large quantities (Fig 148).

For strip-planking with numerous seams, you can apply glue with a felt or rubber coated wheel rotating in a trough of glue. For the large expanses encountered in cold-moulded planking, a mohair roller is ideal.

Get ready The time available for manipulation of a joint after glue spreading is affected by air temperature. Most makers provide details of this—very useful when fixing sheets of plywood, or joints with complicated fastenings. Bore all holes in readiness and remove the burr. Moisture is anathema. Drying surfaces with radiant heaters may suffice for formaldehydes, but with epoxy systems all wood needs to be kept dead dry and the workshop relative humidity below 40% Many craftsmen consider that some makers' suggested minimum temperatures are far too low for perfect results. Avoid using a urea formaldehyde glue below 40°F (4°C). Think around 50°F (10°C) for resorcinol and 60°F (16°C) for epoxy. With an unsuitable workshop, try to glue up certain parts (such as a stem, sawn frame or laminated knee) in the warm house. Remember to bring all parts into the warm several hours before you start gluing.

When gluing in a risky atmosphere, always leave clamps in place for at least twice as long as normal. Avoid stressing such a joint for several days if possible.

Safety Some folk contract dermatitis or other allergies when handling resins and the use of barrier cream and thin gloves is a wise precaution. As hardened resin adheres to skin tenaciously, frequent washing in warm soapy water is advisable. With epoxies, use the special hand-cleansing cream; thinners will damage your skin. After work, lubricate the skin with hand cream, several times. Powdered chalk or talc alleviates sticky skin when the job just cannot be interrupted. Of course, cleaning is much the same for brushes, unless you have a limitless supply of free new ones. Once resin has set, it will probably take force or a paint stripper (Nitromors) to get it off.

The dust from sanding well-set, supposedly inert resins, including epoxy, has been known to cause serious skin and respiratory reactions. This should be prevented by good ventilation, dust-clearing at source, masks and goggles, and long sleeves.

Caulking

Few modern boatbuilders need to acquire the knack of traditional caulking. Its use is restricted almost entirely to carvel plank seams. Even these are often filled with synthetic flexible composition nowadays, and this has long been the norm for those magnificent teak decks.

As detailed in Chapter 11, those types of carvel planking with seam battens, edge-gluing, or splined seams do not need conventional caulking anyway. Strip-planking looks like carvel, even when varnished, yet it has no caulking whatever.

On traditional planking, remember that driven cotton or oakum caulking strengthens a hull and tightens its fastenings, as long as it is not overdone. Modern compositions are little help in that way, though they give when the wood swells and are good sealants. Full details of traditional caulking procedure are to be found in both the previously mentioned companion volumes.

Stopping and Plugging

The many defects commonly found on a new wooden hull, including cracks, nail holes and clamp marks, can be made good with quick-drying hard filler or trowelling cement, available from marine stores. The stopping used over caulked seams is called *paying* and in general this is better if slightly elastic. Fillers are supposed not to shrink on hardening, but if a test shows that this occurs, apply the stuff with a humped surface to allow for shrinkage and still leave a little to sand down.

Plugs Just as planking seams for a varnished finish may be splined with matching wood, countersunk nails, screws and bolt holes may be plugged with dowels of matching wood instead of stopping. These pellets are cut *across* the grain (unlike common carpentry dowels) by means of a plug cutter (Photo 14) which fits into a drill chuck. Having bored closely spaced circles with this tool into the edge or face of a planking offcut, the plugs are freed with a chisel.

One of these may be long enough to fill several holes. It does not take long to set each one in varnish and later chop it off with a sharp chisel. Leave enough proud of the surface to plane down next day. Varnish is better than glue: not only does it cause no discoloration, but it prevents damage to the surrounding wood if removal is ever necessary. Always try to align the grain of a dowel with that of the surrounding wood. This is particularly important for plugs of large diameter.

To withdraw a grain-plug, bore a small hole in the middle and drive in a steel woodscrew. The screw point will bear on the fastening beneath, forcing the plug out.

Ply plugs Cutting the face veneer from plywood offcuts with a fine saw is easy. Then use a sharp wad punch as for veneer plugs. But remember to choose your drill to match the plug size. Test this out before doing any boring.

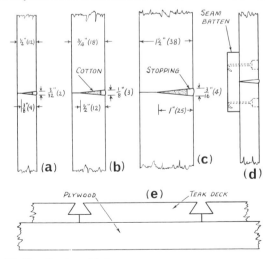

Fig 52 Caulked and false seams

Photo 14 Plug cutter mounted in bench drill

Chapter 7
Tools and Equipment

The range of tools and workshop equipment required for boat building varies enormously according to the type and size of craft. Just a few hand tools will suffice to build a small boat from a kit of parts. To tackle a big deep-sea cruiser requires something approaching a miniature shipyard. In general, fewer hand tools are needed for fibreglass, metal and ferrocement building than for working in wood, though certain power tools and welding equipment may be essential. However, jigs, moulds, mockups, templates, struts and interior work, all in wood, are needed for most projects whatever hull construction is involved.

For small wooden boats, the amateur of modest means with few tools should avoid the temptation to spend money on power tools until all the essential hand tools have been acquired. An electric drill with various attachments can save valuable time; but so can additional hand tools, most of which are comparatively cheap to buy.

Full Lists

The following hand-tool list covers most requirements for building wooden boats of any size, together with their mechanical installations. As few folk are likely to require such a comprehensive array, an asterisk has been placed in front of the items most often needed for wooden boats up to about 18 ft (5.5 m) in length, and for the general woodwork associated with hulls of fibreglass, metal and ferrocement.

Saws

*1 panel saw about 22 in (560 mm) long with 9 teeth per inch (4 per cm)
 1 back saw (tenon saw) about 10 in (250 mm) long with 14 teeth per inch (6 per cm)
*1 coping saw with spare blades
 1 compass saw
 1 keyhole saw or padsaw
 1 10 in (250 mm) hacksaw with spare blades having 24 teeth per in. (10 per cm)
*1 junior hacksaw with spare blades

Planes

 1 jack plane
*1 smoothing plane

 1 rabbet plane with removable nose
 1 circular plane (compass plane)
 1 block plane
*1 spokeshave
 1 drawknife

Chisels

 1 registered chisel $1\frac{1}{4}$ in (31 mm)
*1 bevel-edged firmer chisel $\frac{3}{4}$ in (18 mm)
*1 mortise chisel $\frac{1}{4}$ in (6 mm)
 1 cold chisel about 6 in (150 mm) long with $\frac{5}{8}$ in (16 mm) tip

Screwdrivers

*4 cabinet type with tips to suit screw gauges 6, 8, 10, and 12
*1 electrician's type to fit 3-gauge screws
 3 Phillips type Nos 1, 2 and 3, or similar Pozidrive type
 1 set turnscrew brace bits to fit screw gauges 10, 12, 14 and 16

Drills

*1 carpenter's ratchet brace
 1 expanding bit, $\frac{5}{8}$ in to $1\frac{1}{2}$ in (16 to 38 mm) approximately
*7 Scotch pattern brace bits $\frac{1}{4}$ to $\frac{5}{8}$ in (6 to 16 mm)
 1 countersink rose bit for brace
 1 breast drill with $\frac{1}{2}$ in (13 mm) chuck
 6 twist drills, $\frac{5}{16}$ to $\frac{1}{2}$ in (8 to 13 mm)
*1 hand drill with $\frac{5}{16}$ in (8 mm) chuck
*1 set twist drills, $\frac{1}{16}$ to $\frac{19}{64}$ in (1.5 to 7.5 mm) in increments of $\frac{1}{64}$ in (0.5 mm)
*3 bradawls small, medium and large

Hammers

 1 club hammer $2\frac{1}{2}$ lb (1.1 kg)
*1 claw hammer 20 oz (570 g)
*1 ball-pein hammer 8 oz (230 g)
*1 carpenter's mallet

Punches

 1 pin punch $\frac{5}{16}$ in (8 mm) diameter
*1 pin punch $\frac{1}{4}$ in (6 mm) diameter
*1 nail set $\frac{5}{32}$ in (4 mm) diameter
*1 nail set $\frac{3}{32}$ in (2.5 mm) diameter

1 centre punch
1 set rove punches and dollies if required

Clamps
1 C-clamp or bar clamp 12 in (300 mm)
1 C-clamp or bar clamp 8 in (200 mm)
*2 C-clamps 6 in (150 mm)
*2 C-clamps 4 in (100 mm)
2 sash clamps 24 in (600 m)

Files
*1 hand file 8 in (200 mm) second cut with safe edge
1 half-round file 6 in (150 mm) smooth cut
1 round file 10 in (250 mm) bastard cut
*1 round file 6 in (150 mm) second cut
1 half-round wood rasp 12 in (300 m)
*1 Stanley Junior Shaper

Miscellaneous
saw set, *honing gauge, drill depth gauge, *pliers, pincers, side cutters, tin snips, bolt croppers, *folding rule, steel tape, marking gauge, stubby screwdrivers, marking spike, *adjustable bevel gauge, *try square, dividers, combination drills, plug cutters, *spirit level, cabinet scraper, plumb bob, *oilstone, *putty knife, paint scraper, stillson wrench, pipe grip, full sets of wrenches, gouges, *sanding block, trimming knife, wire brush, bench grinder, *oilcan, *paint brushes, saw sharpening files, straightedge, broom, vacuum cleaner, adze if required, caulking irons and mallet if required.

Tools make good birthday presents. Many handy folk gradually replace cheap tools with good quality ones and extend the range as time goes by. Tools like ratchet and pump-handle screwdrivers can speed work considerably. It all depends on the depth of one's pocket. Good bargains are often found in secondhand tool shops.

Amateurs not fully conversant with the use, care and sharpening of tools should really take a leisure pursuit course first. The all-important safety precautions will then be learnt and many tips on choosing suitable tools to buy. Builders in metal certainly need to be proficient at welding and gas cutting.

Power Tools

Electric drills have been popular for some fifty years and passable ones for light work can be obtained cheaply second-hand. Several old ones often prove handier than a single new one, saving time changing attachments and drill bits. Remember to first check for insulation faults.

Attachments Jigsaw (sabre saw), circular saw and screwdriver attachments especially always need to be mounted and ready for action. A separate thyristor speed controller is valuable when such a device is not already built into the trigger. For fibreglass work you really need diamond or tungsten carbide tipped saw blades and router cutters. Because of the high speed, the router is not a regular drill attachment device, but even a cheap router unit is a superb power tool to have for serious joinery or medium and big size boat building. A bench stand is one of the first attachments one should get for an electric drill—ideal for boring fast, accurate holes through wood or metal, and for cutting mortises dead true.

In addition For big wooden boats, several other power tools will help to make light work, particularly a bandsaw, circular or table saw, belt sander, overhand planer, and perhaps an electric chainsaw with ripping teeth. Although the bulkier machines are often available second-hand, few amateurs have to space them, so the equivalent portable tools must suffice.

Home-made Tools

Making edged tools, extra long drill bits and screwdrivers involves tempering the steel, described in *The Compleat Book of Yacht Care*.

One never seems to have enough clamps, but crude ones are easy to make from scraps of wood and some bolts. A steel sash clamp is expensive, so why not use cheap clamp heads pinned to a batten as in Fig 53a? Alternatives to C-clamps can be made from offcuts of plywood (53b). If all your plywood is thin, several pieces glued together will do. Several examples can be made with varying reaches and mouth openings. A single wedge suits some work, while folding wedges (53b) suit heavy clamping.

The type shown in Fig 53c can be adjusted to any desired opening, with a range of bolt lengths kept handy. With legs of tough hardwood, this type can have a longer reach than any commercial bar clamp. The crudest ones merely have a piece of leather strap or webbing tacked across the end.

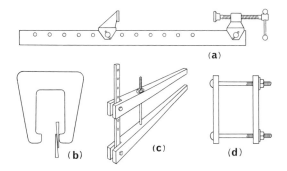

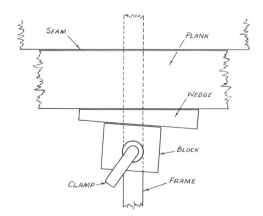

Fig 53 Home-made clamps

Fig 54 Tightening a plank seam

Gripes (see Fig 98 and Photo 37) for lapstrake and strip-planking are made to measure for a certain thickness.

The simple clamp shown in Fig 53d is ideal when gluing hollow masts and spars. Numerous clamps are needed for this job. As they are unlikely to be of use in the future, try to borrow the necessary bolts for a few days.

When laying carvel planks or decking, close the seams before fastening with the system shown in Fig 54, again making use of a wedge. Other improvised devices for clamping include cordage or wire in the form of a Spanish windlass.

Although C-clamps (or G-clamps) are popular and handy, the commercial alternatives, including veneer, joiner's, bar and ratchet clamps, are sometimes better. With all these, remember to keep ready a supply of small plywood offcuts to prevent denting wood surfaces.

The Workshop

The most important piece of workshop furniture is the bench. A boatbuilder's bench should be long, at least half the length of the boat under construction. It need be no wider than about 18 in (450 mm), but if free-standing additional width creates greater rigidity. A small fold-up bench with built-in clamp is most useful to place near a job or even right inside a big boat. A tall worker needs a high bench, but a good average height is 30 in (750 mm). You must have an adjustable bench stop near the left end (if you are right-handed), set about 4 in (100 mm) in from the front edge. This prevents wood from sliding while being hand planed.

A carpenter's vise with wood-lined jaws is best near the left end. It must not protrude above bench level. To enable the edge of a long plank to be planed, be sure to

have an adjustable (but removable) rest fitted to a bench leg towards the right-hand end. A large fitter's vise at the right is invaluable for woodwork as well as metal, but make sure its bolts have butterfly nuts so that you can remove this obstacle in a few seconds.

Your bench can be fixed against the wall or be made free-standing on well-braced legs of wood at least 3 × 3 in (75 × 75 mm) in section. Use full-length boards about 2 in (50 mm) thick. Although drawers are easy to fit underneath (to house planes, drills and other small tools unsuitable for rack mounting), remember that drawers become inaccessible when a plank is clamped across the front of the bench.

A bench hook (Fig 55) is readily made and is of great value when cross-cutting battens, especially when you have no fitter's vise. A wooden tool rack with slots and pegs is simply screwed to the wall. The plastic-coated steel clips stocked by hardware stores are more convenient, but they need to be fixed to plywood or chipboard panels.

Several other items are interesting handicraft exercises. Sawing trestles are almost indispensible and should be about 22 in (560 mm) high. Two trestles will answer most purposes, but four prove ideal when sawing full

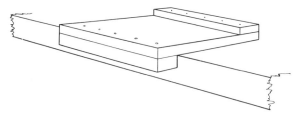

Fig 55 Bench hook

sheets of plywood. The fixed-leg type (Photo 15) is the quickest to make, but folding trestles are more convenient in the confines of a small workshop.

There never seems to be enough shelving or locker space: time spent making these is soon saved later by avoiding the searches for cans, tools and boxes. Clear labels also help to avoid delays.

Good lighting and heating are essential for winter work in high latitudes. Fluorescent tubes mounted on narrow boards are fine for either suspending overhead, fitting to stands, or resting on the floor. The dryness of electrical heating (and the absence of fumes) makes it superior to many other methods. Electrical blown hot air or radiant heat may be directed towards glued joints. A few lamps under a polythene tent will raise the temperature considerably in a big barn.

Wet Heat

For traditional wooden boat building, a steaming box or steam jenny is an essential piece of home-made equipment. Mount it in the open air if possible. Its size depends very much on the type of boat being built.

The small bent ribs for lapstrake dinghies are normally boiled in water rather than steamed. The apparatus used is simple to contrive, often as in Fig 56a, from a length of 3 in (75 mm) steel pipe with an elbow and short leg at the lower end. This end is plugged with mortar, in the absence of a proper screwed cap.

A slope of about 30° is best for such a pipe. Fill it with water and heat the elbow with a wood fire or blowtorch. Oak ribs $\frac{3}{8}$ in (9 mm) thick require about 15 minutes' boiling to become supple, while for $\frac{1}{2}$ in (12 mm) allow 20 minutes. Reckon on 25 for $\frac{5}{8}$ in (16 mm) ribs, and 1 hour per inch of thickness for bigger ones.

Steaming box Not all carvel and clinker planks have to be steamed. Those that do, need it mainly at one end for about one-quarter of the plank length. A box of big section enables one to re-steam a plank end when it seemed unwise to clamp it all the way after one steaming. As some planks are sawn with curvature (as in Fig 99) you might need a steaming box wide enough to take them or indeed one wide enough for a plywood panel!

Rigidity of the box is ensured if the sides are robust, as in Fig 56b. With insufficient plywood for top and bottom, beg some offcuts of thin board from a joinery works and seal the joints with tarred paper or caulking. Although

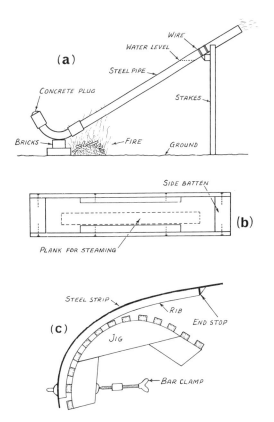

Fig 56 Steam-bending equipment

mounting some 30 in (750 mm) high on legs or trestles is convenient, flat on the ground will do for occasional use. Battens nailed to top and bottom inside at intervals of about 18 in (450 mm) help steam to circulate around a plank. Rag stuffed in the open end keeps the steam hot. The far end can be removable in case the middle of a long piece needs steaming.

Steam raising There is little pressure. A 5 gallon or 20 litre oil drum makes a good pot boiler, bunged at the top with a cork having a hose spigot of $\frac{1}{2}$ in (12 mm) copper pipe through it. A bottled gas ring makes the best heat source. With the boiler half full you will get about $1\frac{1}{2}$ hours of steam. Normally, a $\frac{1}{2}$ in (12 mm) pine plank needs a maximum of 40 minutes' steaming; $\frac{3}{4}$ in (18 mm) about 70 minutes; 1 in (25 mm) about $1\frac{1}{2}$ hours; and $2\frac{1}{4}$ in (38 mm) say $2\frac{1}{4}$ hours.

It pays to soak wood in cold water well before steaming. The heat really does the work, but soaking helps to get this into the core. However, prolonged wetting does entail later shrinkage, so allow for that. Some softening occurs if thin planking or plywood is covered with rag and subjected to a slow stream of boiling water for about 10 minutes. A steam lance as used for stripping wallpaper can be applied on the job as the clamps are tightened. After clamping overnight, further steaming and tightening is possible next day.

Bending Hints

Get steamed parts rapidly into place and clamped. Draping with hot, wet rags helps retain the heat. Being thin, dinghy ribs soon stiffen, so bend them to a bow-shape and tie the tops across with cord before lowering them into the boat. On planks, keep the clamps on for about nine hours and delay driving fastenings until then. In the case of thin ribs, drive a few nails, without the need for pilot holes, while the wood is hot. This eliminates clamping, but the roves must not be put on until the next day. Sharpen each nail beforehand with a few quick file strokes. Pilot holes will be necessary once the wood is hard.

If a piece cannot be clamped quickly after steaming, use a bending jig as in Photo 13 and install the part later. Packing pieces will ensure the bend is correct and side clamps will take care of any edge bend. If possible, verify the optimum steaming time on a trial piece to avoid breaking a long and important part. To allow for spring-back when clamps are removed, exaggerate the curvature on a jig slightly. Over-bending is usually quite easy to pull out: not so the other way. A backing strip of $\frac{1}{8}$ in (3 mm) mild steel arranged as in Fig 56c will reduce the risk of breakages enormously on sharp bends. Hammer the strip straight afterwards ready for future use.

When numerous heavy ribs are to be bent over the same jig, you can remove each one and free the jig after ten minutes, provided two *stay laths* are nailed on, one from tip to tip and one further down, to retain the shape.

No heat As described in Chapter 6, lamination, although time-consuming, makes an alternative to steam-bending for most parts, and is generally stronger than similar bent solid stock.

Care of Tools

Handling and maintenance instructions for wood and metal working tools are available from handicraft books and makers' literature. For the finer points, go to classes

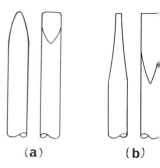

Fig 57 The all-important screwdriver tip

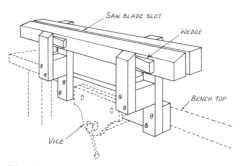

Fig 58 A saw sharpening clamp

or chat to craftsmen. The following points are especially relevant to boat building.

Avoid using screwdrivers as punches and for opening cans. The tips soon get rounded (Fig 57a). Grind them with long tapers, preferably hollowed in the larger sizes (Fig 57b), and ensure that the tips are square in both directions.

Using a blunt hand saw is exasperating. Teeth are bound to get damaged occasionally by careless handling. By all means pay a saw doctor to carry out re-gulleting or straightening, but the average sharpening job takes only about fifteen minutes. You must clamp the blade close to the teeth before filing. A simple saw clamp (Fig 58) is very easy to make.

Planes A wood plane will not always function perfectly after sharpening if the cap iron (backing iron or chip breaker) is not set at the correct distance from the cutting edge to suit the type of wood being planed. For softwoods, this gap can be as much as $\frac{1}{16}$ in (1.5 mm), but for hardwoods it must be less than $\frac{1}{32}$ in (0.8 mm). Many hardwoods have interlocking grain, parts of which tend to roughen when planed along the grain in either direction. To counteract this, set the cap iron within $\frac{1}{64}$ in (0.4 mm) from the edge, plane at an angle of about 20° to the grain, use heavy downward pressure, and keep smearing the plane base with a little boiled linseed oil. Grind and hone the blade edge with a slight forward-facing bulge in the middle and round off the two corners.

A plane always leaves small marks and furrows: on joinery these must be removed with a cabinet scraper or belt sander. Keep planes lying on their sides when not in use to avoid grit damage to the razor-sharp blades—but turn the blades away from you in case your knuckles accidentally touch them.

Safety Precautions

With wood, sweep the floor often, as shavings are a fire risk. Smokers are the main danger, but floor-level heaters or an inspection lamp left unattended are almost as bad. Sawdust is now recognized as a health risk, and commercial workshops are required to capture it at the machine and have air filtering. Very fine dust, e.g. from sanders, can burn explosively and be set off by a spark.

Ground it Electrical extension cables are often too thin for heater supply or power tools. Overheating occurs most rapidly when cables are left partly coiled. Make sure all equipment is grounded or earthed. Preferably have earth leakage contact breakers at all outlets, especially if your voltage is higher than 120. Floors and cabling should be kept dry.

Blade hazards Edged hand tools are responsible for most injuries, especially wood chisels. Unless stored in fitted boxes, such tools should be wrapped in canvas or equipped with protective caps. In use, never let your fingers get in front of the cutting edge, and never use your fingers to dislodge shavings jammed in plane blade slots. Power saws and planers are fairly safe as long as the operator thinks continuously of the possible dangers when using them.

Old-time shipwrights used the adze (Fig 59 and Photo 15) with great precision and speed. Some preferred the lipped adze, gouge adze, or broad axe—tools which are almost impossible to buy nowadays. If you do get to hew heavy timber with an adze, you will come to no harm provided you always carefully remove any shaving which gets impaled on the cutting edge. This could cause the tool to jump off the work and strike your leg.

Hazards with hand saws are mainly when starting a cut (using one's thumb to guide the blade): too hard a push can splinter the wood, making the saw jump sideways. Saws left hanging from nails are dangerous without tooth protectors. Preferably, stow them away well wrapped in oily rag.

Exercises If previously inexperienced, practise using your tools by starting with the workbench, trestles, lockers—and then the smaller units for the boat, such as rudder, drop keel, hatch, table and tiller.

Wood again Various tools applicable to plastics, metal and ferrocement construction are mentioned in the later chapters on these topics. The amateur working in these materials, or completing a factory-built bare hull, will find that he needs to use wood and woodworking tools surprisingly often.

Fig 59 Adze blade and part of handle

Photo 15 Using the adze

Chapter 8
Chine Boats

As mentioned in Chapter 1, the simplicity of some chine designs makes them popular with beginners to boat building. As it happens, this shape is perfect for high-speed powerboats, and is also widely used for small sport-boats (Fig 60), racing dinghies (Photo 19), launches—and sailing cruisers both smaller and bigger than the one in Photo 1.

Well-designed single chine and multichine boats need not look too boxy. *Conic sections* enable plywood to curve a little in both directions, though bluff bows may result which are not suitable for some powerboats. The classic Chris-Craft type runabout (Fig 60a and Photo 16) had attractive concave *flare* to the topsides for'ard and convex *tumblehome* aft, but this was done (and still is) with thin carvel planking, not plywood.

If the amateur is not concerned about pretty curves, he or she will find plywood planking simple and quick. The plywood GP14 racing dinghy (Photo 19) designed by Jack Holt can be built in 400 manhours. The classic Kingfisher 18 ft (5.5 m) carvel runabout, although bigger, takes over 900 hours. Both are fully framed. The type of speedboat shown in Fig 60b must be of light weight and would normally be of frameless plywood.

The 30 ft (9.1 m) Waterwitch auxiliary sailing cruiser (Photo 1) designed by Maurice Griffiths, another fully framed, single chine example, takes some 3000 manhours. The plans show optional plywood or carvel planking. Although of shoal draft, these boats cruise worldwide. A fully framed, robustly-planked craft is more satisfying in mid-ocean than a frameless plywood shell, though the latter construction has proved itself in certain deep-sea catamarans and trimarans when well constructed.

Except for very small boats, single chine framing consists of some sort of keel, a stem, sawn or laminated frames, the two chines, plus the items that even frameless or round bilge wooden boats need: gunwales or beam shelves, stringers, sternpost or transom (see Figs 5–8).

Erecting

Chine boats up to about 18 ft (5.5 m) long are usually built upside down, either on stocks (Photo 16) or with frame extensions (Fig 2) which are eventually sawn off at deck level. Bigger boats are erected right way up, partly because otherwise one's arms are not long enough to reach across to the keel without scaffolding and partly because rolling over after planking could be very difficult.

In the upright position all frames must be strutted from the shed roof. In a tall shed, or in the open air, a central beam or *strongback* must be devised to take the struts. To further ensure that working space beneath the boat is left clear, a solid keel must be supported on poppets, perhaps high enough to enable keel bolts to be inserted from underneath.

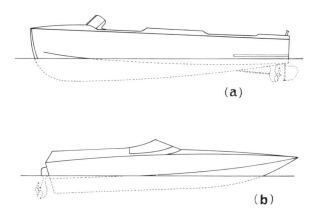

(a)

(b)

Fig 60 Classic runabout and modern ski-boat

Photo 16 Classic runabout in frame

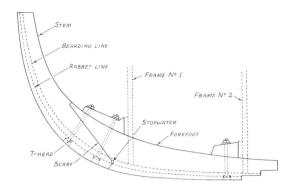

Fig 61 Two-part wooden stem

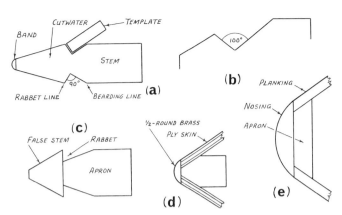

Fig 62 Small-boat stem construction

Instead of a solid keel sawn to shape, some craft comprise two or more strips bent to a curve and laminated together, perhaps with a central fin keel added later. Such strips are mounted on top of a thick plank on edge known as the *building board*, using temporary fastenings.

Backbone

As will be explained later, erection methods similar to the above are also used for round-section wooden boats and for some craft in metal and ferrocement. A complex backbone as in Fig 4 could be applicable to big chine boats as well as for round-bilge types. Having laid down your lines and made patterns, your next move would be to assemble such a backbone as in Photo 7 and erect it plumb on poppets (see Chapter 10).

The stem Most stems are far simpler than the one in Fig 4. That for the Kingfisher runabout (Fig 61) is typical for robustly built chine boats. A single grown oak crook could be used, but as the thickness is only $1\frac{3}{4}$ in (44 mm) it might warp badly after shaping. Also, it would need luck to find a suitably shaped, seasoned piece of wood to use. Using two pieces of straight-grained hardwood scarfed together ensures a sound job. The lower part is called the *forefoot*.

There are other ways. You could laminate the stem from $1\frac{3}{4} \times \frac{1}{4}$ in (44 × 6 mm) strips, or glue seven pieces of $\frac{1}{4}$ in (6 mm) plywood face to face. A number of short flat boards may be glued face to face provided all the butt joints are well staggered. For the Waterwitch, plywood side cheeks are bonded to a core of straight-grained wood.

Work is sometimes simpler if the cutwater (Fig 62a) is screwed on as a separate nosing (62c) after planking. The inner stem (correctly called the *apron*) merely requires bevels each side to receive the planking, and you do not need special T-head bolts for the scarf. The GP14 stem is pictured in Fig 62d. Some chine dinghies and launches adopt a straight apron made from a single athwartship board (62e) to which a broad nosing is later added. With a curved apron, the false stem needs shaping to fit closely. Laminating *in situ* is possible, but prefabrication over a jig is quicker and uses fewer fastenings.

Almost any stem needs a pattern of hardboard, thick paper or good cardboard. For the Fig 61 stem, mark the scarf position on each piece of wood by laying the pattern on top and pricking through the salient points. Resist marking the stem outline until the scarf is cut: whittling away first to get a perfect scarf fit is sure to be necessary.

Stopwaters Further information about scarfs is given in Chapter 4, but the purpose of the *stopwater* shown in Fig 61 needs explanation. This is a pine dowel driven into a hole bored diametrically on the scarf line within the confines of the planking rabbet. If any water tries to leak via the scarf, the dowel swells and checks it from travelling further in. A stopwater is especially useful as a boat gets old, or when the adjacent wood shrinks. A glued scarf should not need one, but it may be wise, just in case! In traditional work, where all scarfs are luted (doped) with paint or mastic, stopwaters are used to seal off deck water—where deck seams run under a pilot-house, or on covering boards—as well as for underwater scarfs in keel, deadwood and stem.

To make a stopwater, choose an ample length of clear, close-grained very dry pine, saw to a square section $\frac{1}{16}$ in (1.5 mm) oversize, chisel into an octagon, then bash it through an exact hole bored in a piece of $\frac{1}{4}$ in (6 mm) mild steel. If required, sand it to a comfortable driving fit. Set the end grain at 90° to the scarf line and drive home. Saw and chisel both ends flush with the rabbet.

Stem Rabbets

The nautical term for rebate is *rabbet*. Most backbone members have a rabbet of varying angle running along each side to house the planking edges. The position of a stem rabbet is indicated on the drawings. This is transferred to the pattern as in Chapter 3. Two lines show the width of the rabbet: the outer one is the *rabbet line* while the inner one is called the *bearding line* (Fig 61).

To set out these lines, tack the pattern to the stem and pierce through with thin wire nails at about 3 in (75 mm) intervals. Keep the nails square and true because to mark the opposite side of the stem you must drive the wire nails through the same holes from the other side of the pattern. This is why a stem pattern should be no thicker than hardboard. Offcuts of planking cleated together would make setting out most troublesome.

Bore for the stopwater before chopping out the rabbets. Make a little template as shown in Fig 62a, the same thickness as the planking (whether plywood or solid wood) and about 1 in (25 mm) wide. First chisel a series of notches about 4 in (100 mm) apart, each notch just wide enough to get the template in. The depth is right when the template will just nestle in flush. Then chisel away the remainder from notch to notch until you have a continuous rabbet, and the template sinks flush everywhere.

Although the angle inside a rabbet is nominally 90°, plank fitting is simplified if you shift the rabbet line outwards a fraction to produce an angle of about 100°, as in Fig 62b. If the planking is to be caulked this will form part of the caulking Vee. Plywood planking is likely to be glued, so the plywood edge would need a slight bevel to make a tight joint.

The leading edge of a stem is normally tapered down into a *cutwater* as shown in Fig 62a. Rough this out on the bench, leaving a little to clean off flush with the planking later. The narrow edge should be protected with *cope*—bronze or stainless steel of half-round or half-oval section. Cope can be as narrow is $\frac{5}{16}$ in (8 mm) on racing boats. Big craft sometimes use heavy flat-section bronze or galvanized steel. Always bend cope to fit before boring for the countersunk screws that hold it on; otherwise you will get kinks.

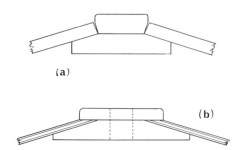

Fig 63 Light keel systems

Bent Keel

With pounding, beaching, trailing and craning, any boat except a canoe needs at least a token keel. The simplest form appears in Fig 63a, drawn in the inverted position as when bent across the erected frames. The wide inner piece is called the *hog*, sometimes the *keel batten*. The other piece is the *outer keel*. The planking rabbet is formed by simple bevels on each member. The arrangement for the GP14 is shown in Fig 63b. The dotted lines indicate the drop keel slot. The outer keel is not fitted until completion of the plywood planking. Marking out and shaping these parts is similar to the procedure given later for the chines.

Looking at Fig 61 you will see two notches below the aft end of the forefoot. One of these receives the hog, the other receives the outer keel.

Sawn Frames

Much work goes into the making of the frames for a chine boat, but they are readily assembled in a small space, perhaps before a place big enough to house the whole boat has been found.

Each frame consists of four short pieces called *futtocks*, two representing the Vee-bottom and two for the port and starboard topsides, joined together by triangular *gussets* at the chines (see Fig 2) and a similar *floor* at the keel.

You could save time by making each frame in one piece, cut from a sheet of plywood. Far less wastage occurs if you just cut one half this way and join the two halves together with a floor. But you cannot drive screws or nails into plywood edges when planking: only epoxy resin saturation would do. Note also that cross-chiselling notches (Fig 115) would be hard. Excellent frames in single units or half units result by laminating thin strips on a jig (Photo 18). Their desirability must be weighed against the higher cost and longer time involved. Straight-grained hardwood such as oak or mahogany is normally fine for chine futtocks, though natural crooks if available might be better on a classic runabout with curvaceous topsides.

Gussets and Floors

When using solid wood for gussets and floors, set the grain parallel to the hypotenuse of each triangle. Marine plywood makes the best gussets, especially when glued to both sides of the futtocks. For extra neatness and strength, glue a filler chock between a pair of gussets (Fig 64). Frames glued to stout bulkheads or a transom may not need gussets. However, floors are useful for attaching a frame to the hog, and for stiffening the whole bottom against twisting and flexing. Extra heavy floors are needed on many cruising boats to receive the ballast keel bolts. There may even be an additional floor knee between each frame. Good plans always show these details.

As seen in Photo 17, the GP14 dinghy has no gussets at all. The bottom futtocks are in one piece right across the hog, secured there with glue and screws. The side futtocks are attached to the bottom piece with flush halved joints, glued and nailed. Without the aid of a table saw or router, these halved joints need the jig shown in Fig 65. Make saw cuts across, just kissing the guide strips. Pare down to the bottom of the saw cuts with a chisel and finish off most of it with a plane.

Photo 17 Ready for planking the GP14 sailing dinghy

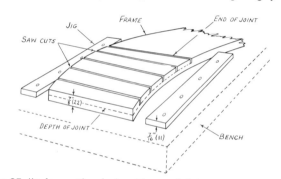

Fig 65 Jig for cutting halved frame joints

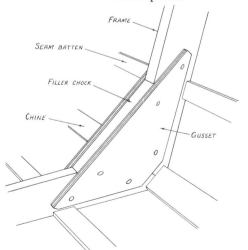

Fig 64 Double gussets with filler chock

Photo 18 Laminated frames including deck beams

As there is very little angle at the chine joints on the foremost frames of some designs, you can make their bottom and topside futtocks as single pieces, attached to the sides of the stem or to floor knees notched across the stem. This method is shown for Frames 1, 2 and 3 on the Waterwitch plans.

Frame Edges

As explained in Chapter 3, most frames have edge bevels to mate up snugly with the planking. Beginners are tempted to plane these off just before planking starts. However, if most of the angle is applied when sawing out the futtocks (on a canting table bandsaw if you are lucky) many hours of working time will be saved.

A springy batten laid fore and aft across three or more frames will reveal at a glance how much the edge bevel needs adjusting. To avoid leaving dirt traps, bevel the gussets as well as the frame edges. The alternative would be to set the gussets well inboard, as in Fig 64. Vertical fairing-in (Photo 17) is also necessary to check the bevels on keel, chines and stringers. Right for'ard the slight double curvature demands a very bendy batten.

Notches for hog, chines, gunwales and stringers should be rough bevelled on the bench, and the *limber holes* must not be forgotten. These lie close to the hog (Fig 2) to allow bilge-water to pass under each frame and floor knee. If you make these extensions of the hog notch, remember to mark the centreline on each frame to assist in aligning the hog.

Make sure you mark the for'ard face of each futtock before applying bevels on the bench. Much valuable wood has been wasted by making pairs of futtocks identical instead of mirror images of each other.

Frame Assembly

Traditionally, single gussets are fixed to the for'ard frame faces. If you wish to avoid having to bevel them as above, set them to face amidships instead.

Aligning Start frame assembly by gluing and pinning one chine gusset into place. Check with the pattern that the angle is dead right, then bore and drive permanent ring nails. Be certain that no fastening will foul the frame edge bevel. To set the opposite gusset, align that pair back-to-back over the first pair. This automatically puts a single gusset on the correct side to make a handed pair.

A floor knee is attached in similar fashion to the above, but the usual half-pattern is not much good, so accuracy is achieved by a measurement check from sheer mark to sheer mark. Take this distance from the table of offsets, but remember to deduct the planking thickness allowance and, if edge bevels have been cut, measure to the bigger face.

Before handling a frame, stabilize it with a *cross spall* or beam tie screwed temporarily across the free ends, as shown for a mould in Fig 3. Set cross spalls accurately when used for erecting frames on stocks (Photo 16). Once a frame is attached to a full bulkhead or transom, or a deck beam is fitted, the cross spall becomes redundant. Note that when frames are to be erected upside down, if each cross spall is fitted on the opposite face to the floor, a plumb line will have a clear run. Once a big boat has been set up as in Photo 2, all cross spalls may be removed.

Frameless Hulls

As mentioned in Chapter 1, a frameless boat has conventional stem, keel, chine and transom members, but no permanent frames. The hull-skin must be of plywood, edge-glued strip-planking, or cold-moulded, with additional stiffness imparted by structural bulkheads plus fore-and-aft stringers glued inside the planking. The same system is applicable to a round-bilge shape, without chines. Nowadays, many more small wooden chine boats are frameless than fully framed. Except for the smallest rowboats, double chine or multi-chine is more popular than single chine. Without an array of frames to clean and paint, frameless boats simplify maintenance work. Their light weight simplifies launching and means that trailer/sailer dayboats and cruisers in wood are no more difficult to handle than their fibreglass counterparts.

For kit boats and certain class racing dinghies, one can hire a self-supporting jig. This is notched to receive stem, transom, keel, chines and stringers. After planking, the complete shell is lifted off the jig.

For a one-off job, widely-spaced moulds or bulkheads are set up in similar style to a jig. All much easier than with frames, as moulds normally need no edge bevels. (See the next chapter for further details.) Remember that chines and stringers will prevent the final shell from lifting off unless the mould notches are shaped as in Fig 73. Alternatively, use woodscrews to assemble the moulds so you can dismantle them easily. Naturally, any bulkheads remain fixed inside the hull at lift off.

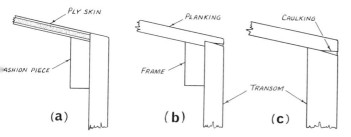

Fig 66 Hood ends at transom

Transoms

As most transoms are raked aft at the deck, they cannot be set up vertical with a plumb line like the frames. The angle is not critical, but a suitable measurement will be on the plans. The Kingfisher runabout transom, for example, is a normal frame planked over. The GP14 transom is a single-width mahogany board with *fashion pieces* (like futtocks) glued to it, set in to form planking rabbets. Note that a frame, or the fashion pieces, must be edge-bevelled before fitting to the transom.

Plywood edges must always be fully housed as in Fig 66a to protect them. Carvel planking may be half-rabbeted (66b), or caulked (66c) as in traditional clinker and carvel work. This corner is prone to damage and protection with stainless steel or bronze angle is never a bad idea.

Some attractive transoms are curved in plan. The athwartships fashion pieces for these are either sawn to shape, steamed, or laminated. Although simple chine boats have transom sterns, you may encounter designs with canoe sterns (Norwegian or double-ender types), or even overhanging counters as in Fig 89. Similarly, chine pram dinghies have small transoms at their bows (Photo 21) in lieu of stems.

Over-powerful outboard motors are popular. Make sure your transom is sufficiently well reinforced to resist the great thrust and torque of such machines. With the transom top cut away to give an outboard propeller good submersion, substantial knees, as in Fig 82, are sure to be advisable. The owner of a small sailboat who is averse to having a transom-mounted motor may wish to install a suitable *well* under the cockpit floor. Unless robustly built, this needs a clamping bearer right across the boat. To reduce turbulence when sailing, a flush bottom panel (removable from inside) is ideal. If the motor is completely encased to combat fumes, do not forget that motors need an air supply!

On the Stocks

For an inverted frame set up without the luxury of extended legs as in Photo 17, nothing is simpler than a pair of 2×6 in (50×150 mm) straight pine balks the length of the boat as in Photo 16. With a curved sheerline the cross spalls are just screwed to little spurs of varying height attached to the inside or outside of the balks.

On an earth floor you drive stakes to support the stocks. On a concrete floor, gluing down wooden pads with epoxy saves boring for anchor bolts or woodscrew plugs. Alternatively, the assembly may be braced like a free-standing table.

For extended frame legs, snap a chalk line as described for lofting and plumb each frame centre above it. Athwartships lines are then set out at the exact locations of the frames. For the centreline between stocks, use a taut wire. For a Photo 2 setup, transfer the station lines onto the backbone and also extend them upwards to the strongback. Much of this setting-up technique applies equally to making a fibreglass plug, or a hull of ferro-cement or steel.

Frame Alignment

The closer together frames or moulds are, the greater the accuracy required when setting them. Otherwise, to avoid a wavy hull surface excessive shaving down and gluing on patches will arise when fairing in.

With the edge bevels already mentioned, most frames have one face wider than the other. The *bigger* one must lie dead on the station line. The exaggerated sketch in Fig 69a clarifies this. Should it happen that on one frame the topside bevel slopes in the opposite direction to that on the bottom futtock, the severest bevel wins. If in doubt, set such a frame centrally on its station, as shown at the point of widest beam.

To avoid having to bevel temporary moulds in frameless construction, set them in exactly the opposite manner to frames, as in 69b. The planking will then kiss each mould only at the station line.

Until you finish attaching hog and chines, newly erected frames are wobbly. To set them rigidly plumb, tack or clamp temporary battens (*ribbands*) along both topsides and bottom.

Look ahead When your boat is in frame, give thought to such jobs as marking out bulkheads, sole bearers, engine bearers, or boring for the propeller shaft—all far easier now than after planking.

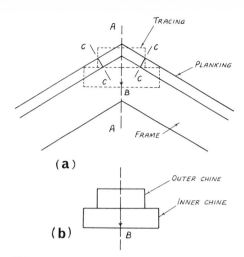

(a)

(b)

Fig 67 Chine knuckle diagrams

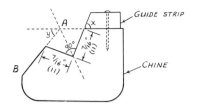

Fig 68 Setting out a bone piece notch

Shaping Hog and Chines

It pays to make separate little full-size drawings of keel and chine knuckles, as the notch depths and rabbet angles can vary quite a lot, especially where the frames have great bevel. A bit of geometry is involved, but Fig 67a makes it clearer. Draw the mitre line A–A, then add the futtocks and planking.

Get some tracing paper and draw on it the hog and keel (or the chine members, as appropriate) assembled together but unshaped, as shown in Fig 67b. Add the centreline B–B and superimpose this tracing on top of the other drawing, as shown dotted in 67a. Keeping B–B in line with A–A, shift the tracing and you will find there is just one position where lines C–C representing the plank edges fit exactly between the sides and base of the outer keel or chine. Prick through the eight salient points marking the frame notch and planking rabbets. Repeat the whole operation for all knuckles which differ.

Keels and chines are usually tapered slightly in thickness and width towards the stem. Shape them accordingly and mark which is which. Pencil the station lines across all of them, then use dividers to transfer the rabbet bevels to them from the little knuckle drawings. Clamp on a thin batten and pencil in the four lines along each member, joining up the divider marks.

Rip with a saw, then finish with a plane. Leave a good shaving more to plane flush with the frames after assembling the hog and inner chines on the boat. Bevel surfaces must be dead flat. To ensure this, tilt the plane to 45° while resting athwart the bevel. Squint under the plane towards the light and any high spot will instantly reveal

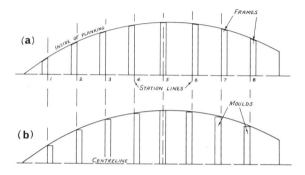

Fig 69 Station line positions at frames and moulds

itself. Scribble with a pencil over the surface. Each plane stroke will erase some of this and show if you are attacking the right spot!

All this bench work saves a lot of time in the end. It also thins down the wood, making it lighter and easier to bend. These members on the Waterwitch are often laminated *in situ* to save steaming, but this means that all shaping must be done on the boat.

Bone Pieces

The GP14 chines are quite different from the above, with certain advantages. There is no rabbet. The plywood planking panels are planed flush with the 90° notch (Fig 68). To finish off, a square sectioned *bone piece* is glued into the notch and then rounded off.

Referring to Fig 68, set out bevel A–B from the frame patterns and shape this on the bench. To rout the 90° notch with a rabbet plane, tack on a guide strip with bevelled edge as shown. Angle y is almost constant from transom to Frame 3, then reducing towards Frame 1 and becoming zero at the stem. When shaping the guide strip, note that angle x always equals half angle y plus 45°.

These chines have well-rounded corners where they fit into the frame notches. Before using saw and chisel to cut a notch, bore a big hole to form a neatly radiused corner—but do remember to aim the drill to follow the frame edge bevel angle.

Conventional frame notches are cut as in Fig 115 when no router is available. Chop along the base with chisel and mallet, working from both sides to avoid splintering. In difficult wood, make more saw cuts. You need a close fit, so keep a stringer offcut as a test piece. Use a wood rasp to enlarge a notch slightly. Mark out a notch on both frame faces (automatically picking up the edge bevel) and make sure that the saw is held parallel to the bevel.

Hog Hazards

If a hog will not bend readily, always steam the stiffest section to avoid distorting the frames. Most will bend cold provided you fix the stem end first. A single length hog bends most easily, so scarf it first if your stock is not long enough. Try to avoid a butt-block joint: this may prevent fair bending and often looks unsightly.

The only tricky bit with a hog is the join with the stem or forefoot. The rabbet bevels on the hog must merge exactly into the stem rabbet. This transition for the GP14 is sketched in Fig 70. Fitting is simplified because the stem has no rabbet, just a bevel, the plywood edges being finally covered with a wide stem band. The position of the outer keel is obvious in the sketch. After fitting it and planing down, you should not be able to detect where the keel ends and the stem starts.

Before fixing a hog permanently, scribe all frame positions on it, take it off, bore the screw holes and clear any burr, put it back, bore the pilot holes, take it off again, glue only the faying surfaces, screw home and wipe away surplus glue. Remember to keep all fastenings clear of the propeller shaft, both for the outer keel and hog.

After the hog and before the outer keel, fit the inner chines to stiffen the assembly. Put these on as a pair in every stage, to avoid any frame distortion.

Drop keel The slot for a drop keel is best cut through a hog after the latter is in place on the frames. This lessens the likelihood of an unfair bend.

Bore a hole at each end of the slot, in diameter equal to the slot width. This produces neatly rounded ends. Bore a line of such holes close together near one end, then with padsaw and chisel, cut out sufficient slot to allow a hand saw to be used for the remainder. A sabre saw or jigsaw will do, but most of these are reluctant to cut dead vertical

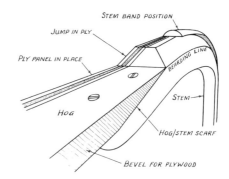

Fig 70 The stem-to-hog joint

through wood thicker than about $\frac{3}{4}$ in (18 mm).

The outer keel will always bend true, with sufficient fastenings. Fit this temporarily, scribe the slot outline through the hog, then remove the keel and cut its slot on the bench. Installing a drop keel casing is easier to do before a boat is planked up. Refer to Chapter 10 for further details.

Fitting Chines

Except for the stem joint, inner chines are fitted, joined and faired off in similar manner to a hog. Some bend without steaming, but twist a lot towards the stem. The Fig 68 type is stiff, but has little twist. To impart twist, clap on a long sash clamp and get a helper to lever on this while the chine is fastened. Although double chine boats have twice the number of chine parts, these bend more readily than single chines and have far less twist.

To make a chine-to-stem joint as in Fig 71a, pull the chine close to the stem, then saw off the tip at the slight angle shown. This allows for the additional bend when the faying surfaces touch. To get it dead right, make a second saw cut using the side of the stem as a guide.

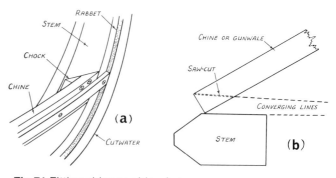

Fig 71 Fitting chine to side of stem

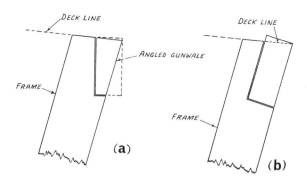

Fig 72 Allowing for gunwale slope

Photo 19 A GP14 under way

Gunwales and Stringers

Gunwales or sheer battens notch into the tops of frames as in Fig 72b and fit to the stem as in 71a. They take more bend and twist than any other part of a chine hull. Unless you laminate them, some steaming is advisable to avoid breakage.

To relieve some twist, angle the for'ard frame notches slightly as shown in Fig 72a. Before fairing off to the triangular shape, glue backing strips on the inside between frames to put the strength back.

With normal notches, leave sufficient gunwale sticking up beyond the sheer line (Fig 72b) so you can later plane it down flush with the deck camber. In a Photo 16 setup, some cross spalls are sure to get in the way and need a bit of notching.

Stringers Plywood planked chined boats nearly always have several stringers running fore and aft between hood and chines and between chines and gunwales, especially in frameless construction. The GP14 stringers are clearly visible in Photo 17. Stringers look fine until you bend plywood planking across them. Towards the stem you will find that the plywood will not touch the stringer between frames. The stringers are too stiff to strut out to closer fit, so thin packing must be glued to them and shaved down until the plywood meets them.

Stress relief Note that all battens to be bent around hull are less likely to break if all corners are chamfered slightly. This is most readily done with abrasive paper, coarse grade followed by a fine one.

Chapter 9
Traditional Dinghies

There is little difference in building procedure between round-bilge and frameless chine boats. Most small round-bilge designs incorporate steam-bent ribs, but when the planking is glued clinker plywood or cold-moulded, all ribs may be omitted. Curves mean strength and in general a round-bilge boat is stronger and lighter than its chine counterpart. A few racing boats have been designed with thin marine ply skins in round-bilge form, the Unicorn catamarans for example.

Most professional boatbuilders find round-bilge construction quicker and cheaper than framed chine. As mentioned in Chapter 1, hybrids using a mixture of chine and round-bilge features have evolved, such as the soft chine and clinker-bilge systems.

Temporary Moulds

Except for those with sawn frames, nearly all round-bilge boats are built over temporary moulds (see Fig 3) or some sort of jig. Inverted construction with the moulds on legs or on stocks is ideal for a dinghy. Bigger craft are usually built right-way-up using roof supports as in Photo 5.

Photo 20 Battened jig for cold-moulding a catamaran

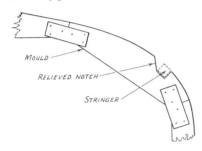

Fig 73 Notches to free stringers on removing hull

Photo 21 Clinker pram dinghy: Alan Buchanan's Lilliput design

For production work, dinghies are built on free-standing jigs which can be stored up in the rafters when finished with. A jig has notches to receive the keel, stem and transom. Internal gunwales (inwales) cannot be fitted until lift-off, but stringers can be built in provided their notches are shaped for clearance as in Fig 73. A battened jig as seen in Photo 20 is best for a multi-skin cold-moulded shell. When such a boat has tumblehome aft, one may have to fit the transom at a later stage to permit the topsides to be sprung apart sufficiently to release the shell from the jig. Cold-moulding is treated in Chapter 12.

Moulds are cheap to make as one can usually scrounge offcuts of planking long enough to be cleated together, as in Fig 3. The thickness is not important, but $\frac{3}{4}$ in (18 mm) is about the minimum. With the clever use of corrugated fasteners (wiggle nails) you may be able to manage without the cleats. Make moulds neatly from planed stock or chipboard if you intend to sell them eventually. Moulds are marked out from patterns as described for chine frames in Chapter 8. Similar surmarks are needed, but no bevel information.

Moulds need no edge bevels if set up as indicated in Fig 69b. If epoxy resin or glue is to be used on the planking, all outer parts of the moulds or jig must be covered with thin polythene sheet to avert adhesion.

Clinker Dinghies

The traditional clinker or lapstrake pram dinghy is the simplest round-bilge type and also the most popular for amateur building. One of these, the 6 ft 6 in (2 m) Lilliput designed by Alan Buchanan, can be seen in Photo 21. Building her takes about 120 manhours. The single mould (Photo 22) is outlined full-size on the drawing, together with the bow and stern transoms. Similar designs with stems involve more work, but are also popular with amateurs, and range from 7 ft (2.1 m) to 20 ft (6 m) for rowing, sailing, and as inboard and outboard launches.

Almost any clinker design is suitable for glued clinker plywood planking, omitting all the steamed ribs. This may take longer and cost more, but produces a light boat with an easy-to-clean interior. Most designs have numerous narrow planks as in Photo 21. In contrast, the Grand Banks dory style uses just a few wide planks each side. With narrow planks, flaws in the stock are easy to avoid. Marine plywood eliminates this problem and is unlikely to warp or shrink much. Silver spruce has been used in Photo 21 with a mahogany sheer strake. Cedar, wych elm and most clear pines are fine for clinker planking.

Photo 22 One mould suffices for a small pram

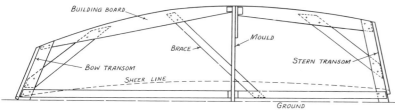

BUILDING BOARD

MOULD

BRACE

BOW TRANSOM

STERN TRANSOM

SHEER LINE

GROUND

Photo 23 Keel plank, skeg and rubbing strip

Fig 74 Setting up pram dinghy framework

Setting Up

The Lilliput pram is set up as in Fig 74. Although the mould has no bevel, the transom edges certainly have, enhanced by the big rake of the bow transom. All this is readily lifted from the drawing onto cardboard patterns. Put most of this bevel on as each transom is cut out, using a bandsaw, jigsaw or compass saw. Leave plenty to plane away when fairing in, as this is easy to do at that convenient height. Guard against rounded bevel faces (see Chapter 8).

Once the Fig 74 set-up is marked out, plumbed, squared, braced and checked, just as in Chapter 8 for chine frames, get a long $\frac{1}{4} \times 2$ in (6×50 mm) batten and fair in the transom bevels. When singlehanded, notch an offcut to look like a tent peg and clamp this to one transom, to hold the long batten there while checking the other transom.

The next job on the Lilliput is to fix on the *keel plank*. This runs from transom to transom on the centreline and is $\frac{1}{8}$ in (3 mm) thicker than all the other clinker planks. The building board in Fig 74 just serves to give the keel plank its true curvature. If you omit this, as in Photo 22, wedge two or three struts from floor to keel plank to do the same job.

Bottom protection Outside the keel plank is screwed a 1 in (25 mm) thick oak strip to serve as the backbone and protect the planking from chafe. Put it on before undertaking any further planking. Steaming makes it easy. If you have no suitable steam box, either laminate it, or soak it in water for a week or two and clamp it over a bending jig with about 2 in (50 mm) more curvature than the keel plank itself.

Sitting on the keel strip right aft is the skeg (Photo 23). Fit this later when the transom knee is in position. The skeg has an opening in the form of a hand grip—useful for swimmers and when lashing the pram down, or for chaining her to a post to stop unauthorized use. The skeg's edge has a brass strip to resist abrasion while being dragged up a beach.

The small bilge keels shown help protect the planking. Attach these with screws from inside to facilitate future renewal. Bilge keels are best cut to shape from thicker stock, but they can be steamed.

Ribbing

Planking a clinker dinghy is fully described in Chapter 11. Once that stage has been finished, the shell may be removed from the moulds or jig, ready for inserting the ribs, or timbers. However, just beforehand, you can save a lot of time by boring all the pilot holes for the rib fastenings. On the Lilliput, there will be one rivet between each rib on each line of planking, fitted during planking to hold everything together. If you forgot to mark the rib positions earlier, do it now. Make a pencil mark on keel and sheer planks for each rib line. Spring a bendy batten around the hull from mark to mark and spike the position of each rib nail.

Drill all these pilot holes as detailed on page 45 and countersink lightly. To make sure your countersinks are not too deep, first make some tests in plank offcuts. A punched nail should just nestle in dead flush. While she is still inverted, round off all plank edges and ends by sanding. If she is to be varnished, erase all pencil marks, fine-sand to remove all the dirty finger marks, then prime with thinned varnish, followed by one full coat. This will help prevent further blemishes.

Do not remove the Lilliput's mould until a strut is fitted across from sheer to sheer (Photo 24). Fasten this with a thin nail each end, through the holes already drilled. (A small piece of hardboard under such a nailhead facilitates later withdrawal.) The fragile shell could be damaged or distort at this stage without the strut.

Timber American elm or Canadian rock elm makes the best steamed ribs. White oak, hickory or ash are good alternatives. Order the stock planed all round, plus 20% spare pieces. Reject any without straight grain, or with knots and shakes. A defect near one end should not matter and a slightly faulty length might do towards the bow where ribs are shorter. Remember to set the end grain as in Fig 35, the top of that sketch being the rib's inboard face, like a leaf spring.

Sharp edges lead to breakage when bending. Lay each strip on the bench and chamfer the two corners which will show inside the boat. If you have time, turn the chamfers into full roundings. Also, round slightly the other two edges and fine-sand each rib all over. See Chapter 7 for details of steaming. Preferably dunk the pieces in cold water for a week before steaming.

Inserting the Ribs With padding on the floor, stand the

Photo 24 Ribbing towards the bow

Photo 25 Showing gunwales, risers and thwart

boat upright on her stern transom, held firm with guys and struts. One person will need to stand on the transom, so cover it well. If possible, arrange for one helper outside the boat and a third hand to attend to steaming, carry hot pieces and help press each rib rapidly up to the planking.

Note that the rib nails which will later also hold the risers and gunwales are extra long ones, so refrain from nailing through these holes and mark them accordingly. The *risers* or *risings* are the stringers seen in Photos 21 and 25 which support the thwarts.

Ribs need not be installed consecutively (the inside operator decides where to place them), but you should pencil rib numbers both inside and outside at the sheer, so the inside operator can call out the appropriate number to his or her mate. Start in the middle of the boat to gain practice on the easiest ribs. If a rib breaks, straighten it out and save it for possible use near the bow.

With ribs only $\frac{3}{8} \times \frac{3}{4}$ in (9×18 mm) in section for the Lilliput, you have just over one minute to get the first three fastenings in place each side before they cool and stiffen up. To save time, tap the anticipated nails into the planking before each hot rib arrives. Sharpened nails will drive readily through a hot rib without boring. The strongest person should be inside, wearing industrial gloves and holding a heavy dolly against the piece. When help is short, slip a bowstring across the tops of a rib, holding it approximately to shape before insertion.

With one nail placed near the keel plank, the dolly is used to press the rib close to the planking at the turn of the bilge. With that nail driven, a matching one is placed on the opposite side. With the piece pressed hard against the planks, next drive a pair of nails a couple of seams above the previous ones, followed by a further pair two seams below. Nails after that may start buckling and pilot holes are expedient.

Once a rib is tolerably close to the planking everywhere, leave further nailing until the next day. In any case, avoid riveting until the wood is dry. Over the keel plank drive a pair of thin ring nails right through into the hardwood rubbing strip.

Canted Ribs

The majority of steamed ribs—even up to $1\frac{1}{2} \times 2$ in (38×50 mm) in a really big craft—align themselves with the planking so that the question of edge bevels does not arise. However, some prove difficult, and the first two at Lilliput's bow need special attention. The problem arises because the keel plank rises sharply towards the bow transom. If these ribs are to run up the topsides vertically (to match all the other ribs) and also lie tight on the keel plank, an impossible degree of twist is involved.

One solution is to fix these ribs flat to the keel plank then strain them for'ard as far as they will go, still leaving them with an aft rake up the topsides. The foremost rib will lean a lot; the second one a bit less. Reduce the lean progressively on the third and fourth, then come back to the vertical at the fifth. This will not look very attractive, so the following method is better.

A glance at Fig 75 clarifies the idea. Set the hot rib vertical in the normal way, driving the minimum number of nails to pull it up close. This will leave a gap one side over the keel plank (75a). Next day, withdraw the nails,

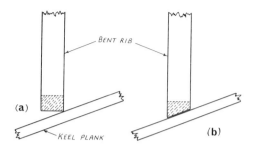

Fig 75 Applying bevel to steamed rib

remove the rib, then bevel the lower part to fit snugly (75b). The earlier nail holes will no longer align, so fill them and bore fresh holes. Re-steaming will not be necessary.

Gunwales and Risers

As soon as the two gunwales (pronounced 'gunnels') are in place, you can saw off the surplus rib ends allowing easy access into the boat. You may not have time to align the gunwales with the sheer planks when hot, so use clamps. Next day, adjust the height, bore and rivet. No problem in nailing the risers hot, but you must first drill through the ribs.

How do you cut the gunwales to exact length before steaming them? Simple: use a pair of *pinch rods*. Choose two thin battens capable of taking the bend easily, long enough to just overlap in the middle when clamped exactly in the gunwale's position. Mark across at the overlap, remove, lay down straight, align the overlap mark again and measure overall. Pinch rods give an accuracy of about $\frac{1}{32}$ in (0.8 mm) under size, which is a good fault. But as the transoms rake, and are also more than 90° to the sheer plank, just make sure you know where the pinch rod ends touch. For a good fit the gunwale ends need a bit of bevel each way: cut small cardboard templates for these angles. Like the gunwale lengths, they may not be the same on both sides.

Gunwales usually terminate at the transoms, with quarter knees to secure them and stiffen the corners (Fig 76a). An alternative arrangement is shown in 76b. More about these will be found later on. The internal type of gunwales on the Lilliput are strictly called *inwales* (pronounced 'innels'). In other designs you will find inwales fixed direct to the sheer plank, so the ribs butt up underneath them. For extra strength and protection inwales and outside gunwales, all through-fastened, are not

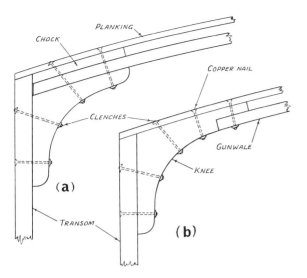

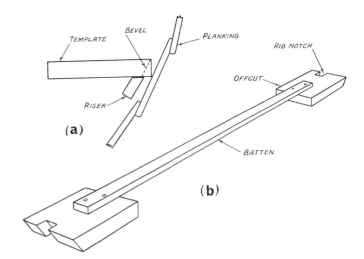

Fig 76 Two types of gunwale-to-knee joints

Fig 77 Templates for fitting thwarts

unusual. In way of the rowlocks, inwales must be reinforced with cheeks glued on the inboard faces, with similar hardwood plates on top to receive the rowlock socket screws.

A smart dinghy or launch often has a well-rounded gunwale capping. This is easy to laminate, but if you can manage steam bending, so much the quicker.

In a pram dinghy, the risers do little except support the thwart and do not need to extend the full length of the boat. Remember to round off the corners neatly before installation; naturally the same applies to the gunwales.

Dinghy Thwarts

The central thwart (seat) in any dinghy is an important structural member, usually well braced with a vertical knee at each end as seen in Photo 21. A stern transom is so rigid that the adjacent thwart only needs a *clamp* at each end (Fig 5a) to hold it in place.

Fit thwarts accurately to butt against the planking, and notch them around any rib which comes in the way. Fitting is almost impossible without a template. Make a cardboard template for each end, at the intended thwart position. Transfer these shapes to short offcuts of plank the exact width and thickness of the thwart. Whittle away until each offcut fits around any rib, and close to the planking. Undercutting is sure to be necessary to match any topside flare (Fig 77a). While holding the offcuts tight on their marks, clamp a batten between them, as in 77b.

Lift the whole thing out, mark and nail the batten and remove the clamps. Hey presto—a perfect thwart template complete with end bevels. This idea has numerous uses in boatwork, when awkwardly shaped parts must be fitted accurately into confined spaces.

Varnished thwarts are visually most important in a dinghy, but they also take much punishment from weather and wear. Even if expensive, teak is worth considering. Iroko and afrormosia also stand the conditions better than the mahoganies.

Knees and Ring-Bolts

Before fixing thwarts, put in the bow and stern knees which brace transoms to keel plank. On a stem dinghy you will find a triangular knee called the *breasthook* bracing the gunwales to the stem. This would be fitted at the same time as the quarter knees mentioned previously. Cardboard templates are essential for transom knees as they must be *joggled* (notched) over one or more ribs, as seen for the Lilliput stern knee in Photo 25. This limits one's freedom to whittle away for a good fit. The choice of woods and fabrication methods for knees is given in Chapter 6. Straight-grained hardwood is fine for a wee pram, but neither this nor lamination is likely to satisfy the traditionalist.

A normal clinker dinghy requires no glue, but as knee fastenings sometimes loosen, the use of waterproof glue or epoxy is not a bad idea. Clenches right through are

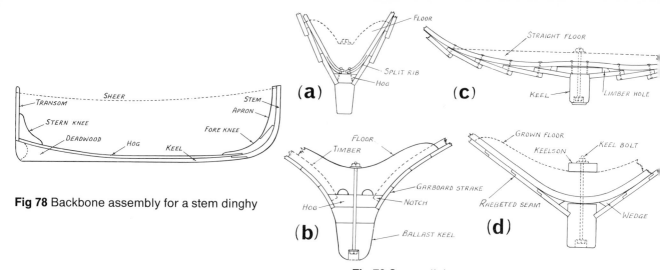

Fig 78 Backbone assembly for a stem dinghy

Fig 79 Some clinker and carvel keel layouts

ideal, helping to stop a knee from splitting. Woodscrews from outside are commonly used, but are best as additions to the clenches.

Thwart and quarter knees are tricky to fit, one or both edges often having considerable bevel. As well as the templates mentioned above, you need separate ones to pick up the bevels. Cut these by trial and error, or use a carpenter's bevel gauge. Remember to cut the bevel in opposite directions on handed pairs of knees! Large knees or webs of strange shape often support the side benches and side decks on sailing dinghies. A good way to make these is from thick plywood with strips of matching veneer glued to the exposed edges. When varnished, no one will know!

Every dinghy needs a ring-bolt to take the *painter* or mooring rope. The ring is generally inside on the apron for a stem dinghy, but is handier outside the bow transom on a pram. A similar ring-bolt aft, as in Photo 21, comes in very useful. (For full details of the care, handling and equipping of dinghies and tenders, refer to *The Compleat Book of Yacht Care*.)

Stem Dinghies

A traditional pulling boat has a solid keel as in Fig 78. Normally a wide hog is bolted on top, but sometimes the planking rabbet is chiselled into the side of a single piece keel. A Fig 78 stem differs from the simple one in Fig 61 as it has wide apron and fore knee backing members to form deep rabbets. It just takes a bit longer to fabricate.

On small motor tenders the propeller aperture is scalloped out of the deadwood, as shown dotted in Fig 78. For powerful launches, the deadwood or skeg ends well before the transom to accommodate a large propeller and perhaps leave space for a *balanced* rudder; one that has part of the blade area for'ard of the pivoting axis.

Assembly Except for the smallest ones, stem dinghies and clinker launches are usually built right way up. Riveting is easier and you get more even illumination. The backbone assembly of stem, keel, hog, deadwood, sternpost and transom is set up on poppets, made rigid, then the moulds are fixed along the hog and well strutted from above. For inverted construction, you set up the moulds just as for chine frames (Chapter 8), then align the hog into its notches and brace the stem and transom.

Incredibly, traditional clinker boats are often built without moulds. The planks are laid from the keel upwards, each riveted to the previous one. Occasional struts are used to correct the shape, and the odd template used to match port side with starboard. There are few quicker or cheaper ways to build a robust sea-going vessel up to about 50 ft (15 m) in length, but one person in the team must possess the necessary expertise.

Big steamed ribs are called *timbers*. With the above type of construction, such timbers are placed after planking, but any floor knees are fitted as soon as sufficient planking is in place. When heavy clinker boats are fitted with sawn frames these are traditionally joggled at every plank seam to fit without gaps.

Single Timbers

Most of the ribs in a stem dinghy are installed just like those for the Lilliput pram. However, near the stem the bend becomes so severe that single ribs must be used, ending on the hog or notched into it. For the former, the single timber is slit with a fine saw (*kerfed*) at the bottom end, so that it bends readily (Fig 79a). With a narrow hog, or the stem apron, you may have to fasten the ends of each pair side by side instead of butted together on the centreline.

All severe bend is eliminated if a single rib is notched into the hog, fore knee or internal deadwood. This method is used particularly towards the stern of yachts built in the style of 79b. Notched-in timbers create a danger point for rot, however. To prevent trapping dirt and stagnant water, filler chocks must be inserted from rib to rib. Set these in mastic rather than glue. Pin each chock with two screws through the planking, plus a screw to hold each rib into its notch. All this is much simpler in bigger boats where the ribs are fitted before planking starts: see next chapter.

Dinghy Floors

Small clinker boats are so light and strong that floor knees (as described for chine boats) are not needed. When glorified bigger dinghies are given inboard engines, to work as tenders, launches and for fishing, sometimes with inside ballast, floors become essential.

All floors should be between ribs, not on top of them. They should reach well out towards the risers. Light floors are steam bent, like extra ribs. Heavy ones are either straight-grained hardwood as in Fig 79c, or like knees as in 79d where oak crooks, lamination or fabricated metal serve best (see also Chapters 6 and 10).

Good floors prevent a launch from breaking up if the keel pounds on a reef or sandbar. They need bolting right through the keel, with screws or copper clenches through all faying planks. Amidships is the weakest region, though dinghy floors can be shaped as in 79a at bow and stern. In extra strong traditional launches a fore-and-aft *keelson* (79d) is bolted on top of the floors from fore knee to stern knee.

A daggerboard or swing keel case needs half-floors, often tied to the case with metal angle brackets (see next chapter).

Limber holes Except where filler chocks exist, bilge-water has a free run alongside the hog. When *wedges* are added, as in the Fig 79d situation, adequate *limber holes* must be left for bilge-water (see also Photo 26). In the Fig 79b situation, each floor has limber holes shaped into it. Alternatively, concave grooves may be routed along the top of the hog in this vicinity.

Photo 26 Wedging up to form limber holes

75

Chapter 10
Traditional Keelboats

Although foam-sandwich, ferrocement and metal hulls have largely superseded wood for the bigger amateur built boats, wood is a friendlier material for the inexperienced to use, and is ideal in remote areas of the world where modern materials are scarce and expensive. When cold-moulded, wood is perfect for one-off high-speed powerboats, racing sailboats and multihulls.

Classic Yacht

A modern wooden sailboat with fin keel, skeg-mounted or spade rudder and retroussé stern is built much like an overgrown stressed-skin, cold-moulded dinghy and ideal for epoxy saturation.

A classic carvel planked sailboat like the Yachting Monthly 3-tonner seen in Photo 29 need not use any glue and is built much more on traditional big-yacht lines, making a good example of many aspects of the art. She measures 20 ft (6 m) overall, was designed by Alan Buchanan and takes around 2400 manhours to build. Even the fixed-keel version is of shoal draft, but Fig 81 is the general arrangement drawing for the drop-keel version which has some interesting complications and optional gaff or Bermudan rigs. We will call her the 'mini-sloop'.

Most big round-bilge wooden boats are built right way up with a solid backbone and either sawn or laminated frames or temporary moulds to obtain the sectional shape. Sometimes two or three bent timbers are set between the sawn frames. In designs with no sawn frames, every third or fourth bent one may be reinforced by laminating a further rib of equal size on top of it, all plank fastenings passing through the double thickness. Composite construction uses galvanized steel frames with all other parts of wood.

Ribbands

You cannot press the steamed timbers of a big yacht close to the planking and nail them rapidly as for a dinghy: there is nothing to clamp to. Therefore, you fit them before planking, fixing fore-and-aft *ribbands* to the outside of the moulds as in Photo 27, then clamping each hot timber to the inside of these. Before removing the clamps,

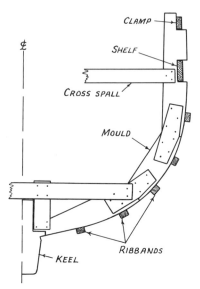

Fig 80 Ribband spacing around a mould

lash each rib to a few ribbands or use screws and washers, driven from outside. Ribbands are removed one by one as the planks go on.

Obviously ribbands need to be strong; but with good overlaps, random lengths suffice. For neatness, join lengths end-to-end using outside butt straps. Nail one piece and screw the other, to facilitate dismantling. For a 16 ft (5 m) boat, ribbands would be of $2 \times 1\frac{1}{4}$ in (50×32 mm) pine. For a 20 ft (6 m) hull use $2 \times 1\frac{1}{2}$ in (50×38 mm), and for 30 ft (9 m), 2 in (50 mm) square lengths, all of planed stock with rounded corners. Steaming is not normally necessary. Set ribbands closer together where hull curvature is greatest, as shown in Fig 80 for the mini-sloop.

Really stout timbers are far easier to bend over the *outsides* of all ribbands: notch the ribbands deeply into the moulds (with any butt straps inside) as Photo 28. As well as being able to install the big-boat versions of inwales (called *beam shelves* or *clamps*) at this stage, you can do the same with the longitudinal stringers, enabling them to be fully fastened as the planks go on.

Fig 81 General Arrangement drawing for the mini-sloop

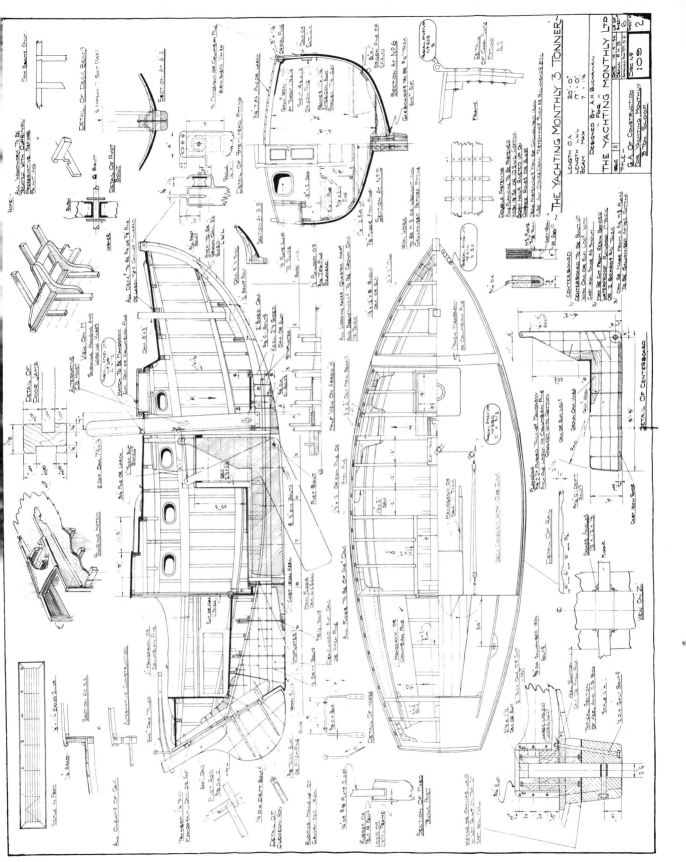

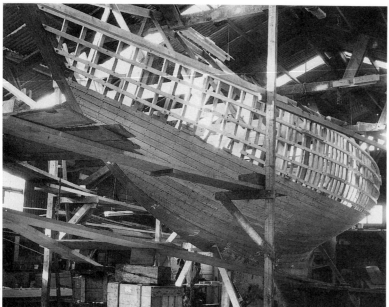

Photo 27 Ribbands outside timbers

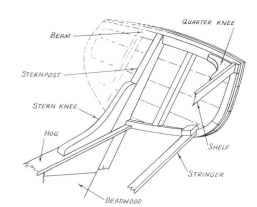

Fig 82 Transom attachment

Photo 28 Ribbands inside timbers

Photo 29 The mini-sloop under way

With notched-in ribbands, you can with ease fill the spaces between ribs in way of shelves and stringers with neat chocks. Before planking starts all faying surfaces may be primed and painted—an important process which is impossible when ribs are fitted after planking as described in Chapter 9.

One little warning: watch that any screws from ribbands to moulds are driven obliquely (or through side blocks) so you can get the moulds out after planking!

Heavy Backbone

The mini-sloop's stem is scarfed in similar fashion to the simple one in Fig 61, but the forefoot bells out to a siding of 10 in (250 mm) where it meets the keel, from a consistent $3\frac{1}{2}$ in (88 mm) the rest of the way up. Hollowing, rounding and tapering such large pieces (including the cutwater) is traditionally done with an adze (Photo 15). Except for certain electric and compressed air chainsaws and chisels, there is still no better implement than the adze for hewing large quantities of hardwood. If you find a dead knot in any exposed face, chisel it out about $\frac{1}{4}$ in (6 mm) deep to a neat diamond profile and glue in a matching *graving piece*.

Although plans must be adhered to as far as possible, the sizes of individual deadwood pieces can be varied slightly to suit the available stock. But the strength of the bolting system must not be decreased.

In very big boats, notches called *tabling* (see Fig 87a) are formed in the faying deadwood surfaces to prevent any movement, even late in life when some bolt corrosion may occur. Alternatively, separate tenon pieces (shown dotted in 87b) can be mortised into each surface.

Thin stock To avoid the need for massive balks, and achieve fault-free timber, thinner unglued, scarfed and bolted stock will do, perhaps with hardwood dowels (like big stopwaters) driven as shown in Fig 88. If you use epoxy for such assemblies fewer fastenings and no crosspinning will be needed.

Sterns

The heel of the mini-sloop sternpost is mortised into the keel. From shoulders to receive the forked end of the hog, the sternpost continues upwards to the transom at reduced width, as shown in Fig 82. For a more massive sternpost, metal *fishplates* might be added each side, inlaid

flush with the surface (Fig 87b).

The lower rudder gudgeon (socket) fitting on a big traditional keelboat is a bronze casting, often made to overlap the sternpost/keel joint completely, bolted right through.

A counter stern (Figs 16 and 89) is an attractive and sea-kindly shape, but not so easy to frame and plank as a transom. Even more difficult is the rounded cruiser stern. The Colin Archer type of Norwegian double-ended stern is not difficult to build, the sternpost being almost identical to the stem.

The backbone of most counters is the *horn timber* seen in Fig 86. In small boats this is a single piece mortised on top of the sternpost. In big vessels the sternpost goes up to the deck, so a horn timber is notched into each side of it. Twin horns may continue right aft to the *archboard* (transom) of a *sawn-off* counter, or to the chock which forms the tip of a *fantail* or full counter.

Alternatively, short twin horns may act as gussets to support a central *midrib* as in Fig 89. Sawn frames are attached to this backbone by means of floor knees or angle brackets to give a counter its shape.

Big Moulds

Our mini-sloop needs only five temporary moulds, at stations 2, 4, 6, 8 and 10. Carcassing softwood a full 1 in (25 mm) thick would be ideal, fabricated somewhat as shown in Fig 80. If the beam shelf and upper clamp go in before planking (as in Fig 80), top sections of moulds should be made for easy dismantling. If you are very clever, you can put in the bilge stringers now—but these must go into extra deep notches to allow the hot ribs to be passed between them and the ribbands. During planking the stringers are pulled tight to the timbers.

Fix moulds to the hog with screws or lag bolts through wooden blocks or bits of angle iron. The lower cross-spall seen in Fig 80 is required only in way of the drop keel trunk. A system of trestles and scaffold planks assist most operations from this stage on. The type of trestle shown in Fig 83 is easily made at home. The minimum number would be four about 5 ft (1.5 m) high and four about 3 ft 3 in (1 m) high.

When laid out flat, most bilge stringers are almost straight, so with a little steam, bending is easy. Even on a design with straight sheer line, a beam shelf or clamp takes considerable edgewise curvature. Unless thin enough to steam bend in both directions at once, such

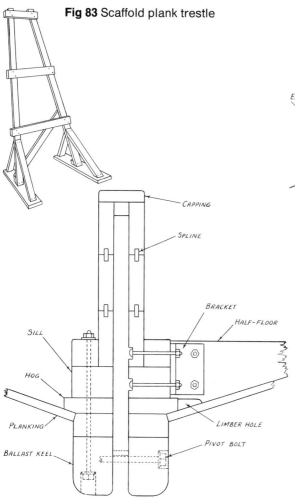

Fig 83 Scaffold plank trestle

Labels in Fig 83 / Fig 85: CAPPING, SPLINE, BRACKET, HALF-FLOOR, SILL, HOG, PLANKING, LIMBER HOLE, BALLAST KEEL, PIVOT BOLT

Fig 85 Drop-keel trunk section for a cruising yacht

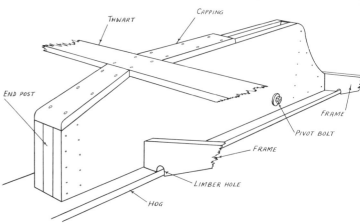

THWART, CAPPING, END POST, FRAME, PIVOT BOLT, FRAME, LIMBER HOLE, HOG

Fig 84 Dinghy centreboard case arrangement

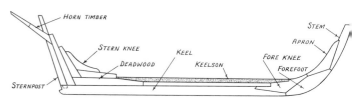

HORN TIMBER, STERN KNEE, STEM, APRON, FORE KNEE, DEADWOOD, KEEL, KEELSON, FOREFOOT, STERNPOST

Fig 86 Backbone layout for *Alhena*

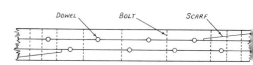

DOWEL, BOLT, SCARF

Fig 88 Dowelled laminations

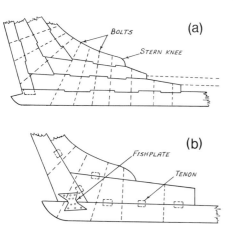

(a) BOLTS, STERN KNEE
(b) FISHPLATE, TENON

Fig 87 Deadwood tabled joints

Fig 89 Traditional counter construction

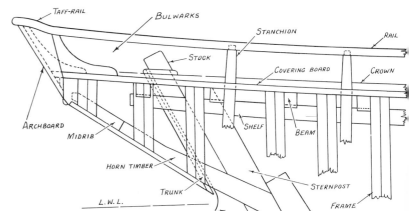

TAFF-RAIL, BULWARKS, STANCHION, RAIL, STOCK, COVERING BOARD, CROWN, ARCHBOARD, MIDRIB, SHELF, BEAM, HORN TIMBER, TRUNK, STERNPOST, FRAME, L.W.L., RUDDER

members are best scarfed end-to-end from two or three lengths. Fitting massive shelves is simplified because they always taper down considerably towards bow and stern. Steaming over a Photo 13 type jig, or laminating, is better than sawing the vertical curvature from a wide balk, then steaming the horizontal curvature *in situ*.

Sawn Timbers

Traditional oak sawn frames are built up from double sets of futtocks with staggered joints as in Fig 90a. Heels register into keel notches and a single oak crook floor is bolted to the side of each frame. Lighter ones are doubled to the turn of the bilge (90b) thence single up to the deck. Lighter still (90c), they consist of just one futtock. Another option comprises doubling in way of the bilge stringer (where the extra strength is advantageous) with singles elsewhere.

Being wide, sawn timbers need accurate edge bevels (see Chapter 3) for the planking. They also need internal bevels to improve appearance, reduce weight, and provide a fair landing for any ceiling or lining. A bandsaw with canting table enables most bevels to be applied with one cut. To reduce the severe for'ard bevels, *cant frames* as in Fig 24 are common.

Only light fastenings are needed to hold double futtocks together. Full strength is attained once the plank fastenings are in place. Trenails through futtocks do not foul plank fastenings, being just wooden pegs. However, bolts or clenches are quicker. Nowadays, rough futtocks are bonded together with filled epoxy resin. Traditionalists might still prefer to lute instead with the old-timers' bedding compo made from white lead paste and auto grease.

Straight-grained stock Neater and lighter double sawn frames result by using short, straight-grained, iroko futtocks, glued and scarfed as in Fig 91. As all these scarfs are the same shape, you need sheet metal templates to mark out and check them. With a little ingenuity a table saw or router and an appropriate jig will make short work of them. Bond with epoxy or resorcinol glue and clamp with bronze woodscrews.

Pairs of straight-grained floors are bonded to the sides of these frames (Fig 92). Sweeter bilges result if intercostal chocks are glued beneath any keelson from floor to floor (92b). The added support enables a thinner keelson to be used.

Undoubtedly the finest sawn frames of all are those laminated from strips, as described in Chapter 6 and shown for chine frames in Photo 18. Unfortunately the method is more costly and time-consuming, although less wood is wasted. With so much glue about, edged tools blunt more quickly when working on them. One unexpected advantage is that when bevelling, the glue lines show up as streaks: wriggly lines mean unfair bevels.

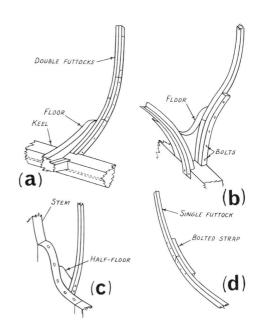

Fig 90 Single and double futtocks

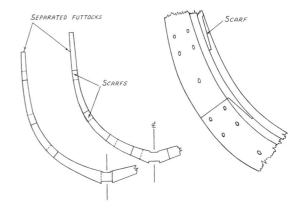

Fig 91 Straight-grained sawn frames

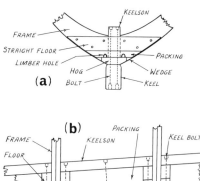

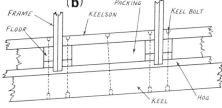

Fig 92 Floors for scarfed frames

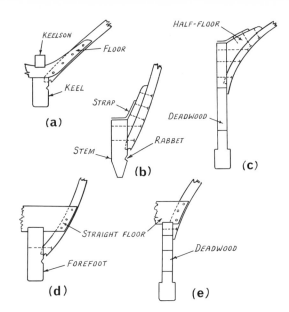

Fig 93 Some floor knee shapes for grown frames

Big Bent Ribs

The mini-sloop plans specify bent timbers $1 \times 1\frac{1}{4}$ in (25×32 mm). As there is no reverse curve to the aft sections, bending is easy after steaming for about 45 min. Unlike the dinghy, here you have 6 min to get a rib clamped home.

Where reverse curvature is coupled with difficult wood, you may need to kerf (Chapter 9) for some distance. A fine-bladed bandsaw does this best; failing that, a very flexible panel saw with almost no set. One other way around this is to use a pair of half-thickness pieces for each such rib, bent piggyback fashion so the join cannot be seen. When using either of these ruses, soaking in rot preservative before steaming is an accepted precaution.

Heavy Floors

It takes a quarter the time to install big floor knees after ribbing as it does after planking. However, accuracy is better the latter way, as ribs can be pulled or pushed a bit as planks are fastened. Best of all, pre-shape floors the easy way and adjust them for final fitting later.

Most floors have edge bevel. Where this is severe you need two hardboard templates, one for each face of the floor. Rough out your templates by scribing alongside the nearest rib. Then get them exact against a spline which is sprung across at least two timbers on either side. When singlehanded, clamp a small chock on the hog and clamp the hardboard to this. The spline must be moved con-

stantly, so a helper at one end is useful. For double templates, if the hog chock is about the same width as the floor thickness, fix the templates to the chock before removal. You then have a perfect replica. To be really fussy, also bevel the hardboard itself.

Full floors (Fig 93a) are easily fitted along all central parts of a hull, passing under the keelson if there is one. Elsewhere, half-floors (93b,c) with metal straps, or deep, straight-grained ones (93d,e) are satisfactory.

Even amidships, half-floors may be needed. They will be essential in way of a drop keel case (see Fig 81) and as engine bearer supports. The blind ends cannot easily be bolted except via bronze or galvanized angle brackets, as seen in Fig 81.

Metal floors Although galvanized steel floors are strong and simple to make, they do get attacked by galvanic action in a copper fastened boat. Bronze floors, either cast or fabricated by brazing, cost more, but are everlasting.

Referring to Fig 94, type **a** in metal fits well under a keelson. Types **b** and **c** bolt on top of sawn timbers or direct to the planking—ideal between steamed ribs and for receiving keel bolts.

Ballast Keels

When you get plans for a stock design such as the mini-sloop, it pays to enquire about a source for the ballast keel

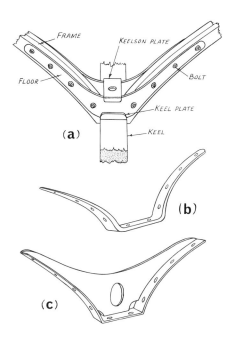

Fig 94 Three types of metal floor

Photo 30 Wooden pattern for ballast keel

or its pattern. Failing this (or in a remote area) a wooden pattern must be made (Photo 30), as detailed in *Boat Repairs and Conversions*. Patterns are similar for iron or lead keels, but concrete ones (usually containing reinforcement and a vast amount of small scrap steel) are cast in simple shuttering boxes. Long ballast keels add a lot of strength to a backbone, but they have been known to fall off in old age!

Whatever the material, apertures for drop keel, towing eyes and keel bolts need to be cast in at the outset. Boring through these materials is painful.

If the casting isn't properly fettled at the factory, borrow an angle grinder to remove superfluous iron or concrete, especially around the top. A Surform plane or rasp will trim lead. Try to get an iron keel grit-blasted and primed at the foundry, after grinding off.

Attaching the keel Instead of jacking the heavy weight under a wooden keel, chock the weight on its side, then bring the backbone up to it while lying on its side. This stage is nothing like so easy to do with a completed hull of fibreglass, ferrocement or metal.

Bore through a backbone with a lengthened drill, using the ballast holes as guides. Alternatively, make a template of the ballast top first. Beware, though: a template will start the holes accurately, but will not indicate their direction. Some holes splay outwards, as seen in Fig 81.

When you have a good fit, paint the faying surfaces thoroughly. If floor knees cannot be fitted until after ribbing, use temporary chocks in place of the floors. This saves having to make shorter temporary keel bolts. Traditionally, a layer of canvas soaked in thick white lead paint came between metal and wood. With modern bedding compound no gasket is required.

Where a fibreglass hull is concerned, you must not whittle away at this to form a tight joint. Either grind off the ballast keel top, or fill any gaps with shims of stainless steel set in epoxy putty.

With the ballast in place, the false keels (fairing pieces or external deadwood) may be added fore and aft, followed by chisel and circular plane to fair them in.

If keel bolts must be withdrawn later, remember to position the poppets to dodge them, and high enough for the bolts to drop clear.

Inside Ballast

Heavily built craft with all inside ballast are attractive for amateur boatbuilders in places where a ballast keel might be difficult to get. Chunks of lead inside ballast are easy to cast. Shaped pigs are useful in deep bilges, but do not allow them to rest against the planking or skin. Pigs cast with rabbeted ends as in Fig 95 are made to rest only on the frames. If pigs are packed between keelson and

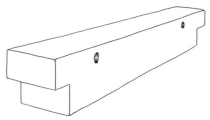

Fig 95 Cast ballast pig

stringer, make sure they cannot shift at great angles of heel or in a knockdown. Wooden packing, wedges and clamping-down battens are referred to as *dunnage*.

Encased inside ballast is widely used in fibreglass boats. An amateur completing a factory-built bare hull can not only save money by installing the ballast himself, but his hull will be much lighter when moving to site.

A lot of resin is required to embed iron or lead pieces into a fibreglass keel trough. The resin needs a correct ratio of filler, and only a small quantity may be placed at one time to avoid heating. Otherwise, enough heat could be generated to damage the hull, or even to burn it. See Chapter 15 for further details.

Drop Keels

The great variety of drop or swing keels, centreboards, and non-pivoting daggerboards, includes twin boards fore-and-aft through the keel, twins amidships to port and starboard, one for each hull in catamarans—even leeboards which are pivoted on the topsides and avoid the structural problems of building a casing in the bottom of the hull.

Through the keel Cutting a keel slot in a big boat is much the same as described for a dinghy in Chapter 8, except that you cannot saw accurately enough along a 9 in (230 mm) or so thickness of hardwood. A complete run of closely bored holes proves best, unless you can get the keel under a power mortiser.

To bore by hand, a jig is essential. Get a chunk of softwood the width of the keel or hog and at least 6 in (150 mm) high. Bore dead through the middle using the intended drill bit. Plane a batten to just slide snugly through the hole. Leave it protruding at the bottom. Using a try-square against this, check the base of the block for squareness. If adrift, plane the base to get it true. Now nail a cheek on each side, so the jig sits firmly astride the keel. Fix it with the aid of a big clamp across the cheeks.

Before using the jig, start all the intended holes along the slot, each to a depth of only about $\frac{1}{2}$ in (12 mm). Use the above mentioned batten to align the jig over a hole. Clamp the jig, then start boring. To reduce any misalignment problems, bore from both ends of the slot to meet in the middle. You will no doubt need to adapt the jig width for the other direction: remember to start with the widest surface!

Use a big chisel and mallet to clean up between holes. To sand the interior, make a square stick slightly thinner than the slot width, then tack some coarse garnet paper around the stick and propel it up and down along the slot. Tack a strip of hardboard sealed with bedding compound underneath the finished slot, then fill it with anti-rot or worm solution and keep it topped up for three days. Pull away one corner of the hardboard and drain the fluid into a pan. A week later, or when fully dry, repeat with priming paint.

Prime or dope with boiled linseed oil all backbone parts after fabrication to minimize warping, shrinkage and cracking. This procedure is unnecessary if you are using epoxy saturation, and in fact oiling will prevent the subsequent use of any epoxy or polyurethane paints or adhesives. However, it is compatible with the traditional type of oil-based primers and paints.

Cases and Trunks

The GP14 centreboard case is the simplest type possible—just a narrow box with sides of solid mahogany glued to spacer strips or *headledges* at each end (Chapter 8). Impregnation, assembly and bonding to the hog with epoxy is ideal, but screw fastenings through the keel are still necessary as well as lateral bracing. A thwart fixed across the top (Fig 84) provides great rigidity. The remainder of the top is sealed with a capping piece, attached by screws to allow future removal.

Before assembly, shape the bottom of each side panel to fit snugly to the hog. Clamp lightly with the spacer strips in place, then support this dead perpendicular on the hog and bed it down with a mallet. Tighten the clamps, remove all to the bench and bore for the spacer fastenings prior to gluing. For a perfect fit on the hog, rub chalk (or paint) on the hog, position the case upright, then tap the top lightly. Marks will be transferred to any high-spots underneath the case.

On bigger craft the headledges often pass right through the keel for extra stiffness. Sometimes the for'ard one goes up to the deck, or is incorporated in the mast tabernacle struts, as in Fig 81.

The largest drop keel trunks are attached to the keel by massive through-bolted balks known as *sills* or *logs* (Fig 85). The bolted side planks have tongued or caulked seams. The top capping must be leakproof as it may lie well below the waterline.

Some wooden boats have galvanized steel trunks, flanged at the bottom. Side inspection panels are easy to fit to these—useful when a stone jams the plate. A flanged steel case also makes a sound job when bonded into a fibreglass hull. A steel case should not be welded direct into a steel boat but bolted to an upstand which is welded to the keel. This way the case can be galvanized inside and out.

Boards and Plates

Galvanized steel plates are more easily made than boards, but they are very heavy to control, and more vulnerable to buckling if left down at the wrong moment. Wood needs weighting to overcome its buoyancy; provided for the mini-sloop by the cast iron shoe seen in Fig 81. Some dinghy boards have friction pads to prevent them floating up; others have a lead weight cast through them. Cast one of these as follows.

Cut an internal groove or Vee around the aperture. Rub chalk or graphite powder into this to reduce scorching. Cool the wood with ice packs, but keep moisture away—it creates explosive steam. Borrow some dirty brass plate to go underneath and make a heat sink. Weight the board down onto the brass. Heat the lead only just enough to melt it, pour quickly and leave it slightly humped. When set, immediately douche with icy water. Trim off with a Surform plane. Work some epoxy resin around it to prevent loosening after the board has dried out again.

The traditional board in Fig 81 is built up from $1\frac{3}{4}$ in (44 mm) planks fastened with $\frac{5}{16}$ in (8 mm) through-bolts and long drift bolts. The oak crook around its inner corner is an important strength feature.

Built up to thickness, plywood might appear ideal for boards and rudders. However, the edges are vulnerable to soakage and damage, while the thin veneers soon chafe through. Some of the veneer layers will be at the wrong direction to contribute strength. Resin-impregnated wood laminates (such as Permali) are much stronger and heavier than marine plywood: although expensive, they make good drop keels, daggerboards and rudder blades.

Racing dinghies and catamarans break boards occasionally, so making a spare one is not a bad idea. A single width mahogany plank serves well for this size of board, but gluing two thinner boards together helps prevent warping. If an airfoil shape is specified, this will entail much tedious planing, and a fragile trailing edge will result.

The pivot bolt must be exactly as specified, complete with nut locking device and water seals. Sometimes a bar or tube is used, held in place with watertight cap plates.

Rudders

Few wooden rudders benefit from being thin: high strength is generally more important. Gudgeon or pintle hinge straps need to extend well across the blade, sunk in flush for high-class work and secured with clenches, bolts or screws. Dinghy drop rudders are interesting to fabricate. All parts need to be shaped precisely to the drawings. Wooden blades generally use shockcord to keep them submerged, but metal plates avoid that complication.

Even when a single plank is used to make a cruiser blade, it pays to cross the grain with drift bolts to deter cracking. Boring for these is detailed in Chapter 6.

Plywood is best utilized in double skin form, glued over a hardwood core or framework which includes a solid wood surround to take the bumps and cover the plywood edges. Gudgeon straps may then be concealed internally. Use WEST SYSTEM resin throughout; then, if leakage should get to the core, it will do no harm.

Foam or balsa sandwich fibreglass construction (see Chapter 14) also makes good rudders. Solid fibreglass proves either too flexible or too high in material cost. A rudder that will float needs gudgeon fittings providing two-way thrust.

To avoid the complication of hollow construction, a metal plate rudder can be reinforced with streamlined external webs. Hollow steel rudders are often filled with oil to add weight and prevent internal corrosion.

Small and medium-sized rudder fittings are standard chandlery items. Those for big craft usually have to be custom built, as described in *Boat Repairs and Conversions*.

Rudder Trunk

One complication of a counter stern is the necessity for a trunk to provide a watertight housing for the rudder stock. On traditional wooden keelboats the rounded leading edge of the rudder fits into a *coving* (concave groove) in the after edge of the sternpost; the stock was a circular wooden shaft integral with the rudder (Fig 89). Metal stocks are now common. Unless the shaft is removable the trunk must be large enough to permit the rudder to tilt for withdrawal.

Small rudder trunks are usually made from copper or galvanized steel tube. A copper trunk has a brazed flange at the bottom, shaped to fit over the planking. The top protrudes above deck and is surrounded by an ornamental chock set in mastic. With steel, a screw-on flange at the base bolts internally to a chock between the horn timbers.

With a wooden stock, the trunk is too large in diameter to be made as above. A tube is formed of wooden staves fastened to the inside of chocks top and bottom. This is lined with lead; with a soldered seam, the lead tube is lowered in, then expanded with a wooden reamer to fit tightly. Flanges are dressed over at top and bottom and secured with sheathing nails.

Chapter 11
Clinker and Carvel

There is nothing particularly mysterious about clinker and carvel planking. Although too time-consuming for mass production, these methods are being used increasingly by specialist boatyards, hobbyists, schools and classic boat enthusiasts. Clinker is attractive not only for its appearance, but because the reinforced seams make the use of incredibly thin planking possible, either traditional timber or plywood.

Lapstrake Pram

The ensuing description of how to plank the Lilliput pram dinghy discussed in Chapter 9 covers most details for all clinker or lapstrake work. The word 'lapstrake' is derived from the familiar overlap between each plank, known as the *land*. The Lilliput's single drawing includes full-size templates showing approximate land positions. Transfer these as surmarks onto the edges and faces of the transoms and the mould.

Most planking starts with the garboard strakes, the first pair of planks adjacent to the keel. Instead of a solid keel, this pram has a keel plank $\frac{3}{8}$ in (9 mm) thick, 9 in (230 mm) wide amidships tapering to half that at the bow and also tapering slightly towards the stern (Photos 24 and 25). To shape this plank, pencil a centreline along it. Mark the width at each end and amidships, then clamp a thin spline into a fair curve, touching each of the three points on one side and run your pencil along. Measure the distance from this line to the centreline at three or four additional points and transfer each distance to the appropriate position along the opposite edge. Spring the spline through all the marks and pencil along. Saw out the shape and plane the edges square.

Fix the keel plank to its marks with temporary steel screws into the transoms. Choose a length of the $\frac{1}{4}$ in (6 mm) stock about 5 in (126 mm) wide for one garboard. Clamp this on the boat so that it overshoots equally each end, and overlaps the keel plank at the mould by the land width indicated by the appropriate surmark. Bend the plank down to touch each transom, slewing it on the central clamp until it lies roughly an equal amount beyond each surmark representing the garboard's outboard edge at bow and stern. Using props from overhead (or L-shaped chocks and C-clamps) hold the plank down to just touch both transoms.

Shaping a Plank

Holding a sharp pencil underneath, scribe a line along the garboard using the keel plank edge as a guide, as in Fig 96.

Outer edge Again on the underside, scribe athwartships lines showing the faces of mould and transom, then transfer the extreme plank width surmarks at these places (see Fig 96). If you partly plane the land bevels on the keel plank as shown in Fig 97 before offering up the garboard, the scribed edge line will be more precise.

Remove the garboard, lay it on the bench and holding the spline in a fair curve through the three outboard edge marks, scribe a pencil line.

Inner edge As we have already scribed a line on the underside of the garboard representing the outer edge of the keel plank, we must now mark off the required land width in a few places and then use the spline to draw that edge. Lilliput's keel plank land width is extra wide most of the way, tapering down to standard width at bow and stern. Marking out is quicker for a design where all land widths are equal throughout, as the spline merely needs to be held parallel to the previous line.

Turn over Saw and plane to both extreme edge lines and you now have one garboard strake of correct shape. All being symmetrical, it should now fit (when turned upside down) exactly in place on the opposite side of the boat. Having checked this, use it as a template to mark out the other garboard.

The Lands

If not done previously, you must now plane the keel plank land bevel (shown dotted in Fig 97) so that the garboard beds down into a close leakproof joint. Clamp the garboard into position on the boat, scribe along the newly sawn inboard edge **A** to mark out the land width on the keel plank, then measure gap **B** at about seven equally spaced positions along the seam and write each value lightly on the keel plank surface.

Remove the keel plank at this stage as planing the land bevel is easier on the bench. As gap **B** is identical to the bevel depth **C**, transfer each of the seven measurements to the plank *edge* and pencil a line joining all these points. Plane a truly flat bevel as shown dotted in Fig 97, but do not go right to the full depth of **C** at this stage, for when the garboard settles right down on the bevel it will lie at a slightly flatter angle than in the Fig 97 position.

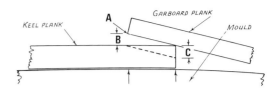

Fig 97 Setting out a land bevel

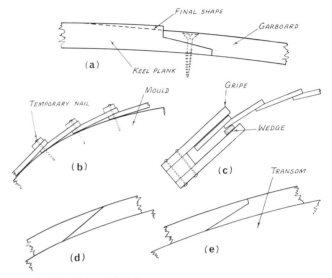

Fig 98 Plank land details

Bevel both lands of the keel plank and replace it on the boat temporarily. Offer up the garboards one by one, mark any highspots, plane these off and repeat the process as necessary. How to plane dead flat is described in Chapter 8.

Land Rabbets

To complete the seams the land bevel must merge into a rabbet starting about 7 in (180 mm) from each end, seen for the keel plank in Photo 31. This permits both planks to become flush at bow and stern. Lesser corresponding rabbets are required under the garboards (Fig 98a)

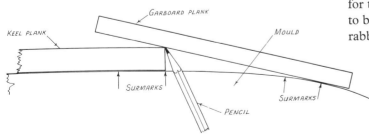

Fig 96 Scribing the Lilliput garboard planks

extending about 4 in (100 mm), to obviate weak feather edges on the keel plank.

Again, these rabbets are best shaped on the bench. Clamp a short guide batten along each line and use a fine saw against this to cut vertically down to just short of full depth. Use a rabbet plane to do the rest, dusting one part with chalk if necessary to test for a good fit. To avoid mistakes have a go with a couple of small trial pieces first.

The method for marking out the next pair of strakes is exactly the same as for the garboards. Clamp the chosen plank from transom to transom, overlapping the garboard by the land width at the mould. Clamp down the ends. Make sure the plank is wide enough to reach its surmarks and that it covers the proposed land width along the garboard at all places. If it will not cover after a bit of juggling, a wider plank must be chosen. Some later planks curve the other way, overlapping greatly amidships but only just covering the land at each end. (See later under Plank Shapes.) Scribe underneath along the garboard edge, transfer all surmarks, then move the plank to the bench for marking out and shaping.

With the plank on the boat again, scribe along its inboard edge and measure off the bevel gaps at seven positions as before. A good way to measure these gaps is to use a set of twist drills in increments of sixty-fourths of an inch or 0.5 mm, recording the diameter of drill shank which will just nose into the gap. Take the garboard to the bench for bevelling and rabbeting, then fix it back temporarily. Where a hull has concave sections aft, you bevel those lands on each *outer* plank instead of as above.

Land Fastenings

Now make pencil lines on the keel plank showing where each steamed rib will lie inside the boat. Midway between each rib a copper rivet must be fitted as planking proceeds. This closes the land joint, preventing dirt from creeping in and stiffening the whole shell.

Use a temporary wire nail at the mould. Later, when driving it hard in, put a tab of wood under the head as in Fig 98b. This prevents hammer marks and also makes withdrawal easier. To hold lands close and to check the accuracy of their bevels before permanent fixing, make five or six *gripes* (98c and Photo 3). Cut them from scrap wood to suit the plank widths and thicknesses, so that a single thin wedge pressed into the jaw of each gripe will do the trick.

Luting

Drill for each nail (see Chapter 6) dead central through the land joint. Remember to countersink outside just sufficiently to house the nail head flush, then remove the plank to clear any burr from the other side.

Traditionally, the faying (contacting) surfaces of lands were left bare wood, so they would swell and *take up* tight when under water. The amateur has time to make perfect joints. To ensure long life, these should always be luted at final fitting. Most dinghies spend more time out of the water than in, so have little chance to take up, and moisture in the land can cause rot. For a painted boat, prime the lands with paint and let this dry, then lute with soft white mastic just before final fitting and riveting. For a varnished hull, prime with thinned varnish and lute with soft buff mastic. Wipe away any surplus which oozes out from both sides, remembering beforehand to erase any pencil marks which might show. *The Compleat Book of Yacht Care* covers suitable mastics.

Final Strakes

Continue planking in pairs using the first one as a pattern for its opposite number, presuming no steaming is required. Surplus length on a plank makes bending easier and prevents splitting when the end fastenings are driven, though early trimming simplifies transferring surmarks. Be careful not to score the transoms when sawing plank ends. No need to feel bashful about using a rope tackle or Spanish windlass to pull a plank down.

As planking proceeds to the sheer, extend the pencil lines marking the internal rib positions to enable the midway rivets to be placed with some accuracy. Do not bore for the rib nails until later, when a thin sail batten can be sprung right around to scribe all rib lines properly.

The last plank is called the *sheer strake*. It measures $\frac{3}{8}$ (9 mm) thick on the Lilliput, made from mahogany whereas all other planking is spruce. This produces a pleasing contrast when varnished, as seen in Photo 21.

Each sheer strake and its neighbour the *binding strake* have considerable edgewise curvature from end to end when laid out flat. Wide boards are specified for these on the materials list. Make sure these wider boards are not used for the wrong purpose. Should this occur, glue narrow strips onto the edges of their replacements, amidships on one side and towards each end on the opposite side.

Traditionally, clinker *stem* dinghies have a tiny rub-rail beading tucked under the sheer strake land for the full length. Fixing is best achieved with 4-gauge bronze screws through the binding strake and into the ribs. Rope fendering hides such beadings, and modern white rubber fendering fixed at the top of the sheer strakes is neater for a yacht's tender.

Planking a Stem Dinghy

The procedure for planking a clinker stem dinghy is much the same as for the pram. However, as the garboards fit into a keel rabbet and the for'ard ends of most planks house into a stem rabbet, work on these parts is just as described later for carvel planking. You may need to screw temporary chocks to the back of the stem to give C-clamps something to grip on.

Not all plans give the plank seam positions on full-sized templates. The method for setting out nicely shaped planks from scratch is described later. Land overlaps are generally about $3\frac{1}{2}$ times plank thickness below the waterline and about 3 times for the topsides. Towards the ends, overlaps should taper down by about one plank thickness.

Instead of forming a rabbet to turn each land into a flush joint at the plank ends as in Fig 98a, some builders just steepen the land bevel angle until the diagonal joint shown in Fig 98d is formed. This method is not recommended as it leaves feather edges on both planks, and is more prone to leakage should the wood shrink. A combination of the two methods (Fig 98e) is popular, being quicker to make than the full rabbet but more reliable than the diagonal.

If possible, utilize surplus planking for making *bottom boards*—never called floorboards by sailors. These look best if the outer ones have sweeping curves, riveted onto cleats into panels of three, as seen in Photo 21. A simple chock amidships at each side with a wooden turnbutton screwed on top takes care of securing the big panels. A pegged brass stirrup through a slot will hold the middle boards.

Glued Plywood

A fine job can be made of any lapstrake dinghy design by using marine plywood for all planking, resin glued (ideally epoxy saturated) at the lands, preferably without fastenings.

Under 14 ft (4.3 m), all steamed ribs can be omitted if the plywood is no thinner than the specified ordinary

Photo 31 Land rabbets on the Lilliput keel plank

planking. A suitable designer should be consulted with regard to scantlings and framing for bigger boats (and those with decks) originally intended for traditional construction.

Clinker plywood hulls generally cost more and take longer to build than their traditional counterparts. The advantages are that marine ply is widely available, and a lightweight hull results with an easy-to-maintain interior. The planks are best scarf-jointed into full lengths (see Chapter 4) before fitting. This saves wastage where planks have a lot of sweep. If very clever, you can hide each scarf line behind a rib, making the scarfs invisible in a varnished interior.

Lands are formed exactly as already described. If your joints are imperfect, use filled epoxy to ensure lasting watertight seams.

Fastenings are not necessary if gripes or other suitable clamps are set at intervals of about six times plank thickness. If cellophane-wrapped stiffening battens (made from the same plywood) are included each side of the joint, clamp intervals may be increased to twelve times plank thickness.

Adequate temperature is all-important for successful gluing. Boatyards specializing in this type of work insert electrical heating strips along each joint while clamping. This avoids delays in getting on with the next strake.

Read on Before planking a lapstrake boat bigger than a pram dinghy, study the following carvel notes. For instance, bigger designs are unlikely to have full-size mould and transom templates with the plank widths marked on them. To produce shapely plank lands, you should tack small battens along all proposed land positions and view these from all angles. This happens automatically if you use the spiling templates described later in this chapter.

Plank Shapes

Whether clinker or carvel, if all strakes were removed from one side of a planked boat and laid out flat in correct sequence, the general shapes would appear similar to the three samples drawn in Fig 99. Planks with downward curvature towards the ends like the garboard shown, are said to *hang*, while planks towards the sheer with upward curving ends are said to *sny*. An intriguing facet of traditional planking is learning to find the most suitable board from which to cut a certain plank by noting how its grain, warp and twist can best be utilized.

Due to the edgewise curvature, straight boards need to be extra wide for cutting out planks near the keel and sheer. The offcuts are often useful for other planks, particularly those which extend along only part of the boat's whole length. Less wood is wasted if the majority of planks are composed of two or more pieces joined end to end. Many planks are almost straight, tapering towards each end. Several of these can be cut from one wide board with minimum wastage.

For a traditional yacht, the garboards would be made wide amidships to permit the for'ard end to reach the forefoot, and for the aft end to climb well up the sternpost (Fig 100a). If a garboard *fishtails* to an excessive width at the sternpost, a *stealer* may be fitted as in 100b. The mini-sloop (see previous chapter) has no planks terminating on the sternpost and no reverse curve to the after sections, ensuring success for the beginner.

Plank Widths

Although schematic plank widths often appear on the G.A. drawing sections, these are only intended to show the suggested number of strakes; not the exact seam positions.

Seam runs Once a boat's framing has been set up, the amateur can have an entertaining time marking out his plank runs. Planks can be made to conform to an infinite variety of seam positions. Although many alternative planking layouts are possible, one particular one usually produces least wastage coupled with pleasing appearance. The aesthetic aspect is obviously more important with clinker work or varnished carvel than for a smooth painted finish with no visible seams. For the ideal layout there should generally be a batch of five or six planks located near the turn of the bilge with very little hang or sny.

To find the location of such planks, get a thin, wide batten the length of the boat—two pieces cleated together will do. Clamp this about halfway up the midship mould, rock it until each end is about equidistant below the sheer, then bend it to touch all moulds. If this looks ridiculous, try it higher or lower until the ratio of mould periphery above and below the batten is much the same at the middle and endmost moulds.

Mark on these moulds where the top (or bottom) batten edge comes. Working each way from these marks, set out the proposed maximum plank widths on the midships mould and divide the endmost moulds into an equal number of smaller spaces. Of course, you cannot include any garboard (or near) plank which terminates before reaching the foremost mould. This automatically sets out the plank tapers fore and aft. For setting out seam positions on all the other moulds, read 'Draw it', below. In practice, planks at the turn of the bilge are always narrower than the others, while the garboards and sheer strakes are often wider than average.

Template strip Having arrived at a satisfactory planking layout on one side of the boat, all seam surmarks can

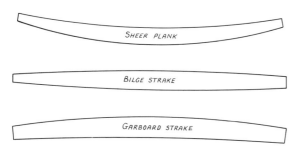

Fig 99 Three basic plank shapes

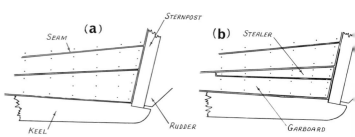

Fig 100 The use of a stealer

be transferred to the opposite side. This is best accomplished by pinning a strip of thick paper around the edge of each mould concerned, scribing the paper at each sur-mark, then shifting the strip to an identical position on the opposite side of the boat.

For the mini-sloop, the sheer strakes would be about 5 in (127 mm) wide amidships, tapering to 3 in (76 mm) at the stem and 2½ in (63 mm) at the transom. The unusual narrowness at the stern is due to the fact that there is no reverse curvature to the after sections. The adjacent binding strakes would be about 4½ in (114 mm) maximum, followed by several strakes at about 4 in (102 mm), reducing to 3 in (76 mm) at the turn of the bilge. From the 8 in (204 mm) garboards upwards, widths might run 6 in (152 mm), 5 in (127 mm), some at 4 in (102 mm), then the 3 in (76 mm) ones again.

Draw it Plank widths can be set out on a diagram as seen in Fig 101, best drawn either full-size or half-size on sheets of hardboard. Make **A–B** equal in length to periphery of Mould 6. Next strike parallel lines **C–D** and **E–F** about 2 ft (600 mm) on either side, representing the periphery of Moulds 2 and 10 respectively. To find the plank widths on the other moulds, measure their peripheries and add them (vertically) to the diagram where their lengths *happen to fit* between the top and bottom lines.

Any plank width can be transferred to its corresponding position on the boat using dividers. The widths at the sloping stem and transom will locate themselves automatically when you spring a spline through each run of seam marks and eye along to make sure all is fair and aesthetically pleasing.

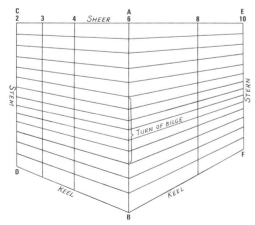

Fig 101 Approximate plank width diagram

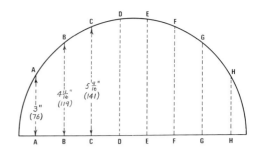

Fig 102 Plotting a fair plank edge

Having cut one edge of a new plank (see below), the widths shown on the diagram at each mould may be transferred to obtain the other plank edge shape. However, this method does not always result in the sweetest curve: the method shown in Fig 102 is superior.

Scribe a semicircle whose radius equals the maximum width of the plank concerned, then fit in line **A–A** equal to the stern width of the plank, and **H–H** equal to the for'ard width. Divide the space between them into any desired number of equally spaced lines **B–B, C–C,** etc. and measure the length of each line as indicated in Fig 102. Now mark the actual plank with the same number of equal spaces and set out the appropriate plank width at each position, as measured across from the one plank edge already marked out. A spline linking all the marks should produce the best possible curve for the new edge, but some marks are sure to need small adjustments to satisfy one's eye.

Planking Order

Garboard planks are invariably fitted first in carvel work, often followed by the sheer strakes. Then planking continues in pairs port and starboard, working towards the turn of the bilge. It makes a change, alternating between working on one's knees and high up on the topsides! The *shutter* plank is the final one to close the gap and generally comes just above the turn of the bilge. Alternatively, the panel of straight planks in this region may be fitted at an early stage and two separate shutter planks used each side.

Spiling With clinker, as all lands traditionally face downwards, you start with the garboards and only stop when you get to the sheer. To obtain the shape of an awkward plank with one edge buried in a rabbet, a sort of template called a *spiling batten* makes life easy. The amateur is advised to make a full-length spiling batten from some fine-sawn pine about $\frac{3}{8}$ in (9 mm) thick and 7 in (175 mm) wide. Hardboard longer than about 8 ft (2.4 m) becomes too supple, but two thicknesses tacked together with staggered joints will suffice up to 16 ft (4.8 m). Professional boatbuilders often manage with a short spiling batten for the for'ard end of a difficult plank, plus a few offsets between a straightedge and the rabbet for the remainder.

Get the batten as close as possible into the rabbet by trial-and-error shaping, to within an accuracy of about 1 in (25 mm). Next, set a pair of dividers to the widest gap and make a series of pricks along the spiling batten, while one point of the dividers rests against the rabbet. Rule pencil lines across the batten as in Fig 103a and follow the direction of these with the dividers. The lines should be closer together on curves and may be widened out considerably where the rabbet is almost straight.

Now tack the spiling batten on top of the chosen garboard strake, transfer all the divider spacings back from each mark (in exactly the same direction as before) and pencil the position of each one on the garboard surface (103b). However, if the dividers tilt (Fig 104a) considerable errors can creep in, so keep the points level by using a small try-square or block of wood as shown in 104b.

The use of a *spiling block* (also called a *dummy* or *dumbstick*) to get the shape of a plywood panel is indicated in Fig 105a. The same idea can be used for a plank and sometimes proves quicker than dividers. The dummy is cut the same width as the divider opening would be. With a pencil held against one side while the other side slides along the rabbet, a continuous shape is transferred to the spiling batten. To get the true rabbet line back to the strake, tack a narrow strip of wood to the block (105b) thus preventing tilt error.

The same spiling batten can be reversed for use on the opposite side of the hull. Provided no steaming is necessary, it may be possible to check whether the actual plank from one side will make a template for its opposite number.

Scribing

Having set out the proposed garboard widths, both edges can be pencilled using a spline, then sawn to shape. Most other carvel planks do not need spiling (except when steaming is necessary or in way of internal obstacles such as stringers or engine bearers) for they can be *scribed* in similar fashion to clinker planks.

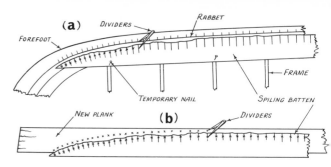

Fig 103 Use of the spiling batten

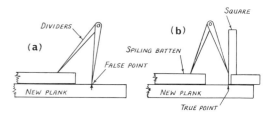

Fig 104 Ensuring accurate transfer with dividers

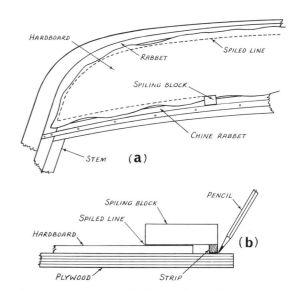

Fig 105 Using a spiling block for plywood panel

To do this, clamp a fresh plank on to the boat so that one edge just overlaps the last plank fitted. The overlap may be considerable in some places and zero in others. The opposite edge of the fresh plank would normally rest against the moulds or frames, but bending is eased and accuracy increased if packing of plank thickness is placed under this edge. Clamps to hold the packing also act as

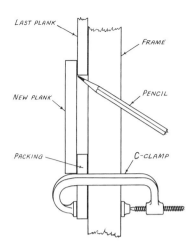

Fig 106 Scribing a heavy plank

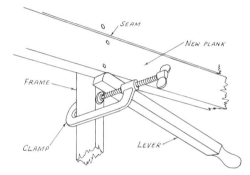

Fig 107 Lever to force plank edgeways

supports when getting a heavy plank into position, especially on the topsides (Fig 106).

Edge set Having done all this, run a pencil along the new plank from inside the boat using the existing plank edge as a guide. Cut to this line and after removing the packing pieces, offer up the plank in its rightful position. There are sure to be inaccuracies at first. Mark the high-spots and plane down, repeating the process until a satisfactory fit is obtained. Planks can be forced edgeways a certain amount by using wedges (Fig 54) or a lever (Fig 107).

Handling Lifting and bending stiff planks around a big boat sometimes proves difficult. In such cases, make up a thin template first, by scribing. Either get this to a perfect fit, or transfer the scribed line on the template to the plank (by driving nails through the template), and then hope

that the plank edge needs minimal planing to fit satisfactorily. Once a plank has been shaped on both edges, removal of the surplus wood makes it lighter and easier to bend into position. This is particularly noticeable near the sheer, where there is great sny. Picking up *both* edges with a spiling batten is therefore a good way to tackle awkward planks.

On a big boat, sheer strakes are most economically jointed from two or more lengths which can be fitted separately. However, with a single template or spiling batten the plank can be jointed on the bench and fitted in one operation. Fit the stem end first, where bend is normally most severe, then pull and clamp progressively towards the stern.

With an element of risk, one can obtain the rough shape of a difficult plank by measuring a few offsets from a wide but thin batten bent around the hull. If the plank is cut to this shape (allowing an inch or so surplus width at both edges) it may become sufficiently light and flexible to offer up for scribing.

Hood Ends

Most of the mini-sloop planks require two copper nails at each rib, with a pair of bronze screws at each end. Wider than average planks will need fastenings in threes, plus screws at 5 in (127 mm) intervals along the keel rabbet.

Plank ends housed in rabbets at stem, sternpost or transom are usually called the *hood ends*. Old-timers revered twisted copper nails for light hood end fastenings. As clamping is often difficult, the amateur is advised to use woodscrews or ring nails.

Soling

When shaping plank edges, use a hand or power jack plane to avoid undulations. Remember to form the caulking Vee (described in Chapter 6) before each plank is fastened. Lazy workers cut all of each Vee on one plank edge only.

Carvel planks thinner than about $\frac{5}{8}$ in (16 mm) warp sufficiently as the fastenings pull tight to conform to the curvature of the hull sections. Thicker planks remain flat. To get a snug fit to the frames or timbers, especially at the turn of the bilge, *soling* may be necessary. This comprises hollowing the back face of such planks (or rounding where sections have reverse curvature) using a gouge, adze or curved plane. Where sawn frames are widely spaced and internal appearance is not important, soling is necessary only in way of each frame.

As clinker planks do not fit snugly to the ribs, they do not require soling. Similarly, clinker planks need little external planing, whereas carvel work must be planed overall to a fair surface on completion.

Ordering To allow for soling and outer shaping, order the relevant boards about $\frac{1}{8}$ in (3 mm) oversize in thickness. It all depends on the maximum plank width adopted: the amount of soling necessary is easily found by measuring from the full-size lofted sections. Remember that outer planing adds no more to the additional thickness required for internal soling (see Fig 108).

Further care in ordering planking must be exercised for certain cruising boats which have two or three extra-thick strakes at the turn of the bilge to act as external stringers. On some boats the binding strake or sheer strake may project beyond the surrounding surface, either as a design feature, for additional strength, or to act as a rub-rail.

Thin carvel (and all clinker) planking is best ordered planed on both faces. This saves much time later and simplifies marking out. For heavier carvel work it might seem a good idea to order most stock with the inside face only planed. However, when choosing a board for a certain plank, reversing the faces might make better use of natural warp and twist. With basically straight frame futtocks, carvel planking for chine hulls rarely needs soling and all stock should be ordered planed both sides.

Plank Butts

There is no harm in joining strakes of planking end-to-end although this may mar the appearance of a varnished interior. Short stock is cheaper than long, and less wasteful when planks with much sny or hang are cut.

Butts must always be well shifted in adjacent planks, preferably at least four rib spacings away. Between the butt in one plank and a similar joint in the next plank but one, the shift should be at least two rib spacings. With heavy double sawn frames, each butt may be located at the centre of a frame, preferably with at least one through-bolt at each plank end (Fig 109). A good fit and sound caulking is essential at such joints, for wood does not swell much along the grain on submersion.

For boats with lighter framing, make all plank joints

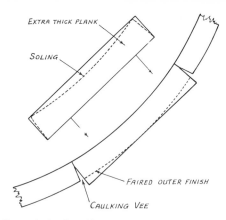

Fig 108 Carvel plank soling

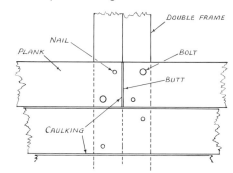

Fig 109 Plank butt on double frame

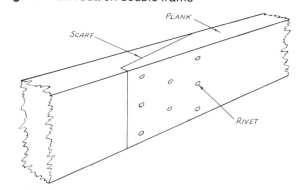

Fig 110 Scarfed plank joint

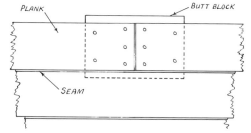

Fig 111 Carvel plank butt block

by scarfing (Fig 110) or by fitting butt blocks (Fig 111) on the inside. Scarfing is almost essential with clinker planking, owing to the lands. It avoids the unsightliness of internal butt blocks, which cannot always be hidden by lockers or linings. With a pattern to work from, sections of a plank can be scarfed together on the bench to form a single strake. More often, final scarf fastening is undertaken on the boat as each section is fitted. Butt blocks are invariably assembled *in situ*, for they must overlap the adjacent planks by about one plank thickness. The length of each block should be about twice the plank width and the thickness about $1\frac{1}{2}$ times that of the plank.

Resin glue or epoxy plus screws generally make a firmer job than mastic and riveted copper nails, for both butt blocks and scarfs. Due to the diagonal joint lines of scarfs (see Chapter 4) screw heads must be embedded in the thinner half of the joint: some screws are driven from inside, some from outside. Scarf joints can be made on top of a frame or in between two frames. Butt blocks must always come between frames with adequate clearance to permit painting. Amidships, blocks generally lie horizontally, so the top edge must be bevelled or sloped to prevent water from lodging there.

Double Carvel

For craft longer than about 30 ft (9 m) a double thickness of fore-and-aft carvel planking (Fig 133b) eliminates the need for steaming, soling or caulking. Teak or similar stable, rot-resistant timber is essential, with bedding compound between the skins. If you propose to use epoxy, it would be wiser to adopt a cold-moulded skin. With bent ribs, rabbeted carvel planking as seen in Fig 79d is more suitable than double carvel. The latter is intended for use with the frames seen in Fig 91, or on any chine boat.

Make end-joins by scarfing *in situ*; lute with bedding compound and fasten with bronze screws, preferably right through into the adjacent skin. For frame fastenings, use ring nails for the inner skin plus heavy gauge bronze woodscrews right through both skins. Outer seams need not run along the centres of inner strakes, but should be roughly parallel to them. The overlap between inner and outer planks should be at least 2 in (50 mm).

Spiling Templates

You can amalgamate the spiling, scribing, setting-out,

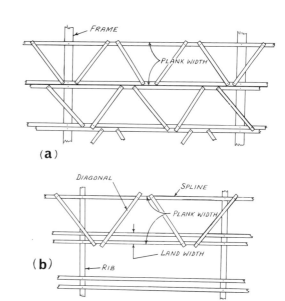

Fig 112 Plank spiling templates

plank width and fairing operations described above into one operation by using *spiling templates*. Thin splines of knot-free wood are needed—lots of them. Suitable offcuts are often discarded as scrap by joinery workshops, sawmills and boatyards. Use $\frac{3}{8}$ in (9 mm) square for a dinghy, $\frac{1}{2}$ in (12 mm) square for a 20 ft (6 m) boat, and around $\frac{3}{4}$ in (18 mm) for a 30 ft (9 m) boat.

Tack the splines around one side of the hull so that each represents one plank edge (Fig 112a). Splines are best in single lengths for small craft, but may be joined (preferably by glued scarfs) on bigger boats. When all splines are in place and appear fair from all angles, glue a lattice of strips of similar wood at about 45° along each template, clamped by means of veneer pins driven while holding a dolly behind. Avoid letting any glue get into the longitudinal joint. Mark on the position of each mould or frame, also each seam for later plank alignment.

Note that the arrangement is slightly different for clinker work (Fig 112b) owing to the lands. Whereas all lattice strips can be fixed before removing carvel templates, clinker templates must be taken off one at a time to allow the lattice strips to be nailed to the next template. To get really accurate clinker templates, block out the lower splines from the moulds by the plank thickness, to simulate the lands. Number each template from top to bottom.

When removed from the hull, spiling templates can be laid flat on the floor to give an exact shape for each plank.

By all means saw out a batch of planks before fitting any, but leave a bit to plane down to a perfect fit when offered up. Transfer carefully the mould positions and the template numbers. Any two (or three) templates can be laid side by side to ensure minimum wastage when cutting planks from wide boards.

Do not attempt to reverse the templates to fit them on the other side—the lattice strips get in the way and the templates may get damaged. Just transfer all seam positions as described under Template Strips on page 90 and use each master plank as a template for its opposite number. If further hulls are to be built later to the same design, store the spiling templates as you would moulds and backbone patterns.

A plank may spring out of shape after sawing, due to grain peculiarities. This will be lessened if planks are fitted immediately after sawing out. A little edge set can be tolerated by forcing. With difficult wood, mark out oversize, let it warp, then re-mark from the template and cut again.

Using Narrow Stock

As shown in Fig 99, most planks for round-bilge hulls possess edgewise curvature which leads to wastage of board width. This happens less with chine hulls, most of which can be planked mainly with straight narrow stock plus a few wide boards.

By setting out round-bilge seams in an unconventional (albeit unsightly) manner, one can make do with boards little wider than the midships plank widths. For a clinker dinghy, by starting the garboard as a small triangular shape, narrow boards can be used for the majority of the planks (Photo 32). But it pays to merge into normal snying strakes towards the sheer as the lands are so prominent.

On a big carvel hull, start with the normally straight planks at the turn of the bilge. Working up to the sheer, continue with straight planks, scribing and shaping each lower edge but leaving the upper edge straight. This results in a plank reaching the sheer amidships while big triangular areas are left fore and aft to be filled as indicated in Fig 113. Having worked downwards in similar fashion towards the keel, you will probably find that mainly the aft garboard area needs to be filled with short boards.

Another method is to transform the top and bottom of the straight bilge planks into pseudo chines by gluing

Photo 32 Economical use of straight planking

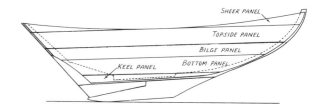

Fig 113 Use of straight planks

strips of plank offcut to the inside between frames to create rabbets. Starting at the sheer, lay the first plank with a downward droop for'ard of about 10°, fill the triangle abaft the stem with short strakes, then continue with parallel planks so that they all end along the newly formed rabbet. Starting parallel to the keel and working upwards, the strakes which end on the lower rabbet will generally do so at a similar angle to those on the topsides, but in the opposite direction.

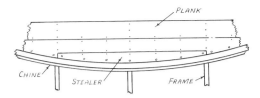

Fig 114 Chine stealer for the classic runabout

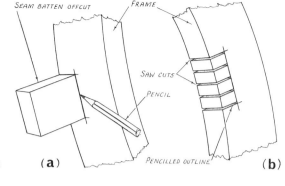

Fig 115 Making notches in sawn frames   **(a)**   **(b)**

Classic Chine

Unless you want to varnish her topsides, a classic runabout (Fig 60a) is simple to plank with narrow stock. Due to the straight sheer-line, even with wide stock the sheer planks only just reach the stem (see Photo 16). As the boat would be set up inverted, bottom planking should be completed first, so you can get inside easily. Spile for the garboards and work across to the chines in pairs. Most planks have considerable twist for'ard and should be steamed. If the chine shutter plank works out a little too wide for the stock available, fit a stealer as shown in Fig 114. This avoids a thin, tapering strip which is difficult to fasten at the ends.

With narrow stock you cannot set out all seam positions on the frames beforehand as described for traditional carvel. One edge is shaped to fit snugly to the previous plank and the other edge is not shaped at all.

Seam Battens

Having planks thinner than $\frac{1}{2}$in (12mm), a classic runabout cannot be succesfully caulked with cotton, so *seam batten carvel* (also called *ribband carvel*) planking is used, as in Fig 52d. A pine batten $\frac{3}{8} \times 1\frac{1}{2}$in (9 × 38 mm) is notched and screwed to the frames to back up each seam. Prime all faying surfaces, smear with bedding compound, then fasten planks to battens with thin, turned copper nails at 4 in (100 mm) centres.

Each seam batten is notched in after fitting a plank temporarily and marking the seam position on each frame. Set out each notch as in Fig 115a using an offcut of seam batten having a centreline drawn along both faces. Be careful to follow the frame edge bevel and the batten direction precisely. Make as many saw cuts as necessary following both angles. Chisel out gently working from both sides.

Chapter 12
Modern Wood

The smooth finish of a painted carvel hull is imitated by several other wooden constructions. Although a few of these have been around for half a century in certain guises, they are modern in comparison with age-old clinker and carvel planking.

Strip-planking

We have already studied the use of straight narrow planks. Strip-planking is a development of this where all pieces are so narrow that they are almost square in section, allowing great edge set without buckling. Before the advent of resin glue, boats were strip-planked (particularly in North America) using softwood with painted seams. Much of the strength was derived from closely spaced edge-nails, each passing through three strips (Fig. 116).

Nowadays, one either uses a stable hardwood with resorcinol glue, or epoxy saturation with almost any type of clear wood. Either method should eliminate disastrous shrinkage. Edge-nails are still necessary but at wider intervals, largely to act as clamps (Fig 117). For a 23 ft (7 m) cruiser with a $\frac{7}{8}$ in (22 mm) skin thickness, each strip

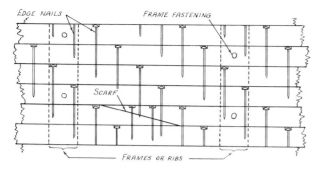

Fig 116 Traditional strip-plank layout

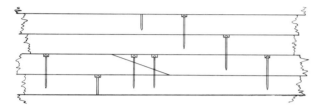

Fig 117 Edge-nails with glued seams

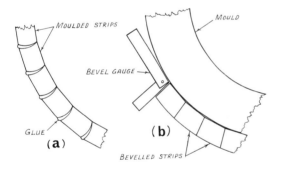

Fig 118 Moulded and bevelled strip-plank edges

should measure about $\frac{7}{8} \times 1\frac{1}{8}$ in (22 × 28 mm), while for a 33-footer (10 m) this might be $1 \times 1\frac{3}{8}$ in (25 × 34 mm).

Two ways One of the two systems shown in Fig 118 is adopted to ensure watertight seams.

a. Strips are spindled at the sawmill with one edge rounded to a radius of about $1\frac{1}{2}$ times skin thickness, while the other edge is coved to slightly smaller radius (Fig 118a).

b. Strips come with fine-sawn edges and both faces planed. As each strip is fitted, one edge is bevelled by hand to meet snugly against the last strip fixed.

System b produces the best results. Although a gives

strong joints, it uses a lot of glue and needs more surface filling. This is shown in exaggerated form in Fig 118a, but in most situations the mouldings fit together closely. You need to use WEST SYSTEM epoxy for this as one of the special fillers will be applicable to any size of gap. The coves should face upwards as far as possible to retain a pool of glue and reduce the amount squeezed out. Also, the edge nails will be hammered on the robust rounded part.

As hardened glue blunts a plane rapidly, always remove surplus glue (inside and out) as work proceeds. Although you can do this with a slightly moist rag after fitting, better to await the gel stage and scrape it off. Using solvents is certain to cause glue starvation. A belt sander (Photo 33) is useful for finishing where glue lines are thick. You may need a suspension spring from the roof to help support this heavy tool.

Strip Layout

If planking proceeds evenly up from the keel it will never arrive parallel at the sheer. This may look queer, but is not otherwise detrimental. By taking the trouble to measure down from the sheer around the periphery of each mould, a neater layout results. This will leave a triangular area at the keel to be filled with short strips or a panel of solid carvel (Fig 113).

With moulds or frames far apart, take care to align strips perfectly and in fair curves, otherwise the surface will have waves which are impossible to eradicate by planing. Make simple gripes as shown in Photo 34, with jaw openings equal to plank thickness. These are faster to slip on than clamps. Remember to cover these with polythene if they need to be left on after edge-nailing. Similarly, moulds must not get stuck to the planking.

Edge Bevels

Although very little bevel is normally needed with method b, a good routine speeds up the job. After a while it can be done accurately by eye.

Only the one edge needs bevelling to match the previous strip. Make a miniature bevel gauge as shown in Fig 118b. Set this to the bevel at each mould or frame and use the same setting while planing the new strip edge at that point. To speed up the process, make a set of five or six small pine or sheet metal test plates to gauge gaps, and give each one a reference number.

Photo 33 Belt-sanding a strip-planked hull

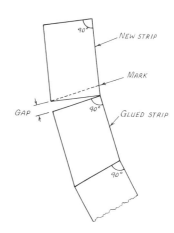

Fig 119 Measuring bevel gap

Photo 34 Trial panel showing use of gripes

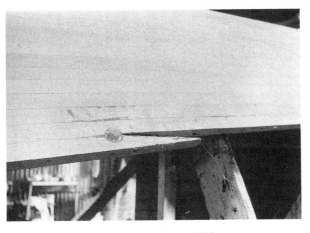

Photo 35 Typical strip-planking scarf joint

To save having to offer up whole strips, dangle an offcut of strip at each mould. Transfer each test plate reading to the back face of the new strip as in Fig 119, then plane your bevel as shown dotted.

On the bench If you have a full-length bench with the mould positions marked along its edge, transferring the readings is simplified. The bench top needs chocks to align a strip for planing, plus an end stop. A wooden drill guide sliding on the strip ensures accurate edge-nail pilot holes without using a drill press.

Joining

Relatively short strips simplify handling. Scarf joints (Photo 35) need a jig for quick sawing and uniformity. Even quicker is a router with suitable jig.

Provided scarfs are well shifted in adjacent runs, their frequency is immaterial. Glued scarf lengths can be as little as three times strip depth. The surfaces do not need planing. To clamp a scarf, use two nails about 1½ times strip depth in length. To avoid splits, make these thinner than the main edge-nails. Drive some edge-nails first to stop the scarf from sliding.

Edge-Nails

Drive sufficient edge-nails to clamp all glued seams tightly, but not farther apart than about 12 in (300 mm). Nail lengths of about 1½ times strip depth will suffice provided the heads are well punched in. For painted seams

(Fig 118a) increase the length to about $2\frac{1}{2}$ times strip depth and set them about 4 in (100 mm) apart.

Ring nails are ideal, though expensive. Square galvanized boat nails have a life of at least 30 years. Edge-nails are so well insulated by wood and resin that galvanic action is negligible, particularly with glued seams.

Pilot boring is essential for edge nails and scarf nails in hardwood, plus a little countersinking. With a strip offered up, but before gluing, extend each hole into the adjacent plank. Additional nails or clamping may be needed after gluing. For extra long holes, spade bits home-made from drill rod work fine. To ensure even distribution and to prevent one nail fouling another, scribe all edge-nail positions on the surface, as in Photo 36.

Woodscrews are generally best for frame or rib fastenings, spaced as in Fig 116 and plugged or stopped over outside.

Photo 36 Keeping edge-nail positions marked

Suitable Designs

Few plans are available specifically for strip-planked boats, but almost any round-bilge or chine carvel design can (with the designer's permission) be adapted readily. Some attractive designs are strip-planked at the turn of the bilge (or soft chine) while all the remainder is planked with plywood.

Generally speaking, if the original carvel skin thickness is retained (or preferably increased by about 7%) with the same framing, all should be well. All strips must be glued to frames, ribs and rabbets. Strip-planking has been used for skins as thin as $\frac{3}{8}$ in (9 mm), but such work is tedious and the shell is prone to cracking. The method is best suited to skin thicknesses between 1 and 2 in (25–50 mm).

For and Against Strip-planking

With the added cost of glue and nails, plus the expense for most amateurs of machining the stock, strip-planking generally costs more than carvel. A 23 ft (7 m) hull can have as many as 5000 nails. With the weight of glue used, strip work can be surprisingly heavy.

On the other hand, strips need no caulking. As they exert very little pressure when bent into position, temporary moulds need not be so robust as for traditional planking.

Strip-planking is well suited to singlehanded work at odd moments, with the help of slings or shockcord to support long strips. If seams are glued in lengths of about 10 ft (3 m), there will be no panic to complete nailing before the glue gels. Short lengths are handy, but where there is considerable twist it pays to scarf into longer lengths on the bench. A sash clamp tightened across a strip makes a good lever to apply twist as nailing proceeds. Alternatively, a hardwood lever with a notch near one end (made a close fit onto a strip) works reasonably well. To accommodate much twist—and around the turn of the bilge, or for a soft chine—narrower than average strips have obvious advantages. Conversely, on the flatter sections, strips as much as double standard depth are feasible, provided the edge set bend is slight.

Remember to ensure that all wood has the low moisture content detailed in Chapter 4, and that the air temperature is amply high when using epoxy saturation or resin glue (Chapter 6).

Using Plywood

Marine ply planking is almost always used for single and double chine boats nowadays. For certain long, narrow hulls such as canoes and catamarans, it can be bent into round-bilge form. You can clad a big chine hull quite rapidly with plywood, but an extra pair of hands is valuable when offering up big panels.

The GP14 sailing dinghy (see Chapter 8) is simple to plank as there are no rabbets. A run through the procedure will explain the problems for most other designs using plywood. A lot of surplus material will be left after planking, but offcuts of marine plywood are extremely useful. Standard sheets of $\frac{1}{4}$ in (6 mm) marine plywood 8×4 ft (2.4×1.2 m) lead to more wastage than 6×3 ft (1.8×0.9 m) sheets, but they are easier to buy.

Scarfing (Fig 30) makes the neatest joints between panels, but most amateurs prefer to make butt joints *in situ* (Fig 29) with wide butt straps made from offcuts glued inside. Note that the outside grain of the butt strap ply must run in the same direction as the outside veneers of the sheets being joined. Spread glue over the butted plywood edges as well the faying surfaces, and fit double rows of fastenings each side unless efficient external clamping is possible.

Bottom Panels

The for'ard bottom panels are always the most difficult to fit, due to the great twist there. They should always be tackled first.

Start by clamping a whole sheet as close to the framing as possible, with the long edge just overlapping the hog and the short edge beyond the stem where the chine bone piece runs out. As C-clamps will not reach across at the forefoot, strut from the roof (or get some help) to keep the sheet near enough to scribe a rough outline. Avoid applying too much pressure as this could distort the framing.

You need lines along the outside of hog, chine, forefoot and stem. Remove the sheet and draw in the bone piece notch line. Do this by transferring a few offsets measured from the side-of-chine line already scribed. Leave a little spare to allow for errors, then cut along the lines. Use this panel as a template for its opposite number. They are a handed pair, so if the plywood has a fairer face one side than the other, place them back to back for marking.

Although clamping will now be easier, it pays to steam the for'ard end with a lance (see Chapter 7) or pour on boiling water for 4 min. Without this, excessive clamp pressure could rupture the plywood.

Final Shaping

Leave a panel clamped as long as possible after steaming to dry out and set to shape. Then drive a few temporary steel screws to locate the exact future position and relieve the clamps. Run a panel saw along the hog surface, cutting the plywood flush and at the correct bevel, but allow for final planing later. Do the same around the stem, using a coping or compass saw. Next saw the vertical jump which occurs as indicated in Fig 70.

It takes some tedious planing to align the plywood to

the bone notch bevel, but this is wiser than trying to saw it. Do not finish-plane any of these edges until after gluing. Now scribe with a pencil from inside the boat alongside all framing members to indicate the exact gluing areas. Bore all the fastening holes which can be readily located from outside.

Panel Fixing

Panels are best attached by woodscrews, perhaps combined with some ring nails. Remove the panel and using the glue lines on the back as guides, bore all fastening holes not so far drilled. Burr from the drill will then appear on the outside surface, to be removed as soon as the countersinks are cut. Before final fitting, trim the after edge of the panel approximately at right angles to the hog, ready to join on the next panel. Before fixing any bottom panels, it pays to mark out the topside sheets. Clamping and scribing are then easier, particularly along the chines.

After steaming or wetting, do not apply glue until all is completely dry. Any two-part resin glue or epoxy will do. Fasten down quickly, starting at the forefoot. Wipe away surplus glue as described for strip-planking.

Joining Panels

Butt straps for the GP14 are about 4 in (100 mm) wide. For bottom panels, glue the ends thoroughly with close fits from hog to stringer and from stringer to chine. If scarfing is preferred (see Chapter 4), it is best done after all panels per side have been roughly shaped, thus making full-length panels.

Having shaped the first section and squared off the edge to be scarfed, draw a line parallel to this on both sides, representing the scarf width. Offer up again and transfer the scarf position on to hog and chine. When marking out the next panel, transfer these marks to it. The parallel line of the previous panel becomes the scarf edge of the new one, and vice versa. Be careful to saw along the *foremost* line! This process should be repeated for any third panel. If done accurately the whole assembly will fit perfectly all over.

If you decide to glue each scarf *in situ*, the same procedure is necessary for marking out. Having shaped all the scarfs on the bench, glue the panels to the boat one by one. Trailing scarfs (see Chapter 4) will not result, but this matters little.

To clamp a scarf *in situ* fit a thick polythene or cellophane covered backing piece inside with temporary steel screws into the hog and chine. Clamp or screw the new panel to prevent sliding. On the outside, pin a thin, plastic wrapped batten along the feather edge. Clamp the remainder of the scarf with wire nails having plywood tabs under their heads to facilitate withdrawal.

With the bottom planked, finish planing the exposed edges flush with the hog, stem and bone piece notch. Add the keel capping, plane that flush, then fit the protective rubbing strips.

Tackle the topsides in similar manner to the bottom, starting at the stem. On completion, fit the bone pieces and stem band. If brass pins are used to hold the bone pieces while gluing, remember to punch these well down before rounding off with a plane. Alternatively, use thin steel screws: remove them later and fill the holes.

Sunken Panels

Many designs avoid the bone piece by letting the topside plywood overlap the bottom, with an external rubbing strip added for protection (Fig 120). As the chine angle becomes zero close to the stem, there has to be a sudden change from lap joint to miter. An exploded view of the changeover is shown in Fig 121.

Designs like our classic runabout have rabbets along the keel, chine and stem. Plywood panels must be cut to drop accurately into these with the minimum of trial-and-error planing. Quite the best way to achieve this is to spile the outline on a sheet of hardboard (Fig 105a). Refer to Chapter 11 for details of spiling. If you cannot utilize a steam-bent panel as a template for the other side, reverse the hardboard and spile again.

Instead of spiling, one can, with a little judicious marking and whittling, make a hardboard template which is an almost perfect fit. One sure (but messy) method of marking this out is to dab spots of paint on the rabbet edges, then press the hardboard on top!

Other Plywood Methods

Some of the simplest plywood chine boats have no framing except for a few bulkheads. The plywood is scarfed into full-length panels which are accurately shaped in pairs from dimensions given on the drawings. Once these panels have been pulled together along keel and chines, a shell of true shape is created. One way to make the joints is

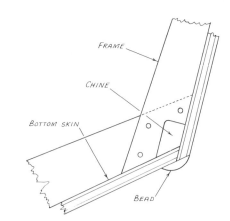

Fig 120 Lapped plywood joint at chine

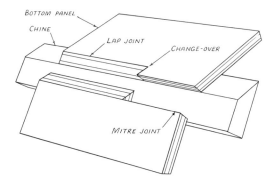

Fig 121 Lap-to-mitre changeover

by using individual stitches of copper wire, then sealing and reinforcing each joint by means of one or more layers of glass tape each side, impregnated with fibreglass resin. See Chapter 5 for further details.

For the long, narrow hulls of canoes and catamarans, a round-bilge form can be produced in plywood in similar manner. One full-length panel for each side is wire stitched and taped along the keel at a specified deadrise angle. When cured, the assembly is forced into a female jig representing the deck outline. This automatically produces the required round-bilge shape. While in the jig, gunwales, bulkhead and decking are added. The jig is then dismantled.

When broad, strip-planked soft chines (see Chapter 1) merge into plywood topsides and bottom, the appearance is very much like the round-bilge form. A double or triple chine frameless hull is easy to plank over temporary moulds and bulkheads with the hog, chines, gunwales and stringers inserted beforehand. Multi-chine skins bend readily without steaming, as three or more panels per sides are sharing the for'ard twist.

A variation of the usual single chine theme is the conic hull shape (Photo 66) mentioned in Chapter 8. This type has considerable curvature to both topside and bottom sections, avoiding a boxy appearance. The lines are developed from parts of cones and cylinders in such a way that plywood or metal will take the curves without buckling.

Cold-Moulding

Double diagonal and similar skins have been in use for nearly a century. Coupled with epoxy saturation, any number of thin skins may be laminated together into a strong shell requiring minimal framing. Factories do it by hot-moulding, applying pressure with vacuum bags and curing in a hot oven to speed things up. By cold-moulding the amateur can do much the same, but in less of a hurry and without complicated facilities.

Dinghies are generally cold-moulded from two or three layers of 2 mm veneer crossing diagonally, with another layer laid fore-and-aft on the outside or in the middle. For light boats up to about 20 ft (6 m) long, three layers of 3 mm plywood suffice, but the method is applicable for hulls up to 100 ft (30 m) long, when seven layers of $\frac{3}{8}$ in (9 mm) solid wood might be used.

High quality plywood offers consistent thickness and lack of defects. For dinghies, diagonal strips about $2\frac{3}{4}$ in (70 mm) wide are popular, laid at around 60° to keel and gunwale. For the outside skin all strips trail aft at the gunwales so that they meet the forefoot roughly at right angles. The inner skin slopes the other way, as seen in Photos 37 and 38.

Veneers have the advantage of easy cutting with a knife or shears and the edges are less hairy than plywood edges. Except perhaps for the first skin, the stiffness of plywood is useful, as fewer temporary fastenings are required to hold it down. For such narrow hulls as catamarans and rowing skiffs, veneer widths can often be increased amidships to as much as 9 in (230 mm), narrowing down to incorporate the double curvature at bow and stern.

(Top) **Photo 37** Cardboard under staples for easy removal

(Bottom) **Photo 38** Tabs stapled across seams in veneer

Especially for the above type hulls, the 'constant camber' system is popular in America. The same radius is used for all sections so the veneers need no edge shaping. A single half-jig serves for both sides. After fixing to the keel the cured shells are pulled in at bow and stern, and propped out to create the desired sheer outline.

Those who want a fuller description and some suitable designs to consider should read *Cold-Moulded and Strip-Planked Wood Boatbuilding* by Ian Nicolson (Stanford Maritime/Nautical).

The Jig The difference in stiffness between plywood and veneer controls the complexity of the jig (mould or plug) required. Similar jigs are used for fibreglass construction (see Chapter 14). For certain catamarans with asymmetrical hulls, a separate plug is necessary for each hull. As such boats often have sealed hulls with little or no accommodation, some utilize permanent framing made in similar manner to a jig.

To prevent veneers kinking, you need a close-battened jig, either strip-planked or with gaps under $\frac{3}{8}$ in (9 mm) wide. Note that impregnating with epoxy makes veneer a little stiffer. When using strip-planking, with a little care it may be possible to turn a tightly built plug into a real boat which can be sold later!

With plywood skins, their stiffness permits an open-battened jig to be used, as in Photo 20. The gaps are about batten width at the turn of the bilge and up to double this on the flatter areas. Square battens are usual, the thickness depending on the frame spacings. Set up three trestles at this spacing. Rest one or two different battens across them. Choose the thinnest one that resists a midspan load of at least 4 lb (1.5 kg) without bending.

To avoid veneer kinks, give a fully-battened plug a skim of decorator's filler prior to sanding. Open battens need light planing and sanding to remove all ridges.

As with most frameless boats, any backbone must be notched into the jig. An outer keel may be added after skinning, as for the GP14, or rabbeted as in Fig 122. If a design has tumblehome aft, fit the transom later. This allows the shell to be sprung outwards sufficiently to get it off the jig. Add internal gunwales at the same time.

The First Skin

To prevent stray glue from adhering to a jig, run a band of Scotch tape along each batten, or cover the whole thing with cellophane or polythene, tailored and taped as neces-

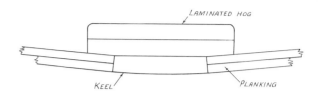

Fig 122 Cold-moulded dinghy keel

Photo 39 Laying outer double diagonal skin

sary. This must not overlap the hog or stem where reliable gluing of the first skin is essential.

A common way to lay diagonal veneers is called the *parrel and wrapper* method. Parrel is really just a contraction of parallel. Starting amidships, fit every other strip as in Photo 39, using strips of equal width with no edge shaping. Ensure that the widest interval between them is not greater than the minimum width of the strips to be inserted later. Lay at an angle between 45° and 60°, depending on the lengths. Using plywood from standard sheets may decide this. Allow a bit to spare at the sheer. There is no need to work to port and starboard in unison.

Multi-skin Fastenings

Glue and fix to the boat's permanent framing with brass pins. Ring nails will later go through all skins. Wipe away surplus glue or the next layer will not fit snugly. Do not glue any edges on the first skin. If veneers miss the jig anywhere, drive a few temporary steel veneer pins or staples. Instead of hammering, use a hollow magnetic pin tool to press in veneer pins.

Photo 40 Cold-moulding a Unicorn catamaran hull

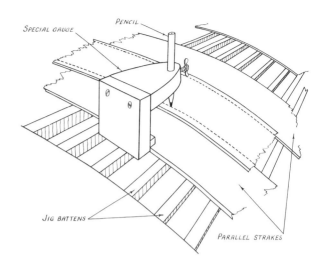

Fig 123 Scribing gauge for alternate strips

To facilitate withdrawal, drive such fastenings through tabs of stiff cardboard. For later skins, ensure release from stray glue by sticking Scotch tape to the underside of tabs or inserting polythene sheet. The tabs pointing downwards in Photo 38 will be hinged across the seam later and a second pin driven.

Staples An industrial stapler (trigger tacker) firing $\frac{5}{16}$ in (7.5 mm) staples speeds work considerably: see Photo 40. Where there is no glue a length of cord under each staple makes it easy to pull them out. Tabs generally apply better pressure. With a compressed air tool, staples $\frac{3}{8}$ in (9 mm) long will tackle plywood or thick veneer. For a jig left permanently in the hull use stainless steel or phosphor bronze staples and leave them in. You need to mark on all the stringer positions for this, or else use an extra thick first skin to prevent any points going right through.

Bagging The rapid pressure provided by the industrial vacuum bagging technique has limited promise for amateurs. With a leakproof floor having a seal around the boat, a PVC bag is smoothed over a net over the glued skin, clamped under the seal, and all air evacuated. Improvising, you need a 6 cfm compressor to get the bulk of air out fast, then a $1\frac{1}{2}$ h.p. vacuum pump to get to -0.7 bar. Laying only a few strips in one session, bagging prevents one from wiping away the glue which oozes out.

Shutter Strips

Having fixed the parallel strips, the wrapper strips need shaping on both edges to fit accurately into the gaps. You can do this with paint spots as described above, but the special gauge shown in Fig 123 does it best. Set the gauge to the width of the fixed strips. While a wrapper is held in position, draw the gauge along both sides as shown. Make sure the pencil is perpendicular to the surface. After cutting out, a little planing should produce a perfect fit. Sanding is better for very thin veneer. Remember, if you fit the wrapper immediately, you will not be able to run the gauge along to mark the adjacent ones! Bevel each edge slightly towards the *middle* of the lamination. This will trap glue in each seam and produce almost invisible joins inside and outside the shell.

Tips for neat work Glue leaking through inner skin seams creates much sanding work eventually. If using WEST SYSTEM epoxy, stiffen some with their colloidal silica or microballoons to fill obvious gaps. A matching filler is best for a varnished internal finish, but few cold-moulded shells clean up well enough to warrant this.

To knife-cut veneer edges you need a steel guide about $\frac{5}{16}$ in (7.5 mm) square which is clamped along the curve. No need to buy dozens of trimming knife blades: each one can be honed on an oilstone about 30 times before renewal. When you saw out inner skin strips, a

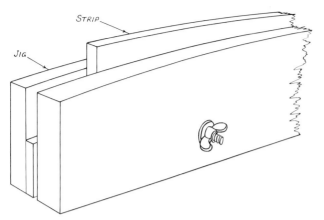

Fig 124 Holding thin strips for edge planing

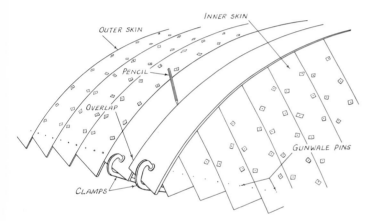

Fig 125 Marking out consecutive strips

Photo 41 Marking the glue line

sabre saw or jigsaw will not roughen the side which faces into the boat: a bandsaw or table saw will. To minimize this stick tape on the inside face. The reverse procedure holds for middle and outer skins.

Accurate planing is troublesome without a jig like the one in Fig 124. This need not be the full length. In fact, with curved edges, keeping a strip well buried in the jig is simplified by moving it along, re-clamping with a quick turn of the butterfly nuts.

Consecutive Strips

Fitting strips one by one (Photo 41) is sometimes more convenient than parrel and wrapper. Working consecutively, each piece has one straight and one shaped edge. Shaping and gluing becomes a continuous process, and well-glued seams are a certainty.

To pick up the shape of the one edge, a strip is no fixed until the following one has been positioned over with edges coinciding at the widest point (or points) an overlapping elsewhere (Fig 125). Draw a sharp penc along the overlapping edge and you have scribed th shape on the previous strip. For better accuracy, sli another strip underneath the overlapping one to preven it from tilting.

Overlapping must create slight error, as both strip are not on the same plane. Offer up, mark the highspot then shave them down. For dead accuracy, once the fit i within $\frac{1}{8}$ in (6 mm) spile with a dummy. To make a guid for the dummy, stack two strips together. It is easier wit some help! On long, narrow boats most strips have ver little edge shape. Trial-and-error planing takes care o this after a bit of practice.

Second Skin

With parrel and wrapper middle and outside skins removing surplus glue to create clean edges wastes a lot o time. Therefore, work in panels of eight strips (fou parallel and four shaped). Number them, mark their seam positions, remove, then glue them permanently in con secutive order. Remember to shape one strip in advance of fitting, for no method of scribing is easily applicabl when all the strips of a panel are firmly glued.

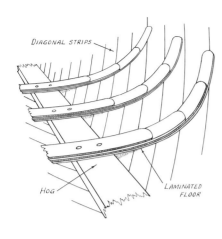

Fig 126 Laminated strap floors

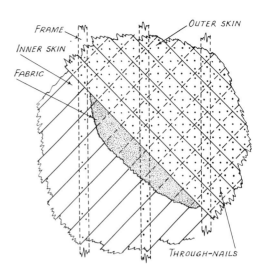

Fig 127 Double diagonal fastening layout

With an open-battened jig, pencil the batten locations on each skin. Keep to these lines when driving temporary pins. Pull cardboard tabs off pin heads before extracting the pins with pincers. Slip a stiff knife under plywood tabs and lever up tabs and pins together. With staples, bend up the middle with a small screwdriver and do the rest with pincers.

Fore-and-Aft Skins

In a three-skin lamination, the middle and outermost layer may be laid fore-and-aft. Such skins take longer to lay than diagonal ones, so avoid them if possible. Whereas diagonal strips need to bend in one direction only, fore-and-aft ones (particularly at the turn of the bilge) need to bend across their widths also. Jig battens are not always just where required for tabs near the strip edges. Much planing and sanding is necessary to obtain a fair external surface, possibly cutting right through the facing veneer of thin plywood.

Fore-and-aft strips need not be full length, provided butts are well shifted and well glued. With parrel and wrapper, be prepared for some weirdly shaped shutter strips, perhaps tapering down to a point at each end.

By using more glue, and where appearance is not important, you can lessen the shaping and double-bend problems—and save a lot of scrap wood—by having strips no wider than 2 in (50 mm). In long lengths these will tolerate a lot of edge set.

If an outer fore-and-aft skin is adopted to enhance the beauty of varnished topsides, set out the strakes neatly as described for carvel planking. Merging with parrel and wrapper is feasible below the waterline.

Finishing Work

Before lifting a shell off its jig, run a pencil along the sheer batten. To transfer this to the outside, drill $\frac{1}{16}$ (1.5 mm) holes at 10 in (250 mm) intervals. Fit temporary athwartships struts to keep the flexible shell steady and to size, before inserting deck beams and/or thwarts. Most cold-moulded dinghies have plywood decking. With some temporary battening, this can be cold-moulded if preferred.

Cruisers On cruising boats, two cold-moulded diagonal skins plus a top layer of fore-and-aft scrubbed teak makes a strong, practical and attractive deck. Cold-moulding can also be used for fabricating well-rounded cabin tops, doghouses and hatches.

Sailboats with ballasted keels need reinforcement in way of the keel bolts. Suitable floors can be laminated *in situ* from straps of thin plywood, arranged as in Fig 126. Similar reinforcement is useful in way of bilge keels, though more often fore-and-aft stringers are bonded to the skin by *in situ* lamination.

Double Diagonal Planking

Although rarely used nowadays, double diagonal planking was highly successful for chine and round-bilge hulls before the advent of cold-moulding. The most noted applications were shore-based lifeboats and a range of naval craft from launches to high-speed gunboats. The method does have merits, requiring no jig and no special long lengths of planking. Two skins crossing at about 90° are fastened to each other with a network of riveted copper nails (Fig 127). A layer of unbleached calico doped with linseed oil is stretched between the two skins (Photo 39) and all faying surfaces are set in mastic. Double diagonal planks up to about $\frac{3}{4}$ in (18 mm) in thickness are normally set out using the parrel and wrapper system, but the consecutive method is equally applicable.

Chapter 13
Decking

As explained in Chapter 8 and illustrated in Fig 72b, you should not trim along the sheer of any wooden hull without first fitting (or offering up) the deck beams. The sheer top bevel must align with the deck *camber*, sometimes called the *crown*.

Dinghy Beams

Some of the GP14 deck beams are fixed to the gunwales using the type of glued joint shown in Fig 128a. Notched centrally into the foredeck beams, a *king plank* runs from stem to mast, rounded to match the deck camber (128b). A square hole through this supports the *samson post* or towing bollard.

Some light-weight racing catamarans have vertical plywood web beams (Photo 42) which are simply glued into saw-cut notches in the gunwales. Some plywood canoe decks are of similar construction.

Launch Beams

Typical classic runabout deck framing appears in Fig 129. The members running fore and aft are called *carlines* (sometimes spelt carlins or carlings), notched and glued lightly into the beams and secured with two screws into the end grain. Each beam end is glued and screwed to the side of a frame, without gussets or knees. Cruising boats need extra strong joints in this position, as described later. Small beams are often cut from straight-grained hardwood or thick plywood. Several beams may be cut from one wide board. Two beams can be parted with one careful saw cut.

Photo 42 Plywood beams grooved and glued into gunwales

To avoid frame distortion, remove cross-spalls one at a time as deck beams are fitted. Alternatively, clamp temporary struts further down.

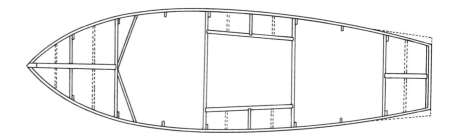

Fig 129 Runabout beam-to-frame joint

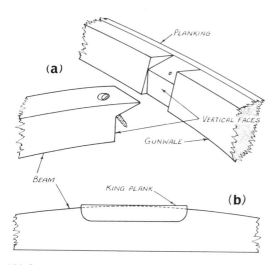

Fig 128 Sailing dinghy deck beam details

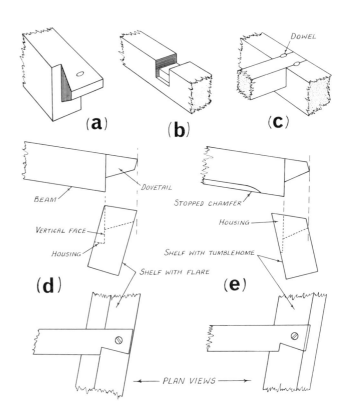

Fig 130 Beam end joints at shelf

Big Beams

Well fitted and strong deck framing is imperative for
cruising boats. Such beams are generally half-dovetailed
to the shelves or clamps (Fig 130a) plus hanging and lodging knees (Fig 8) in way of masts or extra big deck openings. When beams sit on top of the shelves (Photo 43 and
Fig 89) concealed dovetails are used: see exploded view in
Fig 132. Some drawings show the simple half-notched
joint in Fig 130b. This works well with WEST SYSTEM
epoxy and is very secure if dowelled as shown in 130c.

Whatever type of joint, make the male parts on the
beam ends first. Sit the beam in position on top of the
shelves and project vertical lines downwards to get the
shapes of the female parts, as in 130d and e. Whether the
shelves lean outwards (130d) or inwards (103e), always
cut the notches vertically or the beam will never drop in.
Such joints are simpler around amidships where there is
normally little flare or tumblehome.

Always cut half-dovetail mouths to face towards the
stem from amidships for'ard and vice versa towards the
stern. The joints are stronger that way. Slope the bases
upwards as shown in 130d and e, so as not to weaken the
shelves. Do not make half-dovetail necks narrower than
two-thirds of the beam's width; three-quarters is better
on boats over about 30 ft (9 m).

Photo 43 Beam-end arrangement for concealed dovetails

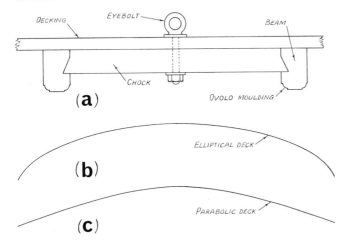

Fig 132 Concealed beam end dovetails

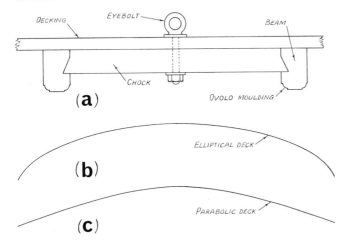

Fig 131 Deckhead chocks and unusual beam shapes

To set a beam dead square across the boat, use a steel tape to measure from a nail in the middle of the stemhead to each end of the beam. The distances should tally within about $\frac{1}{8}$ in (3 mm).

In the full epoxy treatment, dovetailing and notching is replaced by big fillets of filled resin. Most amateur shipwrights enjoy the satisfaction of creating solid traditional joints. Some cost and weight is also saved this way.

Carlines and Chocks

Traditionally, carlines have shallow but full dovetails into the beams. With epoxy, simple notches as in Figs 128a and 130b suffice.

The *partners* comprise one or more chocks between beams to support the mast or tabernacle. Set the grain fore and aft, with two athwartships bolts right through to deter cracking. Mast partners, and the similar chocks to support winches, bollards and eyebolts, are best installed as the beams go in, using notches as in Fig 131a or between carlines as in Fig 144a. For mounting ventilators and low-stress deck fittings, pads are glued underneath the deck and not connected to beams or carlines.

Beam Shaping

Without a source of grown crooks, long beams are best laminated *leaf spring* style. Although numerous thin strips make the strongest lamination, as few as three thick pieces will often suffice for the moderate camber of most beams. Planking offcuts may come in useful here.

An elaborate jig is not necessary. A few chocks screwed to the floor or bench top will do, provided there is sufficient clearance to tighten the clamps. Chamfer or round the bottom corners of all deck beams in cabin boats to soften head injuries. For neatness, stop the chamfers about 2 in (50 mm) from the shelves (Fig 130e). *Ovolo* mouldings (131a) look good in panelled cabins.

Camber

Details of the deck camber are normally shown on boat plans. Particularly for sailing dinghies and launches they are true circular arcs. The curve is easily set out after a little juggling with a long thin wire looped around a pencil at one end and attached to a driven nail at the other end. A length of cord is useless, having too much elasticity. Once the longest beam (or a template) has been shaped, use this to mark out all other beams. Several geometrical methods using splines and trammels will set out curves approximating to true arcs, but these are only resorted to in confined spaces.

For cruising boats, elliptical and parabolic cambers (131b,c) have advantages. Ellipses permit increased headroom without a boxy appearance. A parabolic deck is difficult to distinguish from one with circular camber on a finished boat, yet the flatness at each side simplifies fitting beam end joints and thick plywood decking.

Half-Beams

The narrow side decks alongside a cabin top trunk or cockpit have short beams underneath called *half-beams*. For side decks up to about 18 in (450 mm) wide the beams are often made with no curvature. This simplifies construction and aligns with parabolic cambers on fore and after decks.

The lack of full beams weakens a hull. To add strength fit long bolts or clenches alongside every other half-beam. For neatness, conceal these in grooves routed in the undersides of the beams.

It will be noted from Fig 81 that the mini-sloop has no half-beams, the cabin trunk being an extension of the topsides. This lessens work, gives spacious accommodation and is immensely strong.

Hanging and Lodging Knees

The layout of deck framing knees in Fig 81 is typical of a small wooden cruising sailboat. The various parts are labelled in Fig 8. The horizontal lodging knees could be either grown crooks or laminated as described earlier in Chapter 6.

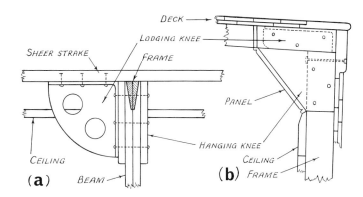

Fig 133 Straight-grained beam-to-frame joint

The only hanging knees are forged from mild steel, shaped to fit around the upper shelf, thinned down towards the tips and galvanized after drilling. Fully laminated frame and beam assemblies (Photo 18) do not need hanging knees. When separate sawn frame futtocks meet beams of equal thickness, the joint can be sandwiched between two plywood gussets.

When using straight-grained wood as in Figs 91 and 92, the beams are scarfed into the frame heads as in 133a, plus two glued gussets. No shelf is necessary as an extra thick sheer plank (133b) makes up for it.

The built-up plate lodging knees shown in 133a are ideal. Although not pretty, they are hidden by the panelling shown in 133b. Further information about deck framing can be found in *Boat Repairs and Conversions*.

Bulwarks

Except on racers, the crews of modern sailboats and powerboats rarely need to go on deck at sea, so bulwarks have shrunk to the size of toerails. Whether 6 in (150 mm) or 18 in (450 mm) high, traditional yachts and fishing craft still need them for appearance and comfort.

Attaching bulwarks to metal or fibreglass boats without creating deck leaks is simple. With wood, unless unsightly metal brackets are used, bulwarks need *stanchions* which pass through the deck. Avoid using extended frame heads as stanchions. A collision could damage the frames, while water seepage could create havoc. Separate stanchions (Fig 89 and Photo 45) are best, passing through square caulked apertures in the deck and bolted to frames or planking. Near the stem, infilling chocks called *knightheads* add strength and provide hawsepipe mountings.

The top of each stanchion is mortised into the rail or capping. Planking is nailed or screwed outside the posts, leaving adequate *scuppers* (draining gaps) close to the deck. A capping across the stern is known as the *taffrail*.

Plank bulwarks sit on deck without stanchions, through-bolted to the shelves (or to chocks) with a capping on top (Fig 134a). *Toe-rails* or footrails are smaller versions (134b) with no capping. To shape the scuppers, clamp the rails in pairs (134c), bore at each end, then saw out between as in 134d. The same method is used when making grab-rails.

Dinghy Decks

Wooden sailing dinghies, launches and runabouts often have varnished plywood decking. Teak veneered plywood with simulated caulked seams is available and can look attractive.

When such decks need to be trodden on, filler beams and carlines (shown dotted in Fig 129) create solidity. With WEST SYSTEM epoxy, webs of $\frac{3}{8}$ in (9 mm) plywood (Photo 42) bonded underneath on completion of the decking work fine. No shaping is needed if they run parallel to the carlines.

Having rotary-cut veneers on the faces, marine plywood never looks quite right when varnished. Sheathing with sliced (*sheer cut*) veneer or thin strips of teak is well worth the time. The same thing applies when plywood is used for joinery.

On the GP14 Start plywood decking with the foredeck. The offcuts may be useful further back. For economy, make a centreline joint. Fit a narrow outer king plank the same thickness as the plywood, forming a rabbet each side. Further economies are possible with a painted deck as offcuts can be scarfed together and the surface grain need not always run fore-and-aft.

Butt joints will do if the framing is wide enough. To achieve this where the side deck meets the foredeck, add a *sister piece* or cant piece, glued on as shown in Fig 136. Deck panels bend easily to the camber while pencil lines are drawn from beneath outlining the gluing areas. Transfer the lines to the outer surface in case extra fastenings are needed after fitting. Deck edges have slight bevel to align with the flared topsides, so allow for this when sawing out. Glued-on beadings later seal the ply edges.

Woodscrews around the edges help to pull a panel down. Otherwise, screws are an embarrassment: sinking

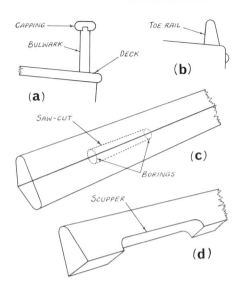

Fig 134 Solid bulwark and toerail details

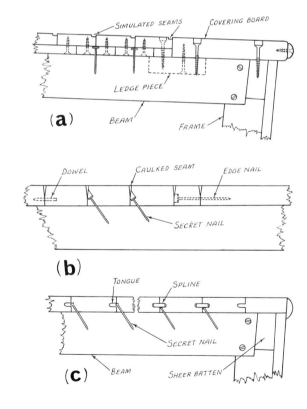

Fig 135 Traditional launch decking methods

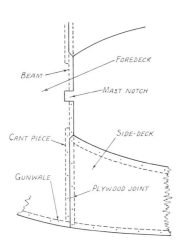

Fig 136 Neat side-deck plywood joint

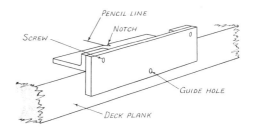

Fig 137 Jig for marking edge dowels

is unwise in thin plywood and flush heads are not very pretty when varnished. Best to remove the screws next day and rely on a good glue. Then sink the holes enough to glue in plugs of matching wood (see Chapter 6).

Between screws and for most other deck parts, brass panel pins suffice. To avoid bruising the surface, use a nail set of correct size (before the pins are flush) to sink the heads for stopping.

Launch Decks

The classic runabout needs a pretty teak or mahogany varnished deck. The ways of achieving this are legion. Teak-faced plywood with simulated seams is a simple answer. Covering standard plywood with teak strips needs no fastenings if weights are used to clamp the glue.

If you have a supply of thin hardwood, a double skin job as in Fig 135a is cheap—either cold-moulded, or laid in mastic and fastened as shown. With thicker stock the methods in 135b and c work well.

Nothing looks smarter than surroundng the dark red decking with a *covering board* of contrasting wood, such as agba or white oak. This may be solid as in 135a, or thin sheathing over a plywood base. Getting fair grain around foredeck curvature is easy with short lengths scarfed or butted end to end.

Recessed false seams (135a) are painted black or white before varnishing. Those in 135b are filled with polysulfide composition as each plank is fitted; the cross dowels prevent driving caulking cotton properly. The tongued or splined seams in 135c are all glued solid. This can lead to shrinkage cracking. Using splines saves wasting wood by cutting tongues. Plywood makes perfect splines; short lengths will do. Set the surface grain to run *across* the seams. Matching grooves are easy to cut with router, table saw or Skilsaw.

Secret nails Avoid surface fastenings like the plague. Skewed secret nails are easy to fit, but require either cross dowels, tongues or splines to anchor the other side. Screws from beneath as in Fig 135a work well with double skins provided the underside is not readily visible. Make up a jig as in Fig 137 to align dowel pilot holes exactly. Put a depth mark on the drill. Galvanized 1 in (25 mm) roofing nails about $\frac{1}{8}$ in (3 mm) diameter with the heads cut off make fine cross dowels. Tap dowels into the fixed plank, points outwards. Force on the next plank then drive the secret nails.

What order? To simplify laying a Fig 135b deck, make the covering boards first. Remove them, lay from the king plank outwards, then replace the covering boards. Many planks taper to zero width at the covering boards, so fit ledge pieces (shown dotted in Fig 135a) to make rabbets.

Canvased Decks

Since the last century, light, cheap and reasonably watertight small-boat decks have consisted of painted canvas stretched over tongue-and-groove boarding, sometimes laid diagonally for added strength. Fore-and-aft TGV (matchboarding) is shown in Fig 81 for the mini-sloop. Nowadays one would more often use marine plywood sheathed with fibreglass, vinyl fabric or nylon.

Photo 44 Straight deck planking payed with hot compound

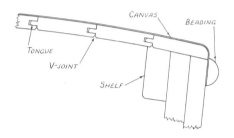

Fig 138 Tongued and grooved deck planking

Photo 45 Swept planks on laid teak deck

When using standard TGV fir or cedar, point the Vees downwards as in Fig 138. This makes an attractive deckhead, camouflaging shrinkage cracks. To get tight joints on top, run a plane along the bottom of each grooved edge to allow for the deck camber. Traditionally, all tongues aim uphill as shown. This deters moisture from lodging in the grooves to cause rot. Start with the king plank, but modify this so that it has a groove both sides.

Clamp boards up tight using the Fig 54 wedge. Traverse with a plane on completion to remove all ridges. Galvanized nails are normally adequate: punch down the heads and fill flush. No covering boards are needed, but round off the top edge generously as in Fig 138: canvas wears through readily on a sharp arris. For canvasing and nylon sheathing instructions refer to *The Compleat Book of Yacht Care*.

Side decks are best laid with athwartships boards. Diagonal planking is more rigid, but is wasteful and time-consuming.

Big-Boat Decks

Scrubbed teak makes the best surface for seagoing decks. Over fibreglass, ferrocement, metal or plywood, teak is usually applied as cladding between $\frac{3}{8}$ and $\frac{3}{4}$ in (9–18 mm) thick. Secondhand deck teak is sold by shipbreakers—if you can dodge the old holes and get it sawn up. Clear rift-sawn pine is a cheaper alternative. Over plywood, fibreglass or nylon sheathing is cheaper still.

For motor cruisers, strips are generally laid parallel to the king plank as in Photo 44. On sailing yachts *swept* decking looks best, the strips running parallel to the covering boards or nearly so (Photo 45). Examine other boats to observe the details of surrounds to pilothouse, masts, hatches and skylights. These items (and ideal plank and seam widths) are not often shown on plans.

Although the procedure in laying the 12 mm or 18 mm plywood base for a yacht's deck is much the same as already described for a dinghy, the material is stiff and heavy, requiring much shaping around obstacles. Avoid small panels. Amateurs often prefer to lay two skins of 6 mm or 9 mm plywood bonded together. Scarfs are useful to couple small panels to big ones and to prevent wastage. Use butts on beams or carlines for all main joints. Glue everything and fix down with ring nails or screws. Always cover ply edges with a beading or rub-rail.

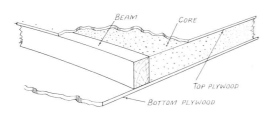

Fig 139 Plywood deck with insulation core

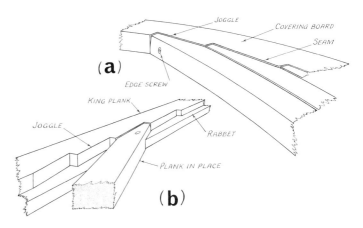

Fig 140 Laid teak deck plank ends

To reduce tophamper weight and improve heat insulation, decking on cabin tops and deckhouses is best made with two skins of about 6 mm plywood spaced apart by a core of end-grain balsa wood or closed-cell foam. By sandwiching the deck beams also, head injuries are greatly reduced (see Fig 139). Glue everything, with a skim of filled resin over the core to ensure that the top plywood bonds perfectly to it. (See also pages 120 and 124.) In way of deck fittings, always replace the core with plywood pads.

Laid Teak

The once traditional solid teak or pine decking is now used only by connoisseurs, on certain fishing vessels and for repairing antique yachts. The steel decks of commercial passenger craft have always been clad with teak at least 3 in (75 mm) thick, laid on bitumastic composition and through-bolted. For modern metal yachts, thin cladding is bedded in mastic and held with screws from underneath. Overhead insulating linings conceal the screw heads.

Wood on ferrocement is bonded with filled epoxy adhesive and no vertical fastenings. Clamping is effected by side struts and weights. Similar bonding will work over fibreglass, but note that polyester resin is not a reliable adhesive on teak. Cladding as for metal decks is cheaper and quicker. Future repair work is difficult with bonded claddings.

Swept Decks

Think carefully before deciding to adopt swept decking as in Photo 45. It will give you incredible satisfaction, but

Photo 46 Partially swept decking

straight planks halve the work and look just as good to most folk.

Whether solid wood or cladding, for a fully swept deck the first plank you fit runs the full length of the covering board. Plank ends are *snaped* (joggled or nibbed) into the king plank or hatch surrounds as in Fig 140. Snaping eliminates pointed ends which could wound bare feet and prove difficult to caulk.

To reduce bending, the partial sweep method (Photo 46) looks inviting. However, it entails a lot of snaping along the covering board as well as towards the

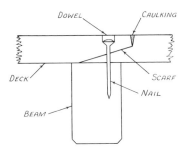

Fig 141 Deck butt joint on beam

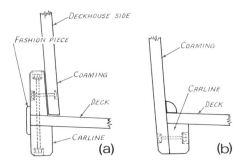

Fig 142 Fitting coamings to carlines

centreline. Bending gets tougher at the Photo 45 stage, as the radius tightens and planks get short. Steaming is not usually necessary, but planks shorter than 4 ft (1.2 m) are sure to need sawing to shape from wider stock. A delightful but troublesome way of easing the bend is to taper most planks uniformly towards bow and stern.

With solid laid decks, planks are butt-jointed as in Fig 141. Snapes are screwed to covering boards as in 140a and rabbeted into the king plank as in 140b. Main fastenings are secret nails plus bronze dowels, much as in Fig 135b.

Again, for solid work, covering boards, king planks and all surrounds to deckhouse and hatches are fitted first. With cladding, fit *last* any such parts which are snaped. Use cardboard templates to pick up the plank end shapes. These parts are easy to cut, being no thicker than the cladding strips.

For thirty years, metal and ferrocement decks have been covered satisfactorily with a screed of resilient composition about ½ in (12 mm) thick, such as Semtex™. This must be laid by specialists who are franchized world wide by Dunlop AG.

Coamings

All superstructures on deck require coamings—vertical or slightly sloping walls—to serve as water bars or to create additional headroom below. On commercial craft, thick hatch coamings stand on deck as in Fig 142a and are through-bolted to beams and carlines. A deckhouse is fitted over such a frame and is thus easily removable when the sideways bolts are withdrawn.

As one cannot caulk efficiently underneath on-deck coamings, a stopwater (Chapter 8) must be set vertically through each seam, just covered by the coamings. These are best driven into blind holes to a depth of two-thirds the plank thickness, or to just below the caulking Vee.

For smart inside appearance, most yacht coamings are fixed inside beams and carlines as in Fig 142b. In way of such coamings, do not chamfer the bottom corners of beams and carlines: the coamings themselves take the chamfer.

Hatch and skylight coamings are best dovetailed at the corners and dropped into place as prefabricated units. Coachroof and cockpit coamings are fitted individually, perhaps needing wedge-shaped packing to give tumble-home. By fitting samson posts inside the after corners of cockpit coamings, great strength is assured. How to frame up big coamings with windows is explained in *Boat Repairs and Conversions*.

Breakwaters

Most deck fittings are simple fixtures set in bedding compound onto pads and through-bolted to chocks or framing underneath. More difficult parts include the fashion piece around a rudder trunk, and the *breakwater* across a dinghy's foredeck. The breakwater is a spray deflector Vee-shaped in plan and usually composed of two hardwood boards leaning forward at the top as seen in Fig 143.

The double angle plus the deck camber makes these parts awkward to shape. Cardboard templates save possible wastage of good wood, but with a little care the actual stock can be spiled direct as shown in Fig 143. Supporting the board on correct line and slope, use a bevel-edged spiling block to draw a line on each face. As always with spiling, roughing out the shape first gives better accuracy.

Solid wood breakwaters are normally glued to the deck and screwed from underneath. A less handsome but easily renewed breakwater of plywood can be screwed to fillets along the for'ard corner.

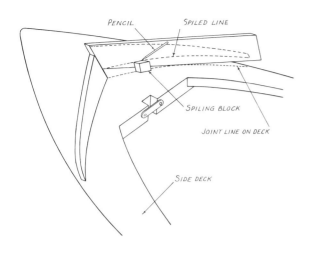

Fig 143 Spiling a foredeck breakwater

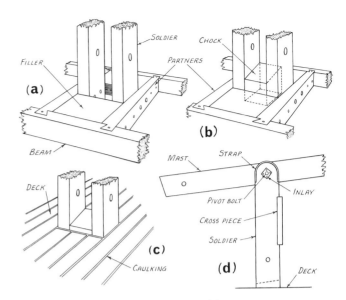

Fig 144 Wooden tabernacle assembly

Tabernacles

Strongly reinforced deck framing is necessary for any through-deck or deck-stepped mast. Strength is often added by means of knees, a steel frame right around the hull, and diagonal flat steel braces running just under the deck. A mast step needs firm bolting to the keelson or floor timbers. Make sure the heel mortice has drainage apertures. Alloy masts are usually aligned at the partners with stiff rubber wedges. Wooden ones are used for wooden masts.

From the smallest to the largest sailboats, masts are often stepped on deck, either in a cup, a bracket or a *tabernacle*. When in metal, such parts are not always easy to fabricate. For popular designs one can usually buy them as stock items. Under-deck support is important for deck stepping. The mini-sloop (Fig 81) has twin plank supports which are extensions of the drop keel case. A tubular steel or alloy pillar is common for a metal tabernacle or cup fitting.

Make It Keep strength in mind if you construct a tabernacle in wood as in Fig 144. The two legs (soldiers) extend all the way, or are bonded to a single stanchion below deck. The cross piece above deck is fitted to the *after* side only, to permit the mast to hinge on the top pivot bolt (144d). The central chock in 144b extends well below deck, its top sloped as shown dotted in 144d to butt against the mast heel. The chock is set in filled epoxy resin. When the deck is laid, normal caulking (144c) or quadrant beadings all around provide a second line of defence against leakage.

At the start, clamp the legs together and bore the pivot bolt holes dead square. Then bolt the legs together with spacer chocks between them, at the exact final width, before lowering them into place. Sink in thick metal plates around the upper holes (see 144d) to take the bolt thrust. Also note the semi-circular straps covering the end grain—so valuable to prevent the legs from splitting.

Chapter 14
Plastics Made Easy

It has taken forty years to prove that fibreglass can be formed into durable boat hulls. Early dinghies were often too thin and soon disintegrated. Boats kept afloat all the time were sometimes plagued with blistering and water absorption. Improved but costlier resins solved that problem. Nowadays, fibreglass or GRP is included in the wider class of FRP (fibre reinforced plastics), as exotic materials other than glass have come into use.

Amateur building Good work in FRP needs a constant temperature between 60° and 80°F (16°–27°C) and relative humidity between 40% and 54%. Even if you get permission, laying up a solid FRP hull over an existing boat is rarely successful. Parting is difficult and you get a good finish inside where it is not required, while the outside is rough. The female hull mould (Photo 47) used in factory production is itself formed thus, or over a special male plug similar to a wooden boat (Photo 48). The ingenious amateur can eliminate one operation by making a female mould—rather like a boat built inside out. However, getting a perfect internal surface in either wood or plaster is very time-consuming.

Solid hulls use vast quantities of costly resins and reinforcement. For a cruising boat having iron or lead ballast sealed inside a hollow keel section, the skin thickness could vary from 2 in (50 mm) near the keel to ⅝ in (16 mm) at the topsides. All solid FRP hulls can sink without trace unless equipped with elaborate buoyancy. This is easy to arrange in a dinghy under thwarts and under bottom boards; and it has also been done for ballasted sailboats up to 40 ft (12 m) long, by losing much locker space and fitting cavity-creating linings. (Building solid FRP hulls is covered in the next chapter.)

Foam-Sandwich

Many of the disadvantages of solid FRP construction for amateurs are eliminated by using the *foam-sandwich* systems. The same idea is used for sailboards and surfboards. Two comparatively thin FRP skins are separated by and bonded to a core of rigid, closed-cell PVC or PU (polyurethane) foam, or end-grain balsa wood. The outer skin is generally thicker than the inner one: both may

Photo 47 Assembling a split female mould

merge into solid FRP where a ballast keel is installed. The core is replaced by extra dense PVC (or by plywood) in way of deck and hull fittings, or by strip-planking at sheer or curved deckhouse roof edges.

Although suitable stock designs are scarce in comparison with other materials, the method can be adapted to most types of round-bilge craft (and certain chine shapes) from dinghies to the biggest world-girdling ocean racers. Two designers in England offering a range of plans are Derek Kelsall at Sandwich Marina, Sandwich, Kent and Alan Newton, 22 Strathnaver Avenue, Barrow-in-Furness, Cumbria (see Photo 49).

When cored construction first started 40 years ago, two shells were moulded and polyurethane poured between them where it foamed. This core suffered from brittleness and poor adhesion. In contrast, the modern version surpasses almost any boatbuilding material known to man, and it suits the amateur well. Cored hulls are extremely rigid, even without internal stiffeners. Collision resistance is very good, while sound and heat insulation is better than for solid wood. Boat factories have been slow to adopt cores (except for decks), as semi-skilled workers pulling solid FRP hulls rapidly from perfect female moulds makes good business sense. Most interior fitments are simple to install using stainless steel self-tapping screws.

For a one-off project there is just one drawback. If you

Photo 48 Making a wooden plug: *a.* light framework, *b.* plywood skin in place

Photo 49 Foam-sandwich in miniature: Alan Newton's Hobo 20

want smooth and shiny topsides, much filling and sanding is required prior to painting. For several identical hulls, factories overcome this expense by laying up inside a female mould. The need for this is exactly what the average amateur boatbuilder is trying to avoid.

Quick Work Although the material costs for a big foam-sandwich hull are higher than those for ferrocement or steel—and in some cases higher than for wood—there is no faster method. Work generally starts with a battened wooden jig, as seen in Photo 50. This is covered with thin polythene or cellophane to prevent adhesion. The foam is tacked in position (Photo 51), then pulled close with stitched twine, or with coarse self-tapping screws through previously bored holes along each batten. Other methods of core attachment are feasible. These may depend upon whether one wishes to keep the jig, or scrap it. Long panel pins driven from outside might do, punched in until the points come through. To release the jig, grips are used to pull each pin right through the core. For a 30 ft (9 m) boat the core thickness might be 1 in (25 mm) with the outer FRP skin $\frac{3}{16}$ in (5 mm) and the inner skin $\frac{5}{32}$ in (4 mm). For a 40 ft (12 m) hull, these thicknesses might be $1\frac{1}{4}$ in (32 mm), $\frac{1}{4}$ in (6 mm) and $\frac{3}{16}$ in (5 mm).

Photo 50 Jig for foam-sandwich construction

Photo 51 Placing sheets of Airex® foam

Skin thickness build-ups for differing weights of fibreglass and numbers of layers are listed in Appendix 4. Woven rovings (often unidirectional and laid diagonally) are usually alternated with chopped strand mat, plus an outermost layer of finely woven cloth. See pages 129 and 137, also Photo 57. Despite the high cost, some layups for racing sailboats and high-speed powerboats demand the use of the so-called exotic materials such as aramid (Kevlar™) and carbon fibre. See the next chapter for further details and laying techniques. With one-off foam-sandwich boats, no conventional thick gel coat is used.

Once the outer skin is bonded to the core and completely laid up, turning over and release from the jig comes next. However, note that if your design calls for solid FRP in way of a ballast keel, you must remember to cover the core with cellophane, plastic sheet or foil (stuck on with contact adhesive) in this region. Before laying up the inner skin, the loose section of core is cut out.

Core Materials

Being light and cheap, balsa wood has until recently been the designers' preferred core material for sandwich decks. However, being porous, it has rarely been used in hulls since outer skin damage could soak the core. The first non-porous, closed-cell rigid PVC foam core material to become available to amateurs was Airex®, around 1965. This is a comparatively soft foam, a property which has given it an excellent track record in collision resistance. But due to that, the maximum thickness in general use is 25 mm. When warmed, Airex® will conform to gentle curves, but Airex Contoured Foam is divided into 40 mm cubes which permit it to bend readily without warming. Airex distributors in England are Impag Ltd of Bolton, Lancashire, and in the USA, Torin Inc in Waldwick, New Jersey.

Divinycell® is a cross-linked, stiff PVC foam which can be worked in similar manner to wood. Eight different densities are in common use, the lowest like balsa wood and the highest like seasoned oak—but very much lighter in weight. Designers can therefore build high strength into the slamming areas of powerboats by varying the core density—but the most dense costs about ten times more than the least! Airex make similar cross-linked foam (but not contoured) in five densities, known as Herex C70®. Termanto® is another brand, with a contoured version called Termino®. Vessels as big as 165 ft (51 m) in length are built with Divinycell cores. Standard thicknesses go up to 80 mm, but laminating to any thickness is possible. Offcuts may be edge-glued together to minimize wastage. Divinycell is marketed in England by Diab-Barracuda Ltd, Gloucester and in the USA by Diab-Barracuda Inc, 315 Sea Hawk Drive, DeSoto, Texas.

Polyurethane foam Although ideal for sailboards, where all curvature is sawn from a solid block, PU foam is too brittle and weak for hull cores. Its cost is attractive—about half the cost of the cheapest Divinycell—so it comes in handy for buoyancy tank and internal stiffener formers. The familiar white polystyrene (PS) packaging foam is attacked by polyester resins and is too soft: high-density PS can be used but requires the costlier though stronger epoxies.

Balsa Although inferior to Divinycell in almost every respect except cost, balsa wood (in sandwich decks) has been used for many years. It must be dead dry when laid up or a pressure buildup will occur on a hot day. Resin soaks into it, so careful workmanship is necessary to get a perfect bond. If water gets in (via a deck fitting or damage to the FRP skin) the balsa swells, weight increases, and freezing or eventual delamination could destroy the deck. Balsa has to be contoured, as each chunk is cut with the end grain towards the faces, all attached to a scrim backing.

Plywood core For a chine boat, the use of a plywood core appears attractive. However, its weight is four times that of Airex. Getting perfect adhesion is a worry. If one did adapt a design, one would finish up with little better than an unduly heavy FRP-sheathed plywood yacht.

Foam Core Construction

You may run foam panels in any direction, but all joints must be bonded together and all gaps filled, making the core a tight, continuous shell in its own right.

For use with contoured Divinycell, a thin blue polyester putty (Divilette) is available to seal all gaps and, in production work with a female mould, to stick the foam onto the outer FRP skin which has previously been laid up completely against the mould surface. A vibrating roller air tool brings the Divilette right through all the slits, eventually creating bridges every 40 mm between the inner and outer FRP skins. This increases the strength greatly and eliminates any possibility of either skin parting from the core. Divilette® contains microspheres making it half the weight of pure resin.

Contoured foams usually have a backing of fibreglass scrim which is compatible with epoxy or polyester resins. The scrim is left in place and does not impede the movement of resin or putty through the slits. Note that for typical hull convex curvature, one lays the scrim to the jig. With reverse or concave hull sections, place the scrim outwards. Even with contoured panels, fitting around the barrel shape of a boat is bound to create gaps. Filling these with slivers of foam and resin is quite strong enough, and much simpler than spiling and cutting. For certain boat designs Divinycell can supply core kits; the numbered pieces fit together perfectly without gaps.

Before sanding the outside of the core smooth and fair, exposed batten stitches must be cut off. First trowel resin putty into all the holes and let it cure. (These will probably be drilled holes, as a packing needle will not readily penetrate the denser foams.) A powerful orbital sander with 60-grit paper works well, followed by a sanding board. This is of 4 mm plywood, 4 in (100 mm) wide by 30 in (750 mm) long, with a handle each end and 100-grit paper glued all over the bottom. If scrubbed lengthwise across the surface in all directions, any flat spots should disappear.

Divinycell is completely non-porous and needs no priming. Other types of foam need priming according to their makers' instructions. Neglecting this is sure to create a poor FRP bond. Balsa wood needs very careful priming and sealing, using a special polyester mix that will set before it soaks right in. Contoured Divinycell gets a type of sealing when Divilette (or similar thin putty) is spread over with a squeegee to fill the gaps, but most of this goes during sanding.

Certain amateurs who prefer wood to plastics will find another method of core construction intriguing. Foam sheets (not contoured) are sawn into strips about 2 in (50 mm) wide. Edges and ends are grooved to receive splines of Formica. A jig with fairly close frames but no battens is then simply strip-planked, all seams and butts being glued with Divilette which also fills any gaps. One big advantage is that all temporary pins into the jig may be withdrawn as soon as the putty has cured: the core shape will not distort. Incidentally, Divinycell is self-extinguishing if burnt, giving off a minimum of noxious fumes. Most modern PVC boat foams are approved by the American Bureau of Shipping, Det Norske Veritas, and Lloyd's Register of Shipping.

FRP Skins

Inner and outer skins to cover a foam or balsa core are each identical to the solid FRP hull construction detailed in the next chapter. Most PVC and PU core materials are compatible with epoxy, polyester, or vinylester resins and putties. Airex recommend General Purpose tack-free orthophthalic polyester. Divinycell recommend marine isophthalic polyester. Epoxies are normally used only in super-lightweight hulls, often with exotic reinforcement.

You may find it advisable to study the next chapter before looking further at this section. From outside to inside, a 10 ft (3 m) dinghy might have: filler screed, $\frac{3}{4}$ oz CSM, 10 oz glass cloth, $\frac{3}{4}$ oz CSM, 12 mm Divinycell, $\frac{3}{4}$ oz CSM, 10 oz glass cloth, flowcoat. A Flying Dutchman may incorporate surface tissue, 5 oz Kevlar cloth, 15 mm Divinycell, 5 oz Kevlar cloth. A 35 ft (11 m) monohull sailboat could have filler, 2 oz CSM, 14 oz unidirectional cloth, 1 oz CSM, 14 oz unidirectional cloth, 1 oz CSM, 20 mm Divinycell, 1 oz CSM, 14 oz unidirectional cloth, 1 oz CSM, flowcoat.

Overlaps To ensure a smooth outer face with minimal filling, use full-length rolls of cloth, mat, woven rovings (WR), composites, aramids or carbon fibre—particularly on the topsides—so that overlapping joins are few. Make full use of unidirectional WR (or carbon fibre, perhaps) as

cloths with the majority of strands parallel do not need overlapped joins. If other types of cloth are butt-jointed, add an extra layer to compensate for the weakness. (See also page 137.)

Overlaps in glass mat are fairly easy to sand or grind down smooth (or nearly so) without too much weakening. But this is best avoided in exotics. When laying up must cease in the middle of a skin, about 1 in (25 mm)—the usual size of overlap—must be tapered down by grinding or sanding before resumption. If the cured join is then again sanded, little hump will remain. How annoying that this procedure cannot be utilized throughout! But interrupted layups are normally taboo.

Overlaps do not matter much on the inside of a hull. You cannot get at the inside until the assembly has been turned over onto a very well padded cradle, and the jig lifted out or dismantled. Slight leakage through of resin or putty may not matter, but any blobs that could create air spaces under the FRP must be ground away. Fill all gaps and screw holes with putty.

Tapering the core Mention was made earlier of fusing inner and outer skins into one solid laminate in way of a ballast keel. The same idea may be adopted along the sheer (see Fig 145) and in way of bilge keels, depending on the designer's specification. The core should never end abruptly at these points, but must be tapered off at a slope of at least 3 : 1. All taper is applied inside the hull as the outer skin must have a smooth surface. To avoid having to cut away expensive foam, you can either substitute with polyurethane foam or build up the jig to outer core level with wood and hardboard.

Core pads Large expanses of high density foam over slamming areas or behind bilge keels and skeg must be inserted when the core is laid over the jig. Small inserts in way of deck and through-hull fittings or chain plates may be installed from inside, just before laying up the inner skin. It may not be possible to scrape away every scrap of foam down to the outer skin, so thickness the inserts accordingly and bed them flush on putty.

Finishing

Keep dust off the core prior to the start of the outer skin layup by covering with polythene sheet, especially when work is subject to long delays. Before turning over, it pays to finish all work to outside surfaces—everything except

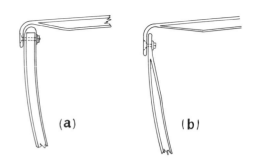

Fig 145 Production methods of attaching deck

the last coat of paint. The hull will never be in a more convenient position.

Fill and rub If you can borrow a good auto body finisher, do so! Only a limited amount of sanding should be done to an FRP laminate for fear of weakening it. Much better to rely on repeated skims of resin filler alternated with use of the flexible sanding board described above. Twelve such treatments is not unusual for a fine finish. Vacuum up dust, and protect your skin, eyes and lungs.

Paint Your paintwork must depend upon the recommendations of the paint maker. Sprayed two-part polyurethane is generally preferred, but your hull finisher may insist on using something else. Whichever is used, several coats of thick primer will prove beneficial, each almost sanded away with wet 400-grit (followed by 600-grit) paper around a cork or rubber block.

Deck mouldings often overlap the topsides, so better not to prepare the hidden parts too well, or to paint them. Similarly, inside the hull, although a flowcoat finish looks wonderful, better to apply this after bonding in bulkheads, bearers, deck and joinery.

Rolling over The hull is delicate at the turning-over stage, so one can rarely risk lifting off the shell while still inverted. Also, removing hundreds of ties or screws is much easier when upright. You need an accurate, padded cradle ready, which will not press heavily on small spots. Fit some cross-spalls inside once the jig is out, after checking that the shell is not twisting or sagging.

Rolling needs space which usually means either dismantling the building shed or dragging the assembly outdoors. If this can be forseen at the start, design the jig to slide easily. Old mattresses are invaluable to avoid marking the outer skin. Once upright, crane out the jig, or dismantle it and scrap it. Dismantling will be inevitable if bilge keels are built in, or there is a lot of tumblehome.

Appendages

One must adhere to the designer's specification entirely when it comes to fitting a fin keel, skeg or bilge keels. If these units are deep and thin, it becomes impossible to lay up an inner skin successfully in conventional manner. Here is one example of the risks in adapting a design not originally conceived for foam-sandwich.

Fin inside out By forming the inner FRP skin on a wooden plug, you can fit this shell on the hull jig, then glue the PVC core material over it—preferably on a bedding of Divilette, which squeezes between the contour chunks—to merge with the main hull core. The outer skin will then flow smoothly over all.

Such an appendage is easily ballasted later, as described in Chapter 15. However, external lead ballast makes a better job: only a shallow stub appendage needs to be formed; the FRP is protected from damage and the ballast is removable to lighten the boat when necessary. Soft lead is easy to shave down flush with the stub, and such a weight is fairly easy for the amateur to cast.

Later on Small appendages are often easier to attach on completion of the hull (see the section on sailboard skegs, below). You might not achieve a perfect finish outside, but this should not matter for a cruising boat. If you do need to cut a slot right through, to bond a prefabricated appendage into a hull, be careful to get it exactly aligned athwartships, and firmly supported, before mixing any resin. Such work is simplified if the core in this vicinity is cut out as mentioned above, making the keel area into solid FRP.

Other ways The diagrams in Fig 146, show two of the many appendage arrangements possible on foam-sandwich sailboats. Some powerboats benefit from shallow bilge keels and full-length external ballast keels; some have built-in spray deflectors along chine and bottom. Blisters for twin-screw shafts are often added (Figs 146c,d). Rudder fabrication is much the same for solid FRP and sandwich construction: see Chapter 15. Some of the appendage configurations described in that section are also applicable to cores.

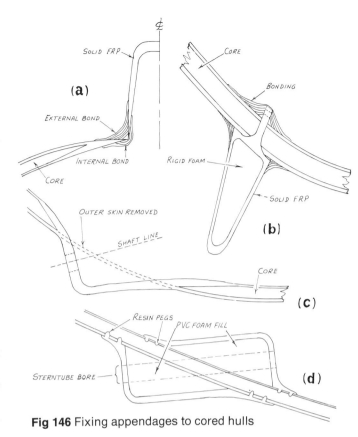

Fig 146 Fixing appendages to cored hulls

Skin-fitting holes through plastic hulls are generally drilled after curing—not at all easy for some amateurs. One more advantage of sandwich is that you can bore an oversize hole in the core, then nick and turn the skins into it, for later finishing with a rasp. Solid pads in place of core foam can be built in at the first stage.

In any FRP laminate, twist drills work well up to $\frac{3}{8}$ in (9 mm), while trepan bits (see Chapter 6) or tank cutters are best up to 3 in (75 mm). Preferably bore from the gelcoat side (if there is a gelcoat) and wedge a block of wood tight against the other side. A ring of closely-spaced $\frac{1}{8}$ in (3 mm) holes is the safe way.

Cored Decks

Without lifting equipment for hoisting a prefabricated deck unit onto the hull, the amateur may need to adopt his or her own techniques.

Exact size The best hull-to-deck joints are similar to those in Fig 145, where both cores meld into solid FRP.

Such shapes usually necessitate a deck jig (male or female) which is dead accurate in outline—in profile as well as in plan. A flanged deck will hardly bend up and down at all. To avoid having to loft a jig to such accuracy, the amateur often goes for the Fig 147 type join, where the deck will snug to the sheer and the outer edges may be shaved down to meet the topsides precisely.

Building it on Further simplification is possible on some designs if you build a sandwich deck direct on the hull. The formwork takes a long time to erect, but no longer than an independent male jig. Temporary carlines are cleated from bulkhead to bulkhead (fitting bulkheads is much simpler with no deck in the way) with a few temporary deck beams or props to stop the longer carlines from bending when stepped on. Deck over with 5 mm hardboard or 4 mm plywood. Cover the outside and edges of each panel with cellophane or plastic sheet to ensure easy release. Do not forget to carry it around the edges and to set all carlines the exact plywood thickness below the sheer and bulkhead tops.

After laying up the deck's inner skin, bed contoured Divinycell in Divilette and vibrate it. Remember to insert solid pads for deck fittings in the core space. Then lay up the outer FRP skin with the desired surface finish. This can wrap over the gunwale as in Fig 147, but the internal bonding to hull and bulkheads must wait until the formwork has been removed.

Preformed An even simpler system is possible for small flush deck areas. Pre-shape the core (direct on the hull or via paper patterns) and number the pieces. Spread polythene sheet over a wooden floor, assemble the core on this and secure with a few partly-driven wire nails. Bond the first layer of CSM over all. When set, pull out the protruding nails, then complete the FRP laminate on that side.

When cured, with the help of a few friends, turn it over and position it on the boat. Some temporary deck beams or props are sure to be needed to get the shape right. Trim around the sheer, force down with weights if necessary and anchor these points with tabs of resin and woven glass tape, then lay up the top skin and bond as in Fig 147.

Superb deck assemblies are made in female moulds by boatyards and factories, incorporating anti-slip surfaces, cockpits, coamings, anchor lockers, cabin tops and pilot-houses. Many incorporate balsa wood cores. However, amateur sandwich decks can have great flexibility of style

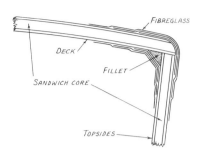

Fig 147 Sandwich-to-sandwich deck joint

plus superior Divinycell cores. Both skins may be of plywood, the top one finally clad with attractive teak strips. A sandwich pilothouse can have varnished teak-veneered ply skins.

Prelude For the beginner, starting a boat with the deck is a wonderful way to learn about cored FRP. Unfortunately, few will have enough workshop space for this, though a flush deck might be hung overhead if well supported. Leaning a completed deck up on edge, for storage, or hanging it, can cause even a well cured structure to take up a 'set'. This warping can be troublesome to deal with. You need accurate lofting to ensure that the deck will fit the hull and vice versa. With a Fig 147 joint you need no hull thickness deduction from the lines drawing in *plan*, but a full deck thickness deduction in *profile*.

Sandwich Building Tips

The two most tedious operations connected with foam-sandwich construction are the temporary attachment of the core to the jig, and smoothing down the outer FRP surface to produce good topside paintwork. Some of the ideas so far used with success to ameliorate these chores are as follows.

The former problem has been overcome by factories needing to produce from four to ten identical hulls in a hurry. They make a plug exactly as in Photo 48, lay up the inner skin over that, then apply the foam by vacuum bagging to make a beautifully even and secure bond. The outer skin is applied in the normal way.

Nearly all the pain is taken out of core fixing *and* final sanding by using the Kit Panel Method devised by Derek Kelsall (see page 126). Although this is ideal for chine boats, Derek prefers the looks of round-bilge. A pioneer

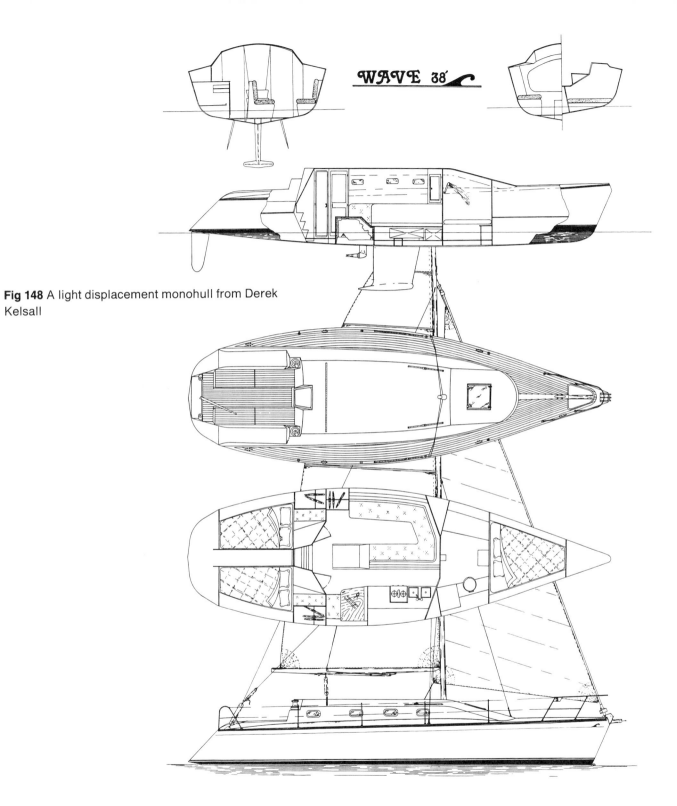

WAVE 38'

Fig 148 A light displacement monohull from Derek Kelsall

of Airex one-off boats, he now uses this method at his own boatyard as well as for amateur one-off designs worldwide. Some of the designs are equally suitable for solid FRP or epoxy/plywood construction. Using computer methods, accurate dimensions are produced for all panels and jig frames, eliminating the need for lofting. Drawings for the ultra-light displacement Wave 38 are shown in Fig 148. The Tonga Tini 27 catamaran is seen in Photo 52.

The simplicity centres on the constant camber design at the turn of the bilge. Only one female mould, generally between 2 m and 3 m long and 500 mm wide is required in which to lay up all the laminates for these high-curvature regions (Photo 53).

The topside and bottom panels go on with glassy smooth outside surfaces. Each is laid up on a table surfaced with cheap melamine veneered chipboard, or formica, usually the full length of the boat up to about 6 m and half the length up to 12 m. All panels are often made before the simple jig of rough wooden frames is set up, on which the hull is erected. The outer FRP skin is laid up on the waxed melamine. The core is vacuum-bagged to this (see page 105) followed by the inner skin. An industrial vacuum cleaner is sufficiently powerful to evacuate such a bag to −0.3 bar. It will overheat in 10 min, so have a standby ready!

Panels are just sufficiently flexible to take up the double curvature in topsides and bottom. For well cambered decks you must wait until the panel is placed before adding the top skin. How the panels are joined together is not only simple and neat, but is very strong. Place strips of film-wrapped hardboard (precision sanded if necessary to match the FRP skin thickness) on the table, all around the marked out panel area, set inwards enough to leave a rabbet all around. With panels butted together on the jig, strips of tape or mat are glassed into the rabbets flush with the surface.

Filling and sanding these narrow patches (and any holes for temporary jig fastenings) is then all the major surface finishing one needs to do before painting obliterates all trace of any seams. As interior appearance is not normally critical, all inside joins are backed up with the familiar humped fibreglass strips, similar to bonding a bulkhead as in Fig 149.

Photo 52 Foam-sandwich catamaran: Derek Kelsall's Tini 27

Photo 53 Turn-of-bilge moulds for the Kit Panel system

Making good use of Foam

Once set up for foam-sandwich construction, one might as well extend its uses to the limit, ensuring that few core offcuts and other materials are wasted.

Bulkheads and panels Foam-sandwich bulkheads can then be cheaper than plywood ones, with a considerable

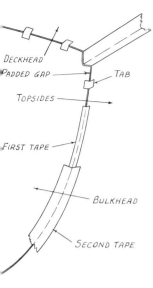

DECKHEAD
PADDED GAP
TAB
TOPSIDES
FIRST TAPE
BULKHEAD
SECOND TAPE

Fig 149 Bulkhead bonding procedure

saving of weight. Provided you leave access to get them into the hull, bulkheads are easy to prefabricate on a table, or even on the floor. With light foam in stiff sheets, offering up to check the fit is simple, prior to laying up the skins. Vacuum bagging is ideal for bedding the core down tight.

If it's not highly stressed, you may clad the core of a bulkhead with various other stiff materials instead of FRP. However, almost all bulkheads, not just the obvious ones near the mast and cockpit, have a structural role, even partial bulkheads incorporated into the furniture. It is the complete bonding of both outer surfaces to core that provides the strength of foam-sandwich, not the core alone. In case of doubt, build an FRP skinned foam panel first, then add decoration. Formica and any number of decorative laminates are easy to bond onto stiff foam, preferably with a solvent-free contact cement, weighted down or vacuum bagged all over. Or fix on thin knotty pine stripes or other decorative wood, using resin glue.

Smooth finish To eliminate the surface finishing chore of FRP on a one-off foam-sandwich boat, some amateurs who are allergic to resins have used double diagonal cold-moulded skins instead. Epoxy glued strip-planking has been used for the outer skin. Start thinking of all the possibilites!

Undoubtedly the use of a good female mould to provide a sandwich hull with a smooth pigmented gelcoat would be the wish of many an amateur. Making such a mould in foam-sandwich (as described under Sandwich Building Tips) looks fairly easy, but it should not be forgotten that the insulation properties of the foam prevent some of the heat from dissipating when laying up the final hull—particularly when this is to be solid FRP. It also adds to time and costs, unless the mould can be sold or rented out.

Polyurethane core The comparatively soft and brittle PU foam is good enough for filling boxed parts where the core is not under stress or likely to flex, such as engine bearers, hull stiffeners, buoyancy tanks and floors. Bulkheads, with their thin skins, big area and vulnerability to flying bodies and flexing, are best cored with Divinycell® PVC.

Sometimes one needs to fill a cavity with poured PU foam. Two liquids are whisked together and after about two minutes expand forty-fold into a rigid foam that adheres well to FRP laminates. Do not expect the surplus to spill out through a $\frac{1}{2}$ in (12 mm) hole: pressure could build up. A 3 in (75 mm) vent is better. Keep away from the fumes. Avoid pouring into a space bigger than about a 10 gal. capacity, owing to the great deal of heat which is emitted. Check that the way is clear for the foam to expand and push air out as well, or voids and damage will result.

Bearers Light engine bearers and cabin sole bearers are often bonded to the inner skin (see next chapter). Heavy engine bearers must fuse with both skins; the core is tapered away to create solid FRP in way of such bearers. Likewise, there should be solid FRP at propeller shaft logs, at rudder posts, and at stems with sharp or semi-sharp cut-waters.

Sailboard Building

With the variety of possible sailboard shapes and sizes, there is great scope for fascinating experimentation and cost saving. The same applies to surfboards, which are constructed in similar fashion.

The common sailboard shape with upswept bow and flat bottom amidships is the easiest type to make, but the amateur can progress to a hollow or stepped bottom or the latest fashions. A 10 ft (3 m) board can be 6 in (150 mm) deep in places: a lot of buoyancy is required unless you really want a sinker. Commercial boards are made in moulds from polyethylene or ABS, often filled with poured PU foam. The makers of custom boards (and most amateurs) use FRP/polyurethane foam-sandwich. One can buy ready-shaped cores for numerous standard types, or get an oversize block of foam from which to sculpture a special shape. Clark or Burford blanks are of fine quality. With epoxy resin and extra cloth, you can use the cheaper, lighter and softer high-density polystyrene which would be attacked by polyester resin. This is safer to shape by hot-wire cutter: PU gives off very toxic fumes if melted or burned, and must be sawed or planed.

To prevent buckling or snapping, most sailboard cores are stiffened by vertical web *stringers* of 3 mm or 4 mm plywood. Standard ply sheets are not long enough. To obviate scarfing, use red cedar, which is also lighter, or glue up thinner veneers. Surfboards should not need stringers but beware rocks! As most boards need skegs, fins or daggers up the middle, two stringers are convenient, set 3 in (75 mm) to either side of the keel line. Saw the core lengthwise and glue the webs between. To add some decoration underneath using clear resin, artistic builders may stain the stringer edges black or bright red, and tint the foam itself.

Advanced designs strengthen blanks by inlaying 12 mm Divinycell in way of mast and fin boxes. Sometimes the whole footstrap area has 3 mm PVC foam let in. A blank made from offcuts of Divinycell (hopefully gotten gratis!) around 80 kg/m³ glued up as in Fig 150 is heavier than PU but needs no stringers. PVC shapes cleanly like softwood; PU is dusty, noxious and brittle. A portable power planer shapes PU well: a hand plane is useless. A heart of PU surrounded by PVC has possibilities if the bonding is secure. High-density PVC makes excellent stringers.

Stringers cut to the final shape serve as templates for the fore-and-aft profile. Once glued up, sand a PU core flush with the stringers using 40-grit paper at first. Make five or more hardboard female templates to check the athwartships shape. With its longer setting time and better adhesion, epoxy (creamed with added microspheres or microballoons) is ideal glue for stringers. Spread this on both sides of each web, with none on the foam.

Light pressure is all you need to clamp it all up. Five padded cords or straps tightened by Spanish windlass, bungees or shockcords work better than sash clamps or wedges. Rest the foam on two athwartships bearers

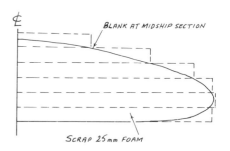

Fig 150 Divinycell® can be glued into any shape

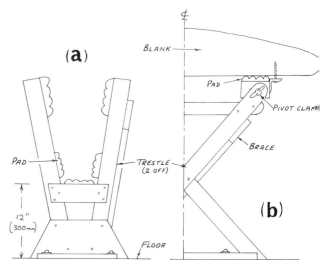

Fig 151 Sailboards are difficult to hold without stands

covered with polythene sheet with a few weights on top to prevent bulging. Cords will cut into foam unless you wrap thin cardboard around the edges.

You need two separate, well padded, racks to support a board conveniently at various stages of construction. The one shown in Fig 151a is to clamp one edge while the opposite edge is shaped: you need two of these, set about 5 ft or 1.5 m apart. A pair as in 151b is invaluable when shaping top and bottom, also when tailoring and glassing the cloths. The board is held by four self-tapping screws: such holes are easy to fill invisibly afterwards. Omit the screws later when putting on deck fittings and polishing the bottom.

Smoothness As with foam-sandwich yacht work, the quality of core finish is transmitted to the final surface. The long sanding board and strips of sandpaper will get id of all humps. When not needed, wrap your core to lessen dust and fingermarks.

Skin Layup

The boardsailing magazines advertise suppliers of kits, materials and fittings. *Sailboards Custom-made* (Stanford Maritime/Nautical) is the book that covers the whole process. Friendly enthusiasts often know the best sources—suppliers willing to advise the amateur.

Preparation Whatever reinforcement you use, and especially if it's one of the exotics, first try out its fitting and layup behaviour on a curved piece of spare foam, especially wrapping it around edges. Then find the best stage in the setting process to trim off the rough edge before it goes too hard, and smooth it off later. Practise mixing resin and getting it well into the glass with the excess squeegeed off, and measure the time before setting starts. If doing the whole surface in one go looks impossible, get helpers, cool the room off a little, and consider cutting the cloth into smaller areas if you must.

Cloth By eliminating CSM, no filler need be used to produce a beautiful finish. Plain weave E-glass cloth weighing about 225 g per m² is popular, the roll width of around 600 mm leading to minimal wastage. Thinner S-glass is available, also carbon/aramid (Kevlar) weaves, unidirectional carbon fibre and a carbon/glass hybrid, all in 1 m widths. These exotics are normally used only for superlightweight boards with epoxy. Certain class rules forbid them.

Over a PU core one normally uses two layers of the E-glass on the bottom and three on the deck. On a *wave board* or over a polystyrene core, you need one extra layer all over. Epoxy adds considerable strength. If carbon strands are incorporated, do not go for a transparent laminate: black can absorb too much heat in the sun. If carefully laid up with no air bubbles, three layers of E-glass weave looks much the same as a clear gelcoat!

Laying-up To reinforce vulnerable bow and stern edges, start by bonding single layer patches on these parts. Cut darts to avoid creases. First test that Scotch tape used to anchor stray ends and for masking will not rip the foam surface many hours later. When sanding patch edges, avoid scuffing the soft foam. A big patch is

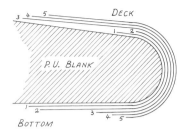

Fig 152 Lay-up sequence for sailboards

often used in way of the footstraps, usually just beneath the final cloth layer.

Most laminators glass the bottom first. They mask the deck with paper and tape, the latter taking a sweet curve about 2 in (50 mm) in from the edge. Place the board on padded Fig 151b stands, bottom up. Stretch cloth over the bottom and trim off about ½ in (12 mm) beyond the masking line. Cut bow and stern darts where necessary to let the cloth follow the curvature. To facilitate cloth alignment during layup, make about 20 tiny pencil marks across cloth and masking tape. Make other reference marks over each stringer, centrally and near each end. Tailor the second cloth over the first one and trim it off about 1 in (25 mm) smaller all around. Mark the stringer positions on it.

A big board uses some 12 lb (5.5 kg) of resin. Apply it fast with a rubber squeegee on the flat areas (as in Photo 54) and with a brush around the edges. Unless you get help to bed the cloth around and underneath the edges while you work, the gelation time could beat you. Do not rely on much more than 10 min for polyester, or perhaps 25 min for epoxy. When the cloth goes invisible, no air bubbles remain and surplus resin has been squeegeed off, you are truly wetted out! Prick out any small whitish bubbles with a sharp awl.

Follow straight on with the next cloth. Trim the rough edges to the masking line when the resin is semi-hard at the green or toffee stage, then strip off the tape and surplus laminate. When hard, sand any rough places on the bottom and sides before turning the board over. Mask as before, this time on the bottom (Fig 152). Proceed as above, but with a third cloth layer ending 1 in (25 mm) outboard of the middle one. Carefully sand away all edge ridges.

Photo 54 Fibreglassing over a sailboard blank

Motifs

Graphics showing through clear laminates may be the hallmarks of specialist one-off custom boards, but all-white resin is quicker and cooler, perhaps with some artistry or decals beneath the final varnish. An anti-slip surface makes graphics less sharp, but limitless decoration is possible on the bottom where a glossy finish reduces friction.

If you paint directly onto the foam, make tests on offcuts first. Acrylic water paints are bright and easy to use. With an airbrush one can spray fade-out edges, or merge one shade into the other. Aerosol car paints are less precise (use a stencil) and may react with resin. Make sure any masking tape used is the fine line type for striping cars.

Art experts spray a coat of fixing lacquer over graphics to ensure that brushed resin will not smudge anything. Spraying with layup resin thinned with 30% of the appropriate solvent will do, but continue the layup soon after it sets.

Finishing The surface cannot be completed until all the fittings have been built in. Mask any fittings which are not removable. You can only sand the laminate lightly for fear of damaging the cloth and Kevlar roughens badly if sanded. If the board has been touched by fingers, wipe over with degreaser. Brush or spray on clear flowcoat (or epoxy finishing resin, as appropriate) and when hard and non-tacky sand this thoroughly, always wet, starting with 150-grit paper. Recoat if necessary and use ever finer

grades of paper up to 600-grit, until you get a fine, frosted, even finish. Where the deck is to get an anti-slip surface less time is needed. On bottom and sides apply two coats of two-component PU glossy varnish. With any luck this will not need burnishing. Anti-UV properties in a varnish do nothing but good. Refer to *The Compleat Book of Yacht Care* to find out how to brush on a blemish-free coat of varnish.

Except around the sides, a glossy deck is dangerous, so mask off and spray Intersurf (or a similar anti-slip finisher) on the rest. This will not graze your knees like a traditional sand-on-wet-varnish surface. For a transparent finish over graphics you need sheet nylon Peel Ply. Spread this over wet varnish and peel off next day to reveal an evenly embossed roughness like that on production polyethylene boards. Lacking this, with a few trials a certain grade of table salt or sugar sprinkled over wet varnish may produce just the roughness you prefer.

Fittings

Plenty of footstrap nut inserts give more scope for adjustment than permanently bonded straps. Similarly, removable skegs (fins) slotted into moulded plastic wells are more practical than fixed ones. Many of these items can be home made, including mast steps with their sockets or tracks, though all can be bought separately. One can lay up FRP skegs and daggerboards over glass or plywood, then profile them and grind them into airfoil shapes.

Slots A router is ideal for gouging out the deep recesses for the boxes which house fittings. They are then glassed in. Knives and saws can be used instead. Keep to just a slack fit, or the vast amount of epoxy resin or resin putty will overheat. If a fin is to be a fixture, bevel back the FRP skin at 45° at the mouth of the slot and run a fillet of rovings all around with a strip of glass cloth over that. Standard plastic boxes usually need solvent cleaning and external sanding first to ensure secure bonding into the core.

This chapter was entitled *Plastics Made Easy* because building boats around rigid foam cores is so much more suitable for amateur work than the familiar solid FRP system described in the next chapter—but a lot of the information there is needed before you can start sandwich construction.

Chapter 15
Solid Fibreglass

In comparison with foam-sandwich construction, few amateurs ever build solid FRP hulls, whereas the majority of production boats utilize this latter method. For amateur one-off hulls, given the right materials and working conditions a sandwich design is bound to succeed. And if a cruiser, the resulting yacht will always be more comfortable than its solid-skin counterpart. Without a proper female mould, a solid FRP job could finally prove unsatisfactory. (So much exotic reinforcement material goes into skins nowadays that the word *fibreglass* can be a misnomer: FRP or fibre reinforced plastics is the more correct as a general term.)

If you can borrow a mould, solid works out cheaper than sandwich. A smooth, glossy gelcoat is said to be another merit of solid FRP, but a sandwich hull can have this from a female mould. While laying up a solid FRP hull over a male plug is possible, the outside surface will need an awful lot of filling: the thicker a laminate the more irregular the surface tends to become. There is one big advantage of solid: if you do get into trouble, scores of boatyards in every sailing area are competent to carry out good repair work. An advantage of building any hull in a female mould is that one never needs to roll it over, especially where the mould is designed to dismantle.

The Plug

When it comes to making a plug, on which to build a good female mould of GRP, the accuracy required necessitates extensive filling, sanding and painting of the upside-down shape. Most amateurs prefer wood, sometimes in conjunction with plaster or similar filler. The starting procedure is much the same as for a cold-moulding male jig, described in Chapter 12. You can use braced hardboard or plywood to make a flat transom. As in all FRP work, round off the corners generously and fit wooden backing to support quadrant beadings or resin putty nosings. The plug in Photos 48a and b has a single skin of 4 mm plywood stapled to the stringers, later to be stopped over and painted. By continuing this into cold-moulding (or by using strip-planking), you would get a better plug with the added advantage of eventual sale as a brand new wooden hull ready for fitting out. By using epoxy satura-

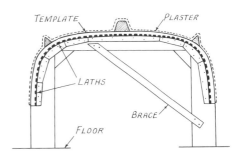

Fig 153 Making a hull plug with wood and plaster

tion you do not need expensive hardwoods for strip-planking.

If you hate wood, use the plug method shown in Fig 153. If a hull $\frac{1}{16}$ in (1.5 mm) bigger than intended will not matter, cut a temporary plywood frame to represent each station line and make no deduction for skin thickness from the lines drawings (see Chapter 2). The frames will be coated with a $\frac{1}{16}$ in (1.5 mm) skim of plaster. If pine is used instead of plywood, the plaster will crack. A piece of $\frac{1}{16}$ in (1.5 mm) diameter wire stretched around the periphery of each frame and stapled at each end enables the plaster skim to be floated off accurately. Before the plaster hardens, peel away the wire; fill the groove the following day.

Bevelled edge frames are best. Tack laths from frame to frame, as in Fig 153 leaving gaps averaging $\frac{3}{8}$ in (9 mm) between them. Alternatively, heavier battens with 2 in (50 mm) gaps, then cover these with burlap (hessian) or plasterers' metal lathing. Or again, instead of battens, tension 14-gauge wires fore-and-aft, notched into saw-cuts in the frames and cover with mesh etc.

Plastered Plug

If this is not your trade, better to hire a good plasterer for a few hours. For a base, mortar made from $2\frac{1}{2}$ parts of builders' sand to 1 part of Portland cement comes cheapest, though it needs 24 hours to go off. Hessian will only stand an initial $\frac{1}{8}$ in (3 mm) skim, due to the weight.

Once this hardens, a thicker layer will go on painlessly. Remember to scratch each layer with a comb just before it sets, to ensure a good bond with the next coat. To avoid any highspots, spring a thin batten across several frames, building up the mortar to within about $\frac{1}{4}$ in (6 mm) of this.

Regular wall plaster (or plaster of Paris) is ideal to bring the surface up level with the frames. For the final skim flush to the periphery wires, use decorators' filler which has a longer working time. Shave this down where necessary with a Surform tool. Use fine filler paste for the hundreds of small low spots you are sure to find and sand with 240-grit paper.

To show up unevenness, wait until dusk, then shine a light along close to the surface. A glossy surface shows this best, easily achieved by spraying with pale car paint. Thin smears of car filler and further fine-sanding will no doubt prove necessary. It takes a long time, but slight waviness below the waterline is permissible on certain types of hull.

Female Moulds

Unlike epoxy, a polyester laminate shrinks slightly on curing and is thus easier to part from a female mould than from a male plug. By making the female mould in two halves bolted together along the centreline (see Photo 47), or even more sections, parting, future storage and transport are simplified. This could be essential for a design with bilge keels. A removable transom on a mould may suffice to accommodate parting a hull with tumblehome.

Strong flanging is needed to bolt mould sections together. To form this on one half-mould, clamp a temporary vertical board to one side of the dividing line along the plug. Having laid up that part of the mould, remove the board and you now have one flange. Cover this with cellophane, Mylar film or some other release agent and lay up the mating flange and mould against it. Bore for the flange bolts at this stage.

Before glassing on supports as shown in Fig 154, allow the shell to cure. If glassed too soon, stretch marks will show on the gelcoat. Leave the plug in position while bonding on wood, metal or FRP box section supports. Brace the supports solidly together into a cradle. A poorly supported shell will twist and sag.

For a production mould, skin thickness is often 50% greater than that of the final hull. For a one-off dinghy you can get away with a mould 30% thinner than the boat, using cradle supports 30 in (760 mm) apart.

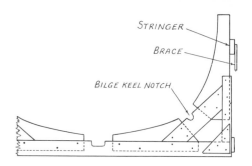

Fig 154 Cradle detail for female mould

To avoid the need for walking about inside a big but fragile one-off split mould, one can lay up the boat itself in two separate halves and glass these together later! In fact this is not an uncommon procedure for Divilette® sandwich production work. Allowing for the above extra stress, the mould for a one-off 17 ft (5 m) launch could have a skin 20% thinner than the boat's skin, with supports 39 in (1 m) apart. For a 30 ft (9 m) cruiser, try 30% less with supports at 4 ft (1.2 m) intervals. If the mould still seems frail, wait for full cure and then bond extra mat or ribs outside, perhaps only over certain areas.

Commercial moulds sometimes have thin electrical heater strips in the laminate to speed up the hardening time of each layup. Putting heaters inside an inverted plug is not normally necessary and could cause damage.

Release from a stiff plug after laminate contraction is not always easy. If you bore beforehand several $1\frac{1}{4}$ in (32 mm) holes through the plug's keel (duly sealed with cork and patches of Scotch tape), pegs jacked up through the holes take the weight of the mould, while the outside of the mould is tapped with rubber mallets. The shape has to allow withdrawing the plug, or else it has to be dismantled from below: plan this beforehand.

Factories build nozzles through female moulds, for compressed air. At the turn of the bilge such openings (lightly plugged and covered) cause no gelcoat defects which cannot be readily made good.

Keels and Appendages

Even without compressed air, you should not have too much bother releasing a split mould from its plug (or releasing the final boat shell) when bilge keels, fin keel, skeg or shaft blisters are incorporated, provided it has been designed correctly.

The only tricky bit is a drop-keel slot. A well rounded entry for this should be included on the female mould, as in Fig 155a. Make the plug indent as deep as you dare, but taper the sides for easy release. Cut the unwanted blank out of the final hull shell (155b) before bonding on the internal trunk. A stubby fin with external lead ballast bolted on makes moulding easier and the centre of gravity is lower. Much the same applies to ballasted bilge keels. To simplify later checking for tightness of inaccessible keel bolt nuts, equip the nuts with tubular extensions.

Whether ballasted or not, deep hollow appendages are bad medicine, for osmosis blistering could start, especially if condensation or any other sort of fresh water gets in. Best to fill with poured (see page 127) and glass over the top: if such glassing is made as a heavily webbed plate, keel bolts may be brought right up to that level. It all depends on the designer.

Fitting separate appendages as shown in Figs 146a and b saves making a complicated plug and female mould, but loses the perfect gelcoat. Skegs or fins are best fitted as in Fig 156, unless they have to be bolted on. Almost any added bonded-on appendage may be built in foam-sandwich, like a sailboard. Using this method can save having to make a special plug and female mould.

Rudders need to be made from two FRP shells stuck together, enabling you to encase within the rudder a metal stock with straps welded to it that extend at least halfway across the blade. Airex PVC foam (or similar) will help take up the spaces; but fill every tiny void with polyester microsphere putty (such as Divilette) before the two halves are brought together. Such putty produces very little heat when in a big mass, but if you use this lightweight type make sure your rudder does not float. There is little difference between rudders for solid FRP and foam-sandwich hulls. The fabrication of metal stocks, gudgeons and pintles for rudders is detailed in *Boat Repairs and Conversions*.

Building the various appendages onto a plug is best done using a combination of solid wood, laminated wood, laths and plaster, and boxed plywood.

Laminating Resins

It took 30 years to find out that certain cheaper standard polyester resins could be a contributory factor towards the osmosis damage which affected some 30% of fibreglass hulls left permanently afloat. More costly isophthalic, iso-NPG and vinylester resins have appeared to

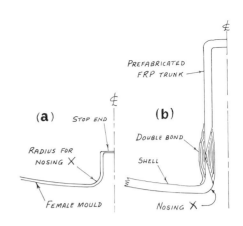

Fig 155 A drop-keel slot must be formed in the mould

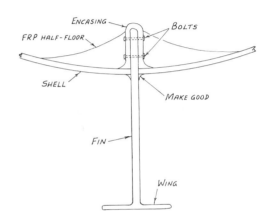

Fig 156 Metal fins are adaptable to FRP construction

help combat this problem, though impeccable laminating workmanship is still of paramount importance.

Epoxies For ultra-lightweight hulls using exotic FRP, most designers consider expensive epoxies the best resins. For bonding to wood (as in deck sheathing) and for bonding wood (or separate FRP mouldings) to cured fibreglass, epoxy has better adhesion. Epoxy does not wet out mat so readily as polyester. It takes longer to gel and to cure, especially with fillers added, and is not normally used in the form of a pigmented gelcoat, as solventless epoxy enamel is brushed or sprayed on instead. The absence of styrene fumes is an added bonus but some people do become allergic to either resin or its dust.

Buying It pays to buy resins in bulk when a big job is to be completed fairly fast. A dinghy might need 100 lb (40 kg) of resin, and for a 30 ft (9 m) cruiser, 1500 lb (700 kg). Most chandlers can get what the amateur needs and mail order suppliers advertise in the practical boating magazines. Professional moulders will sometimes supply small quantities, or recommend a good source.

Make certain you get resin of the exact specification for your working conditions, method of construction, and chemistry of mat or cloth. Cheap offers, surplus or out-dated stocks, are not worth risking for boat work. Good suppliers know whether you need E-glass, R-glass or S-glass, and whether the coating it comes with is compatible with your resin. Unless in metric units, mats come in oz per sq ft while wovens come in oz per sq yd: see also Appendix 4.

Additives The correct marine grade resin of low viscosity usually contains a thixotropic agent (to minimize downward seepage) plus enough accelerator for average conditions. Having to add more of the latter is a nuisance, with some danger (see below). You may have to add it in cold weather: do so after catalyzing. First study the maker's technical literature clarifying all such matters and ask their advice.

The only other additives likely to be encountered are pigments, fillers and fire retardants. Nothing will make resin or laminates fireproof, however.

Fillers Titanium oxide or dioxide makes the best white filler, though powdered chalk or talc is cheaper. All fillers are considered taboo for hull layups, but up to 15% of powder by weight may not be detrimental for moulds and furniture, reduced to 5% for the gelcoat. Special black gelcoat resin is available for female moulds, to aid polishing and waxing. Lamp-black powder or black pigment paste in the resin gives the same effect.

Large amounts of lightweight fillers such as ground coconut fibre or microspheres are added to make resin putty. You can also make a putty by cutting oddments of mat or rovings into $\frac{1}{4}$ in (6 mm) lengths and mixing these into your resin.

When making putty, add the catalyst first. To save time when mixing small quantities, keep a stock of resin to which about half the total amount of filler has been added, then catalyze a portion of this when needed, followed by the remainder of the filler. No putty adheres as efficiently as a straight resin, especially when very stiff. Epoxy putty

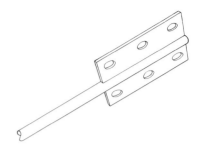

Fig 157 Home-made resin mixer

adheres best, but if the bond is critical always apply priming coat of straight resin first.

Mixing Resins

If stored in a cool, dark, fireproof place, resins and the hardening catalysts could remain good for a year Absence of any accelerator increases the shelf life; pigmentation decreases it. Once a quantity of resin is catalyzed its pot life (working time) is brief. A large bulk hardens more rapidly than a thinly spread coat—and gets very hot. Refrigeration will delay hardening, but this is rarely of any practical value. Gelcoats must be at room temperature before application.

Liquid catalysts mix more readily than the powder variety. With an electric drill capable of low speed, the sort of mixing paddle shown in Fig 157 will stir effectively. High-speed mixers often entrap air.

Watch eyes Wear goggles. Catalyst in one's eye can injure it badly. The usual remedy is instant douching with cool fresh water for ten minutes. If pain persists report to a hospital. Catalyst is also a skin irritant. It can ignite wood and paper, so dunk any swabs contaminated with it into a tub half-filled with water.

Bang! If you need to add extra accelerator, keep it well away from any catalyst. If the two chemicals meet, an explosion is likely.

Setting time Additional catalyst will speed the hardening process, but try to avoid doing it. Resin makers issue chart listing the volume or weight of catalyst to add per pound or kilogram of resin at various temperatures to give the permissible range of setting times. Epoxy resins demand far more precise mixing ratios than polyesters.

Science marches on. Actinic resins are available which harden under a strong light. This eliminates mixing and enables delayed curing to be effected where necessary.

Sagging Rarely should it prove necessary to add extra thixotropic agent. If drooping occurs, you may have the wrong sort of resin, too much for the reinforcement, or the working conditions are unsatisfactory. Excessive use of this additive makes a resin more likely to entrap air.

Tinting Mix pigment pastes with a little resin before adding to the full pot of uncatalyzed resin. At least 1 oz per lb of resin (63 g to 1 kg) is needed to ensure opacity. The maximum ratio is about 50% more than this. Try to avoid the complication of mixing special tints, or else make up the whole batch of mixed pigment at once.

Pigments are now considered to worsen the waterproofing and adhesion properties of a gelcoat. To prevent problems, the wise amateur buys gelcoats and flowcoats pre-pigmented at the factory. Epoxy layups do not normally have pigmented gelcoats at all, but to start with a polyester gelcoat and continue a layup with epoxy is considered very bad practice.

A clear gelcoat is ideal below the waterline where antifouling paint will be used. This is impervious and also helps reveal air pockets in the lay up: cut these out and build up with further resin. Copper-rich gelcoat resin now available is intended to provide antifouling properties for some 15 years.

Safety A notice forbidding smoking should be displayed on your workshop door and inside. The same applies to all naked flames in the vicinity of resins, including propane space and water heaters (which also create moisture) and radiant electric heaters. Cleaning solvents are all volatile and flammable, as well as giving off fumes that should be removed from the work area.

Equipment

A suspended spring balance is useful. Once the weight of resin held by a certain pot is known, you should not need to weigh every mix.

If the mat or cloth to be used in one session is weighed, you can estimate the approximate weight of resin required by assuming a $2\frac{1}{2}$: 1 resin to CSM (chopped strand mat) ratio by weight, or $1\frac{1}{2}$: 1 when using WR (woven rovings) or cloth.

Dispensers A calibrated medicine cup will measure catalyst, but a dispenser pump is not expensive and saves much time. A large bore tap or faucet for resin drums is quick in use, but the special dispenser pump to fit through the top hole of a drum is cleaner and more accurate for small quantities.

Cleaning Styrene is the thinner to use for polyesters and xylene for epoxies. More than these, you need a lot of industrial acetone for cleaning tools. Never use acetone on your skin — resin-dissolving creams are made for that. Use barrier cream before you start. Talcum powder is useful if hands do get sticky. Get accustomed to wearing rubber gloves and long sleeves.

You can break hard resin out of a plastic pail or half a flexible ball. Leave a lot in and it could burn up! For cleaning brushes and rollers you need two pails of acetone: one with clean solvent for rinsing brushes, the other for acetone contaminated with resin. Before this starts to solidify, dump it and refill with the contents of the other pail. Plan how you will achieve safe, and legal, storage and disposal of such solvents.

Have enough brushes so that they can be washed and dried before further use. Failing this, dunk them in styrene monomer to get rid of any lurking acetone which could affect the resin.

Applicators Cheap, white fibre, throwaway flat paint brushes about 4 in (100 mm) wide are ideal for applying resin. If necessary, stiffen them slightly by cutting about $\frac{1}{2}$ in (12 mm) off the bristle tips. Long-handled 7 in (175 mm) paint rollers are useful in big hulls, but troublesome to clean. Some throwaway foam rollers are attacked by resins. Rubber squeegees work well for spreading flowcoats and fillers. Metal washer or vane rollers (Photo 56) are essential for dispersing air bubbles.

Laying Up

Having made a suitable mould, a factory might employ sophisticated methods to build up a thick FRP shell, including the use of a *chopper gun* which sprays resin, catalyst and short glass strands in one operation. The amateur and the small boatyard is restricted to the *wet layup* process. This gives perfect results if carried out conscientiously, using reinforcement which is completely dry and staying within temperature and humidity limits.

Designers do not always refer to skin thicknesses; more often they specify the number of layers and types of mat or cloth. The information in Appendix 4 is a guide to the likely build up with the more common materials. Trial panels made from offcuts during the hull layup process are valuable. A hacksaw cut will give you the thickness, while testing to destruction will verify whether or not you have some faulty material.

Keep the air moving when laying-up with polyester resin: the styrene fumes given off could make you ill. In addition, stagnant fumes delay gelation. Being solventless, most epoxies avoid these problems.

Gelcoat Having prepared the mould or plug surface as described above, the wet layup operation starts with the application of an unreinforced, maybe pigmented, resin gelcoat at least 0.015 in (375 microns) thick, brushed or rolled in one pass evenly (and with no air bubbles) over the release agent. This represents about 10 oz per sq yd or 350 g per m² of resin. Half as much again is ideal if you can spread it evenly in one pass. Special highly thixotropic resins are marketed for the job. To further deter sagging, place a layer of fine surfacing tissue gently onto the resin (Photo 57).

Flowcoat Standard polyesters do not harden fully when exposed to the air. If such resins are used as final coats on sandwich hulls (or for any internal finishing) you must exclude air. To do this, spray wax over it, cover it with polythene film or add to the resin an exact amount of wax dissolved in styrene, as specified by the makers. Note that polythene film wrinkles badly when in contact with some resins. Aerobically hardening *flowcoat* resins are also made. The problem doesn't arise with a surface laid into a female mould, of course.

Impregnation

As soon as the gelcoat feels firm, brush clear resin over the area to be covered by the first reinforcement, often CSM. If coarse woven cloth forms the next layer, there should be no risk of its pattern showing on the topsides. Thick CSM

Photo 55 Inner skin layup over Airex® core

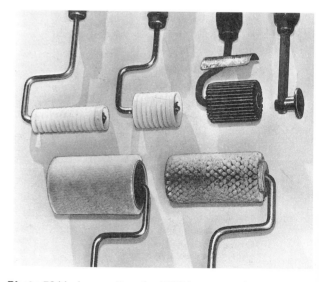

Photo 56 Various rollers for FRP impregnation

can be troublesome to bed down on curves and corners: tease out the strands a little. For your first attempts, don't lay up too large an area.

Mat takes a few minutes to become saturated. After that, careful rolling (from the middle towards the edges) with one of the tools illustrated in Photo 56 is essential to remove every pocket of air. Whitish blobs indicate bubbles under the mat. If these are not squeezed out, a porous, brittle laminate will result. Every ten minutes, brush or stipple more resin over any recent patches which appear starved. Air bubbles are invisible in opaque resins, so avoid pigments and fillers for all except essential topside gelcoats, decks and internal flowcoats, especially in major hull layups.

Except for unidirectional materials all adjoining pieces of reinforcement should overlap by about 1 in (25 mm). A good moulder can tease out the edge strands of CSM with deft twists of his brush, thus minimizing the final surface humps. Your design will probably specify layups where CSM alternates with WR or exotics in adjacent layers. This gives strong, impervious wet layups. Epoxies dislike CSM. Most exotics are troublesome to wet out with *any* resin.

Glass cloth or woven rovings (Photo 57) take longer to wet out than CSM, except at the cut ends. The same applies to the combination mat and cloth which is stitched into one fabric at the factory. Driving air bubbles towards the edges of cloth is often more easily done with the brush than with a washer roller. Beware of resin starvation after a short time has elapsed.

Remember to end a laminate 1 in (25 mm) beyond the sheer, to give full strength when trimmed. Exceed this and the laminate will sag. Trimming each layer at the *green* semi-hard stage (which lasts about 15 min) is possible with a knife. However, cutting the full thickness after curing (using a diamond-impregnated fast disk) gives better strength. Kevlar resists cutting much more than glass cloth.

Inside It seems a good idea to get the sticky resin on the hull's final inside surface covered with flowcoat at an early stage. However, this is best not done over any parts where deck, bulkheads or other major attachments will be bonded. Where flowcoating is delayed 30 hours or more you will need to sand the laminate with a 60-grit disk.

Decorations

Contrasting stripes and motifs are seen on some cruisers, as well as on sailboards, canoes and racing craft. Temporary flashes are easily applied using waterproof tape. You can build permanent decorations into the gelcoat, or apply them later with two-part polyurethane paint or tinted flowcoat resin.

When preparing a female mould surface, forgo the use of PVAL (see page 140) as a releasing agent where a motif lies, as the masking tape will peel it off. Just rely on thorough waxing. Outline your motifs with tape and brush on some brightly pigmented gelcoat. Peel off the tape immediately and leave to gel before applying the main gelcoat around and over it.

To stripe a finished hull, first clean off any PVAL or other release agent with hot water. Next wipe over with warm white spirit (mineral spirit), changing rags frequently, to remove any wax. Mask around the desired shapes, then carefully sand the area to be painted with dry 300-grit paper. Apply the paint or resin, then peel off the tape.

Tailoring

Provided overlaps are well staggered in adjacent layers you can lay CSM in convenient panels no longer than 6 ft or 2 m. Overlapped joins make tailoring easy, but it pays to make paper templates so the whiskery mat is moved only once from bench to boat. Attaching reference numbers is easier on paper than on mat. Templates keep a record of where joins lie on hidden layers—particularly useful when work is deferred for a long time.

At places of great hull curvature, both paper and mat tend to crease. Scissor cuts (darts) will turn the folds into overlaps. Cloth conforms to most curves without cutting, especially once wetted out. If necessary, tease out the strands of thick CSM when wetted. Remember, glass causes itchiness: wear gloves in the cutting room.

Designers often specify unidirectionals to run diagonally or athwartships. Impregnation is a little more leisurely in the latter direction—see Photo 58. Tailor a fore-and-aft cloth to the boat's full length. Tape it in place. Roll up from one end to midway. Impregnate that half before rolling up the remainder and impregnating the other half.

Films and cloths incorporating carbon fibres and Kevlar (or other aramid) strands are not difficult to

Photos 57 Glass mats and cloths: *a.* surfacing tissue, *b.* chopped strand mat, *c.* woven rovings, *d.* unidirectional rovings, *e.* scrim, *f.* glossy black carbon twill, *g.* Kevlar carbon hybrid cloth.

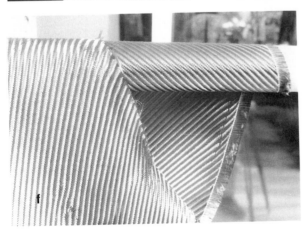

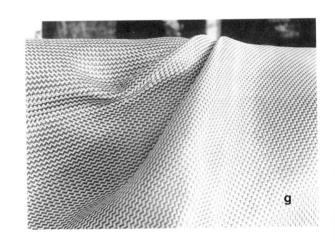

tailor, except for the tough cutting. Impregnation is a different matter: they don't soften and lie down meekly like glass. Carbon fibre is particularly non-absorbent and it must be kept in straight lines. Hybrid cloth containing Kevlar and carbon is often used with epoxy resins. Fortunately, few designs for amateur work use exotics at all, except perhaps for local strengthening. Designers are now specifying the knitted triaxial glass for some economical high-strength layups.

Before cutting woven rovings, stick a strip of $\frac{3}{4}$ in (18 mm) masking tape along the proposed line, to stop fraying. Cut down the middle with a sharp trimming knife or scissors. Half-width tape is more easily removed during impregnation than a full width strip. To avoid having to tailor fabrics on the floor, set up some sort of cutting table. Materials come in heavy rolls, so set up a horizontal steel tube mounted on trunnions to hold them. Never let your materials meet moist air—in store or on the axle.

Keep going When layup must be restricted to short spells, avoid full-length cloths. If a single length has been tailored, keep going, otherwise the extra overlap might ruin the fit at the far end. Continuous impregnation makes the best quality layup. But if you pile layer upon layer too quickly, you get a damaging heat buildup. When one layer follows on top of another, you must catch the *primary bond* limit of some 10 hours for polyesters and 15 hours for epoxies. After any longer delay, scuff the surface with a coarse disk sander to ensure a good bond. Of course, you must grind off all protruding strands however little time has elapsed.

The team A well-organized team of helpers speeds FRP work greatly. On any boat longer than about 10 ft (3 m) you need a full-time helper to deal with resin mixing, cleaning brushes and carrying materials, while a third operator deals with tailoring and edges.

Internal Bonding

In general, you will never have time to catch the primary bond deadline when fitting engine bearers and major stiffeners inside a hull. If you manage to catch it with wooden inserts and pads, glass these on, then carry the final hull or deck lamina over them, making a neat job.

With internal reinforcement, be sure to learn whether the design is based on lengthwise *stringer* stiffeners or

Photo 58 The outer skin: laying cloth athwartships

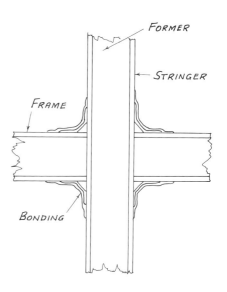

Fig 158 Unimpeded run for a major stiffener

frame (rib) stiffeners. Even if both are specified, with the former system the longitudinals must be continuous, with the frames acting as intercostals (Fig 158). With the latter system, the frames will not be interrupted, but the stringers will.

The cores for small stiffeners are best made from paper rope or metal top-hat sections (Fig 10). Rigid poly-

139

urethane foam formers are best for engine bearers and big stringers, stuck in place with contact adhesive. Use a circular saw to cut up random blocks of foam. Chamfer the arrises generously and stick fillets along the bases as in Fig 161. Moulding a bundle of rovings into a corner will create a fillet, so will resin putty or wood of triangular section. Avoid making sharp corners or edges. Fitting formers accurately takes a long time. Beforehand, scuff thoroughly all hull surfaces to be covered by the wide glass patches. Remove dust with a vacuum cleaner, then wipe with frequently changed rags soaked in styrene for polyester work and xylene for epoxy.

Deck joint Structural joints such as the important deck-to-topsides as shown in Fig 147 often need a buildup of four or more layers of mat or tape both sides where bolts cannot assist. Each layer should overlap the last one by at least 1 in (25 mm). A putty fillet plus three layers would just about reach the heat barrier. If details of such major joints (and bulkhead-to-hull joints) are omitted from the plans, consult the designer or a boatyard expert.

Pre-doped To obviate getting resin in your hair when working overhead, use strips no more than 1 m long and wet these out on the bench over a piece of sheet metal covered with cellophane or polythene. Slide it (with the cellophane) onto an offcut of plywood, carry this to site, stipple it onto a prepared coat of resin, then peel off the cellophane. Mat becomes fragile when fully saturated.

Woven tape has limited uses for bonding, as widths greater than 6 in (150 mm) are hard to get. Joining is in order provided the usual overlap is included. Having a selvage on either side, tape remains stable when wetted out.

Joists The subject of cabin soles is dealt with in *Boat Repairs and Conversions*. Wooden sole bearers suit some FRP boats well. The easy way to bond them to the hull is with permanent CSM patches. Much better to bolt the wood to FRP brackets which are bonded to the hull. Removing a bearer for hull maintenance work or replacement is then not difficult. Slip a pad of foam between all bearer ends and the hull to reduce point stresses. Do the same where bulkheads abut the hull.

Bulkheads Small tabs of tape as seen in Fig 149 will steady a bulkhead to simplify bonding. Polyester is unreliable on a teak faced bulkhead. Epoxy is better, but if the teak is veneer, stop this at the limit of the bonding. To be doubly sure, bore $\frac{3}{4}$ in (18 mm) holes at 6 in (150 mm) intervals through a plywood bulkhead. This gives the strapping something to grip.

When the small tabs are hard, glue on the usual fillets. If you wish to use up CSM offcuts, cut them to make the first layer. Tape is better for the second or final layer if appearance is important. Keep dirty finger marks off plywood by covering it with paper and masking tape; just leave bare the margin to be bonded. While the resin is still green, run a razor knife down where the masking tape starts. Peel off the masking, taking all surplus laminate with it.

As for cabin sole bearers, if a bulkhead is ever likely to need shifting, perhaps to remove the engine, bolt it to FRP flanges duly bonded to the hull. The plans should indicate where particular bulkheads are structurally important, needing extra strong bonding.

Releasing

Prepare the surface of a plug or mould diligently to make sure that the applied gelcoat will release freely. Wax-free polishes are available, but they must not contain silicones. Pure carnauba wax is the most popular. Apply this thinly with a circular motion, using clean, damp stockinette—mutton cloth, not nylon. Polish off with a soft lint-free cloth or gentle power mop. Always work in a warm, dry atmosphere. Repeat the whole process at least three more times.

To make release doubly sure, lightly spray a thin coat of PVAL (polyvinyl alcohol) all over. This dries in about 30 min. Then spray it again to eliminate any holidays. If you put it on by hand with a sponge, do not go back over it or apply a second coat. Beware of run marks. Try to get tinted PVAL rather than the type that looks like gin: coating evenly is then much easier.

Some release agent will get transferred to the gelcoat. Whether or not the hull is to be painted, clean this off. Use warm water and detergent to remove PVAL. One of the patent cleaners marketed will tackle pure wax. After laying up a hull (or any component) over a *male mould*, remember to clean off the inside before attempting to bond in bulkheads, tanks etc. Sanding will not reliably clear away all wax.

If a mould will dismantle (Photo 47), you should need little persuasion to strip it from a completed hull shell—particularly if wedging slots were formed along the langes, and you remembered to run Scotch tape over the joints inside to prevent resin from percolating.

One-part moulds are more troublesome. The longer he job is postponed, the easier it becomes! If rolling over is not feasible, glass a couple of temporary steel bars across the keel trough, enabling the hull's weight to be taken by sheer-legs or a hoist while the mould is dropped away.

Pushing metal tools between the two skins could damage the gelcoats. If both hull and mould will flex slightly at the gunwales, strips of cardboard can be inserted. Tap lightly with a rubber mallet further down, then run hot water into the gap. Industrial laminations are sometimes *pulled* by means of compressed air.

Once parted, drop the hull back in for bracing across the beam with a few temporary cross-spalls. Glass their ends, but keep them below deck connection level. Do not attach the deck while the shell rests in its mould: resin could get between and damage both gelcoats. Clarify the sheer-line location at this stage and cut along the sheer as previously described. Any coarse tool may chip the gelcoat. A sabre saw or jigsaw which cuts on the up-stroke must be held on the opposite side to the gelcoat. Fortunately, most dinghy gunwales and yacht decks cover the sheer-line, so a little waviness or edge damage may not matter. Don't be in a hurry to finally remove the shell from the support of its mould. Curing goes on for some time, and until you can set it up true and braced all around, there is a risk of its warping and getting a distorted 'set'.

Attachments

Professionals use a lot of wood on FRP yacht interior work and deck trim. This costs more than the basic bathtub look, but fortunately most amateurs can find the time to emulate the best. Attaching joinery to a foam-sandwich hull is simple: see page 118. With solid FRP you must bond plywood pads or metal inserts inside the hull, to support screwed-on battens which in turn take the fastenings from built-in or prefabricated joinerwork.

Before glassing in metal inserts or brackets designed to receive bolts or machine screws, scuff the buried parts with a power wire brush, then degrease. Light duty inserts and pads need not be glassed in as in Fig 159: good epoxy putty will bond them adequately. You are unlikely to be tooled up with CSM which is compatible with epoxy, so cover plenty of surface area when polyester bonding is

Fig 159 Bevel-edged insert glassed into hull skin

used to attach an important moulded component inside the hull.

All glassed-in pads and backing pieces should be bevelled on all edges, as in Fig 159. This not only eliminates fillets but lessens the stress point effect. Big pads, as for outboard motor mountings, need extra thick glassing. To prevent vibrational delamination, bore $\frac{3}{4}$ in (18 mm) holes in a pattern of 2 in (50 mm) intervals for the resin to penetrate. To glass in pads, CSM squares cut with corner darts will lie down best: two layers minimum, each overlapping the previous one by about 1 in (25 mm) all around. Long lengths of CSM alternated with unidirectional WR is often specified for structural stiffeners.

Even on solid FRP hulls, sandwich decks are common. As described in the last chapter, the standard foam or balsa core must be replaced by plywood in way of most deck fittings. You also need a pad or backing plate inside the hull, but this need not always be glassed over. If you forget to harden the core, do so later by cutting away the inner skin and core. Finally, thicken the new skin with overlapping mat and fit a large backing plate.

Self-tapping screws on solid hulls are mainly confined to attaching light parts to flanges, hollow boxes and cored stiffeners. If wiring cables must be clipped to solid FRP without mounting battens, fit a depth stop on the pilot hole drill to make sure that self-tappers do not penetrate much more than halfway through the laminate.

Built-in buoyancy The simplest tanks are built into the bow and stern of a dinghy or launch by making a plywood mould with one corner (Fig 160). A single sheet of 16-gauge metal (bent around a piece of tube or bar) is even better. It can be reused, and the panel can be laid up with the gelcoat on either side. Use polythene sheet for releasing. Make the laminate oversize, then trim it to a template before bonding to the hull.

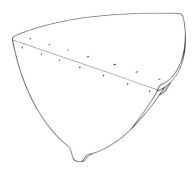

Fig 160 Plywood former for bow buoyancy tank

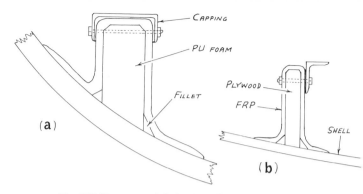

Fig 161 Heavy and light duty FRP engine bearers

Some launches and rowboats lend themselves to the useful device of a double bottom—a buoyancy compartment with a flat surface for the bottom boards. Internal stiffeners are advisable, though a poured foam fill adds stiffness.

Tanks Unless lined with solventless epoxy enamel, built-in tanks can give drinking water a foul taste for more than ten years. But these, with fuel and sewage holding tanks, can strengthen a hull greatly. Remember that the hull surface inside a tank might not have a proper gelcoat, and osmosis damage is most severe under fresh water. How to make separate tanks is described in *Boat Repairs and Conversions*.

Flat FRP panels bend easily, so big tanks need internal baffles, webs or ribbing to resist the great loads. Foam-sandwich structures are greatly superior to solid ones for tanks, baffles, bulkheads (Chapter 14), bunk boxes, cockpit lockers and suchlike.

For engines Powerboats need stiff engine bearers of considerable length, capped with galvanized steel channel (flanges downwards) in way of each engine (Fig 161a). Galvanized angle is common for small engines (161b).

In auxiliary sailboats, motors may reside on grillages (see *Boat Repairs and Conversions*), basically of plywood duly glassed over. When flat galvanized strips are screwed or lag-bolted on top, be careful to set these in mastic so that no water can penetrate to the wood. Have a dry run with the alignment first, to get the engine mountings welded on (or stud holes tapped) prior to galvanizing. Make full use of epoxy saturation for a grillage. For thick parts you can then use pine instead of hardwood—much cheaper and lighter. Continue with epoxy resin for the

FRP encasing, to give the best bond possible to wood an hull skin.

Ballast

The advantages of an externally ballasted keel were dis cussed in Chapter 10, but many an amateur is attracted t the idea of pouring all ballast into a sealed keel trough Many types of sealed ballast are possible: iron or lea pigs, lead shot, shaped-to-fit castings, steel punchings se in concrete, bitumen or resin. But make sure it will not fa out if the yacht should turn turtle!

Concrete or mortar relies on the inside surface rough ness for adhesion. To be sure, epoxy-bond a 1 in (25 mm diameter thick-walled steel tube every 18 in (450 mm across the keel trough, about 3 in (75 mm) below the to of the concrete. For a resin-and-sand matrix, again adhe sion could be poor, so it pays to roughen the shell b bonding on a small pat of epoxy putty every 6 in (150 mm in both directions.

A mass of concrete gets warm while setting: a mass o resin gets hot enough to burn. Therefore, embed ballas with filled resin in layers no thicker than $1\frac{1}{2}$ in (40 mm adding no more until the surface is quite cold but wel within the primary bond period.

Water lurks in bilges, even if only via condensation stern gland drips or over-filled water tanks. Build in small pumping sump and try to give the ballast surface fall towards the sump from all directions. A screed of ric mortar makes a dust-free surface for concrete, but a thic skim of flowcoat serves well for most matrices— preferably pigmented white. Bitumen or pitch is not eas to keep clean.

Bedding the keel You cannot bolt on external ballast until you have a fair fit—kissing the FRP in at least ten places after coating one surface with chalky water and ringing the parts together. Do not cut away any FRP: instead, use an angle grinder on the iron or a flat bearing scraper on lead. Paint iron with epoxy tar or similar. Bed in mastic, not resin putty: a ballast keel should be removable without too much hassle and flexible mastic is a better sealant.

Small Parts

Where appearance is not a problem, components made from solid or foam-sandwich FRP find uses with hulls of almost any material. They include hatches, pilothouses, spars, cockpit lockers, bath or shower tray, buoyancy compartments, tanks, furniture, ventilators and engine casings. There is great scope for individualistic design and practising on small parts is a useful prelude to the costly hull layup. Fabrication procedure is much as already described for hulls. If a female mould must be made first, forget about FRP and look to wood or metal. Take your time over small thick parts, for the heat build-up could cause damage.

Sheathing Another facet of FRP work is the bottom (and sometimes topside) sheathing of wooden hulls. You may meet various reasons for sheathing, such as designed-in strength, reducing the painting frequency, adding an impervious membrane, or hiding a lot of defects. Details and costings for most sheathing processes are given in *The Compleat Book of Yacht Care*.

Sheathing a plywood deck is much easier to do. By using scrim cloth (Photo 57) a tolerably good non-slip surface results. Do not apply the final pigmented flowcoat with a squeegee: brush it thinly and touch up the worn areas as time goes by. Make sure you get materials formulated for sheathing. For instance, International Paint supply epoxy resin and cloth for decks. The special wood primer, cloth, polyester resin and finishing coats by Bondaglass-Voss in England and Bradson in America should be available through any good chandler.

Chapter 16
Ferrocement Hulls

As the material costs for a bare hull can be as little as one-third those for any other method, ferrocement—although not attractive to all amateur boatbuilders—is not to be despised, particularly for boats over 40 ft (12 m). Needless to say, there are snags. The weight compared with other materials is greater for certain designs, so that ferro is generally unsuitable for multi-hulls, light displacement sailboats and racing powerboats. Although most ferro boats are of round bilge form, the method is quite suitable for curvaceous chine designs, particularly for powerboats.

Much of the work can be done singlehanded, but several expert plasterers are essential to apply the mortar, backed up by a large team of amateur helpers. Due to this, in some remote locations wood or steel construction is often a better choice. Internal condensation is a problem in some climates, but can be overcome by the use of anti-condensation paint or panel-covered foam plastics bonded on. Plenty of floor space under cover plus good headroom is needed for ferro work. Good illumination to all parts is essential, especially during the plastering operation.

Properties

Two small ferro boats, one of which still exists, were built in France in the mid-19th century, shortly after the general introduction of Portland cement. The idea was forgotten for almost 100 years, while ferro-concrete made great strides for structures ranging from bridges and ships to pipes and fence posts. The latter material gets tensional strength from thick steel reinforcing bars (*rebars*) embedded in concrete, which is a mixture containing more crushed stone than cement mortar.

Ferrocement is a more costly material suitable for thin shells, for which it is also used on land. The reinforcement consists of an armature of thin wire mesh, layers of which are so tightly packed together that there is just room to force rich cement mortar right into it, with only a thin skim hiding the steel (see Photo 59). A thin fer-

Photo 59 Armature before final wire tying

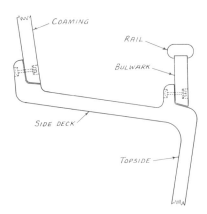

Fig 162 Rabbet to house bolted coamings

rocement panel possesses magical properties which bear little resemblance to those of ferro-concrete. It has considerable elasticity and will vibrate when struck with a heavy mallet. A curvaceous boat hull of ferrocement is immensely strong. In collision only local surface crushing is normal, repaired by re-plastering the original armature after removal of all damaged mortar. The fire-resistance is superb.

Whereas rebars in conventional concrete are never placed closer than about $1\frac{1}{2}$ in (38 mm) to the surface, to prevent possible corrosion, the rich mortar in ferrocement is so waterproof that cover of only $\frac{1}{8}$ in (3 mm) is sufficient on the outside; often even less inside.

Panels about $\frac{5}{8}$ in (16 mm) thick are the thinnest practicable for normal boatwork, suitable for hulls 26 ft (8 m) long or so. However, with great care hulls have been built as thin as $\frac{1}{2}$ in (12 mm). Test panels are easy to make. Skin thicknesses are always detailed on plans for ferrocement boats. Although the keel trough is usually thicker, $\frac{3}{4}$ in (18 mm) is common for the remainder of a 40 ft (12 m) cruising yacht. Up to about 50 ft (15 m), 1 in (25 mm) is used; with $1\frac{1}{4}$ in (32 mm) up to about 70 ft (21 m).

A $\frac{3}{4}$ in (18 mm) ferro skin is roughly comparable to $1\frac{1}{4}$ in (32 mm) of planked teak, $\frac{1}{2}$ in (12 mm) of fibreglass, $\frac{1}{4}$ in (6 mm) of mild steel, or $\frac{5}{16}$ in (8 mm) of light alloy.

Designs

There is no scarcity of good ferrocement designs, such as those of Benford in the USA, Samsons in Canada, Hartley in New Zealand, and Tucker Designs of the UK. They range from power to cruising and racing sailing yachts, in many sizes. In view of this, it would be pointless to risk adapting designs intended for other materials.

Most ferro boats have integral framing and are built upright, but some are built upside down over a plastic-sheeted, wooden male plug. Web frames are then normally added later to short bars left protruding through holes in the plug and tied in to the shell armature. Similar stubs are left to support the deck and any bulkheads which are not attached to a frame. Having rolled such a hull over after curing, the plug is stripped out and all staples used to fix the armature to it are ground off flush. Temporary wooden formwork covered with polythene sheeting is erected underneath the deck level. Then construction is continued as for the hull.

Good plans will give a schedule of materials and the essential details of armature and skin thicknesses, rudder, ballast, engine bearers, and joints for bulkheads, deck, floors, superstructure and furniture. Time is saved if the positions and sizes of apertures for through-hull fittings, rudder fittings, chainplates, wiring, plumbing and propeller shaft are indicated on the drawings. The cement mixtures should be specified, also the steel mesh type and size. Not all designs utilize ferro for every part. Wooden cabin coamings may be bolted into rabbets as shown in Fig 162. Similar bulwarks or toerails are often preferred to ferro ones. Some boats have decks and bulkheads entirely of wood or foam-sandwich, or superstructures of light alloy. Teak cladding on a ferro deck adds great style (see Chapter 13). Bonding internal parts is covered at the end of this chapter.

Ballast arrangements are similar to those for fibreglass boats. External ballast prevents the ferro surface from

Photo 60 Typical web frames with mesh in place

Photo 61 Web frames suspended from overhead strongbacks

Photo 62 Galvanized strip edging screeds

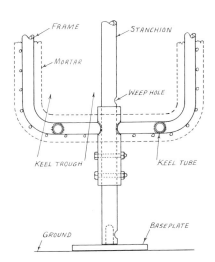

Fig 163 Keeping the keel clear of the ground

grinding on a beach. It also leaves the keel trough free inside to house tanks, a bilge sump, or cans of beer. Scrap steel embedded in concrete makes cheap inside ballast.

Framing

In the most popular building system the boat's shape is derived from right-way-up permanent frames of bent steel tube (Photo 4), or of lattice girder type (Photo 60) welded up from thin bar, sometimes with deck beams or temporary cross-spalls. Frames and struts must be strong enough to withstand the great weight of the hull after plastering. To allow easy access to all parts for plastering, avoid bilge struts from the shed floor. Either use overhead strongbacks as in Photo 61, or fit base tubes as in Fig 163—preferably both. Each base tube is bolted to a central tubular stanchion reaching from floor to roof.

With similar fixings at deck level, you must also hang each frame head from above with rebar rod to prevent sagging. On completion, jack up the hull enough to fit chocks under the keel and bilges, remove the stanchions, burn off tubes and hangers with a cutting torch and make good with mortar.

Making frames Tube frames are best made from standard untreated steel water or steam pipe, varying from $\frac{3}{8}$ in (9 mm) bore for the smallest craft, through $\frac{1}{2}$ in (12 mm) and $\frac{3}{4}$ in (18 mm) to 1 in (25 mm) for 70 ft (21 m) boats. Corresponding stanchion sizes would be $\frac{3}{4}$ in (18 mm), 1 in (25 mm), $1\frac{1}{2}$ in (38 mm) and 2 in (50 mm) bore. Frame

145

shapes are determined by patterns taken from the lofted lines as described in Chapter 3, taking care to deduct the skin thickness which lies outside the frames.

Some design agencies can supply pipe frames bent accurately to shape. Plumbers' pipe-bending machines are almost useless for this job. Up to $\frac{1}{2}$ in (12 mm) bore, steel tube can be hand-bent around a jig with comparative ease. If proper bar rolls cannot be borrowed to deal with the larger sizes, it proves best to send patterns and pipe to a suitable engineering plant and pay them to bend a pair of pipes to each shape.

Lattice frames are readily bent at home, but with so many welds they require much time. A jig needs to be adapted for each one, holding the main bars to shape while the cross members are tack-welded. Finish welding off the jig. Blast-weld galvanized strip on the inner edge to form a screed: see Photo 62 and below.

Although frames must be braced fore-and-aft during erection, such supports are not needed once the armature is started. Keel, stem, sternpost and counter shapes are derived either from thick tube or lattice fabrications. To form bulwarks, tube frames are often extended above deck. All surmarks for sheer, waterline, bilge keels, etc., should be transferred from the patterns and nicked into the frames with a hacksaw or file. As these marks will be hidden by the armature and mortar, it pays to take a vertical measurement from the floor to each surmark.

Note that pipe frames must be completely sealed at each end eventually, to prevent internal corrosion. Even better, after plastering, fill each pipe with oil and seal it.

The Armature

Thin fore-and-aft, high tensile steel stringer bars are clipped, laced or welded to the frames and faired in by eye to complete the hull shape, plus rib bars at right angles for the bigger boats (Photo 63). Common mild steel reinforcement bars tend to kink at each frame, failing to produce sweet curves. Deck bars are best bent parallel to the gunwales.

Stringers Full-length bars are ideal, but joints can be tolerated if overlapped at least 12 in (300 mm) in line with the skin and tack-welded at three points. Most stringers are $\frac{1}{4}$ in (6 mm) diameter bars at 2 in (50 mm) spacings; sometimes $\frac{5}{16}$ in (8 mm) at 3 in (75 mm) spacing for larger boats. Rib bars are usually the same diameter but 6 in (150 mm) apart. On an inverted male plug, stringers and

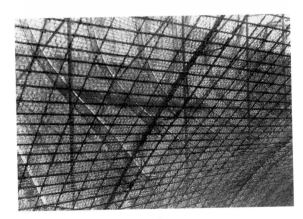

Photo 63 Stringer and rib bars

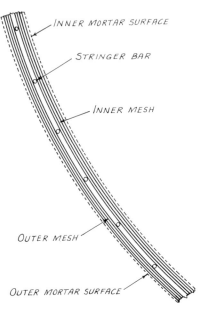

Fig 164 Mesh arrangement for a ferrocement hull

rib bars are stapled to the wood for speedy weld-free work.

Inner mesh To complete an armature or *basket*, layers of wire mesh must be laced tightly to each side of the bars and frames (Photo 62). With a male plug, the inner mesh is laid before the bars. The same thing applies when a keel stands flat on the ground or on a baseboard as in Photo 64. Strong ferro needs compacted mesh all through. The central void shown diagrammatically in Fig 164 must almost disappear when the mesh is pulled in tight. Having no rib bars helps this greatly. Mortar without mesh is just unwanted, weak weight.

Alongside frames, poke short U-shaped prongs of 18-gauge (1.2 mm) soft steel wire through the basket from outside, at about 2 in (50 mm) intervals. Twist tightly inside and hide the ends back in the basket. A common quick-pull tool (a *twistle*) will wire rebars, but needs an improvised clamp to grasp mesh prongs. Elsewhere, wire lacing in vertical rows is quicker. Make sure netting edges are well secured. One person inside and one out can weave a long wire into tight stitches very quickly into a in (75 mm) grid for all sizes of boat.

Lastly, settle all humps with a rubber-faced mallet. Draw a fairing batten systematically across every surface, ensuring that no wire breaks surface during plastering.

Wire Mesh

After 40 years of successful ferrocement boat building by amateurs and professionals, some details have altered. Web frames have largely superseded pipe frames, and the once popular $\frac{1}{2}$ in (12 mm) hexagonal mesh (22-gauge 0.7 mm) chicken wire has been largely replaced by $\frac{3}{4}$ in 18 mm) spot-welded square mesh of 19-gauge (1 mm) birdcage wire. However, only chicken wire will hump neatly over pipe frames inside a boat, or fold around web frames. With many layers of chicken wire used, an outermost layer of weldmesh helps to create a smooth finish Photo 59). Builders' expanded metal lathing is not suitable for ferro work.

Chicken wire is only available galvanized in most countries. Black wire is less likely to react with mortar than galvanized, but for prolonged working outside galvanized wire is preferable, to obviate excessive rusting. A *thin* layer of rust on steel bars and tubes improves the cement bond and gets rid of mill scale. Hosing down an armature when under cover assists the process. Galvanized mesh should be left to weather before plastering.

Six layers of mesh are normally required to make a total skin thickness of $\frac{3}{4}$ in (18 mm), three layers outside and three inside (Fig 164). For a 1 in (25 mm) skin you need eight layers divided equally, and for a $1\frac{1}{4}$ in (32 mm) skin twelve layers. The design may show additional thicknesses built up in way of keel and gunwales, requiring strips to be cut with shears. As with fibreglass, all edges and corners—particularly those at stem and transom—must be generously rounded to relieve stresses, aid mortar penetration and minimize future damage.

Mesh or netting is usually laid fore-and-aft quite loosely, but is sometimes vertical. Stagger all joints by introducing cut strips of varying widths, tied just sufficiently to keep all panels in place. Avoid overlapping joints which could cause surface bulges. Work is speeded if all netting is folded double longways on the floor before placing, but in unequal parts to stagger the edges. Weldmesh may need darts.

Deck armatures are fabricated in the above manner, but the plans may specify thicknesses and bar spacings quite different from those of the hull. Provided deck openings are adequately large for plastering access, and there are places to stand, it may pay to wire hull and deck baskets one straight after the other. Lay heavy plastic sheet over the inside of the hull once it's smoothed, so that dropped mortar does not stick and can be cleaned out easily.

Mortar Ingredients

As the use of correct mortar ingredients is critical, the amateur must take great pains to ensure that he buys the right materials in perfect condition and stores them carefully until needed.

The sand will cause most difficulty. It must be sharp, washed, silica graded sand, all passing a $\frac{3}{32}$ in (2.36 mm) mesh sieve. Quartzite, limestone or mica sand will not do, nor beach sand. The nearest suitable sandpit could be hundreds of miles away. It pays to send samples of the possible choices to a concrete laboratory for tests, having specified the purpose for which it will be used. All sand must be stored on clean boards or sheeting, convenient to the mixers and covered over to exclude dirt and rain.

Although more expensive than common Portland cement, sulphate resisting cement is best for ferro work, and essential for use in the tropics. All bags must be closed, fresh and soft, kept dry during transportation and stored off the ground with waterproof covers. High alumina cement is not recommended.

Ready-mixed dry ingredients are available in some countries (such as Renda-Flor Yachtmix in Britain) and the amateur not trained in concrete techniques would be sensible to pay more for the reliability and certainty of such materials. Because of settling, good mixing is still necessary. Huge quantities of mortar are needed—up to 6 tons for a 40-footer (12 m), 10 tons for a 50-footer (15 m) and 20 tons for a 70-footer (21 m).

Mixing

Using separate cement and sand, two buckets of cement are mixed with three or four of dry sand, depending on the sand grading and the mix specification. If the sand is moist its volume should be increased slightly. The extent of this may be found by taking two samples and drying one of them.

Clean, fresh water is essential, stored in open tanks near each mixer and filled from hoses. After trials by an expert plasterer, only the exact amount of water must be added to each batch—see below. Soft water is better than hard. If necessary, hire a big commercial de-ionizer for the duration of plastering, one with a good throughput.

In general, no additives such as pozzolans, rapid hardeners or waterproofers are necessary, but a set retarder may be beneficial in very hot weather. A plasticizer or air-entrainment agent could be handy to avoid having to add the extra water which might otherwise be necessary to make the mix sufficiently workable to force through a great thickness of mesh, or when a concrete pump is used. Avoid any chloride-containing additives.

Consistency Within limits, the less water added the stronger the mortar and the less liable to crack and shrink on setting. Reject any mix which is sloppy: it could drip out of the armature and is certain to delay finishing work. It should never be necessary to produce a slump of more than 2 in (50 mm) by the cone slump test. Slight variations in added water are inevitable, as the moisture content of sand normally varies through a stack. The ideal ambient temperature is about 60°F (15°C). Under such conditions, do not use any mortar after 45 min from the start of adding water to the sand/cement dry mix.

Mixers Horizontal paddle mixers produce the best mortar in the quickest time, but the popular half-bag tilting drum type is quite satisfactory. A reserve mixer is essential in case of breakdown. A good stock of fuel must be ready at hand. For hulls between 40 ft (12 m) and 55 ft (17 m) in length, two mixers will be needed almost full time. For bigger boats you will need three.

Mixers need to be close to the armature, but unless they are powered by electric motors exhaust pipes must be extended outside a shed, or lengthened upwards by about 10 ft (3 m) when in the open air. Some sort of roofing must be provided if there is any possibility of rain. There will be no time to clean mixer drums until work ends. Self-cleaning is generally assured by starting each

Photo 64 Keel on baseboard with meshing in progress

new mix with a good proportion of the total water, followed by any necessary additive.

Fit a large plywood *banker board* in front of each mixer, attached to an 18 in (450 mm) high vertical back board. Each plasterer will also need near him a banker board about 3 ft (1 m) square, raised on legs or an old table. Deliveries of mortar are then dumped on-to this surface.

Vibrating Poker vibrators are necessary to ensure well compacted mortar in the thick keel, stem, stern, gunwale and frame sections. Electric vibrators on long cables have obvious benefits over the flexible shaft varieties. Keep the tip moving or you may find mortar dripping right through the armature. Even vibration is necessary when using a male plug to ensure the mortar gets right through without voids.

Photo 65 The right height for a lower staging

Scaffolding

Strong staging should surround a boat at every 6 ft (1.8 m) of height, three scaffold boards wide throughout, with toe-boards, rigid guardrails and fixed ladders (Photo 65). A clear space of about 12 in (300 mm) should be allowed between scaffolding and armature. You should already have this for the meshing stage, but the plasterers may have some suggestions.

Inside, a similar suspended platform can be clamped to the centreline stanchions if the hull is deep. Scaffold bridges across the ship near hatchways enable mortar buckets to be handled without walking on the deck. Simple sheave hoists can be hung above the bridges. Hooks on the ropes save time tying knots. Buckets should never be brim full, to reduce spillage. Have plenty of spare scaffold boards or odd ply panels to lay inside the hull and on deck.

Pargeting

Feed all the mortar to the armature from inside. One plasterer outside can oversee the progress of two pargeters (pronounced 'parjet-ers') inside, making sure the mortar is forced evenly right through the mesh. The plasterer trowels surplus back in and screeds off flush with the wire.

Inside, the pargeting is best done largely with gloved hands, starting at the keel and working gradually upwards to the sheer. Stroking the inner surface lightly with a damp sponge in a circular motion produces an ideal final finish, with a thin layer of mortar covering the wire (all to be painted later). Where ballast is to be bonded into a hollow keel, scoring the surface with a stiff brush is best. The same treatment produces an anti-slip deck surface. Plasterers' coving tools and old spoons are useful in creating neat fillets where web frames, beams and deck meet the hull.

In stages For ideal results all plastering should be completed in one day, but on a big boat this proves almost impossible. In such cases, tackle the thick keel, stem and stern sections at least seven days beforehand. Coat the hardened edges with epoxy concrete adhesive just before plastering is resumed. This ensures a homogeneous bond.

Decks may have to be tackled at a third session, after similar jointing. A popular deck procedure consists of plastering a thin finished skim on the whole inside surface. Leave this for about two weeks to cure, then parget the remainder from outside. By using this method for the *hull*, less hired help is needed. However, one can never be sure about the hidden bond: the adhesive will not flow in as reliably as on a level deck. If sprayed, much of it bounces back. Also, the cement is not quite as compacted on the first side as it would be if being pressed in from both surfaces. With the male plug system, *shotcrete* (sprayed mortar) has been used, but hand pargeting generally penetrates better.

Exterior Skim

During pargeting the expert plasterers must not get too tired, for as the mortar starts to set—some six hours after mixing, according to ambient temperature—their work begins in earnest. Returning to the starting point, they use a long rubber *darby* (scraper) to strip back protruding mortar to the bare mesh, then, using a steel float they plaster a $\frac{1}{8}$ in (3 mm) skim of mortar on top. The surface is stroked alternately with a steel and a rubber float, going back over it as often as possible in the time available, until an even finish is produced. Waviness shows up clearly in a powerful light shone close along the surface. Any part of the skim coat thicker than about $\frac{1}{8}$ in (3 mm) is liable to *spall* some years later, so major humps in the armature cannot be hidden by extra mortar elsewhere.

If small trowel marks persist, grind these away with wet carborundum stones about two days later. No further finishing should be needed. Etching with dilute muriatic acid (hydrochloric acid or spirits of salts) prior to painting is a good idea: then flush off thoroughly.

Curing

Perfect plastering could be ruined by cracking if post-set *curing* is skimped. The goal is to prevent any drying out for at least ten days, followed by slow drying from the inside over a period of about four weeks. If drafts cannot be excluded, cocoon the hull completely with polythene sheeting as soon as the mortar has set enough. During curing, the cement develops full strength and hardness, which will not happen if it dries out fast.

Wait for a day, then put a shallow pool of water into the bilges and hose down inside and out at least four times a day from then on. Keep all parts continuously moist for ten days or more, ideally with a system of sprinklers or wet steam. Adequate drainage from the hull and the ground beneath is essential. A simple siphon pipe will take water out of the hull for free, but keep watching in case it sucks dry and fails.

Brushed-on liquid membrane coatings simplify curing, but one likes to have full control. Membranes are difficult to remove completely and form a barrier to paint adhesion, but they may be worth while if there is difficulty in keeping the hull damp, or perhaps on the underside of the deck.

No mortaring or curing should be contemplated if the air temperature could fall much below 40°F (5°C). Freezing must be prevented. A constant 60°F (15°C) is ideal.

Cracks Hair cracks which need magnifications to show up are not normally detrimental and disappear after painting. Localized deep cracks could be due to faulty mixing and may lead to tedious repairs. Deep cracks over much of the surface, usually due to faulty curing, could mean complete failure.

All Hands

The following table shows approximately the number of hands required for plastering various sizes of boat completely in one day.

Hull ft	Length m	Plasterers	Pargeters	Mixers	Helpers
26	8	2	4	1	2
35	11	4	8	2	2
45	14	5	10	2	3
50	15	7	14	4	4
55	17	9	18	4	5
60	18	11	22	4	7
65	20	13	26	6	8
70	21	15	30	6	9

In some countries, teams of plasterers specializing in ferrocement work can be hired for the big day and will travel to any site. The plasterers recommended by big firms of contractors will be perfectly competent, but you must employ at least one ferro expert to take charge of the team.

Hands for mixing may be reduced by using ready mix, while a big reduction in carriers is possible if a concrete pump is used to feed a continuous supply of mortar to the pargeters.

You will need one heavy-duty rubber bucket for each mixer and two for each helper. The pargeters will need industrial gloves (plus spare pairs) and other workers may also need gloves. Allow at least one shovel per mixer.

Apertures

Ferrocement and its armature can be bored with masonry bits in a hammer drill, but above 1 in (25 mm) diameter a diamond-coated hollow concrete coring bit should be used. When boring inside for woodscrew plugs (to hold joinery, cable clips and linings) always keep a depth gauge on the drill to avoid puncturing the hull.

Hole planning To reduce drilling, every conceivable aperture should be thought out before meshing and plastering. Chunks of thick cardboard tube are ideal to form limber holes and hull apertures, while oiled wooden dowels suit smaller holes. To locate these later, take measurements in two directions. Polythene-wrapped wooden disks make simple blanks for portholes (Fig 165).

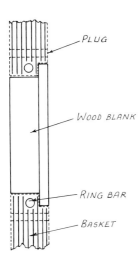

Fig 165 Wooden blank for porthole aperture

hawse holes, ventilators, drainage holes and skin fittings. Rabbets for countersunk fittings are easy to incorporate. Dowels will form the flange bolt holes. Tiny holes in each blank allow it to be held to the armature with copper wire ties.

Each large aperture requires additional reinforcement, usually a peripheral bar with radiating rods welded to it in star formation.

Through-hulls A sterntube should be removable. To hold it, cast into the hull a bronze liner with brazed end flanges, plus a few bonding stubs along the outside surface. Most designers specify bronze skin fittings, especially under water, though good plastic ones have been available since 1965. Electrolytic insulation from the armature is essential, so make size allowances to enable all apertures including bolt holes to be lined with epoxy putty at least $\frac{1}{32}$ in (0.8 mm) thick.

Screeds

Plastering an accurate exposed edge to a bulkhead, web frame, or toe rail is almost impossible unless an edging screed of wood or metal is attached to the armature. Screeds can be temporary or permanent; often the latter along the sheer. When half-round light alloy or hardwood cappings are to be added eventually, a temporary wooden screed may be nailed to dowels wired into the armature. These dowels later serve as inserts for woodscrews. For a

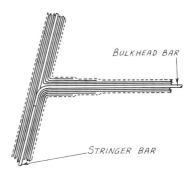

Fig 166 Ferrocement structural bulkhead attachment

bulwark rail the dowels can be bored out and expanding anchor nuts put in.

Temporary wooden screeds need doping with mould oil to ensure easy removal a few days after plastering. Permanent wooden screeds should be well wetted so they won't suck water out of the mix, and to prevent them expanding and stressing the mortar. Stub bars may be welded to metal permanent screeds to anchor them into the matrix. To avoid the expense of galvanizing, a good operator can blast-weld through the zinc on the six standard sizes of builders' cheap *water bar*.

Bulkheads

One is normally limited to the designer's specification regarding bulkhead construction. Important structural ones are built into the hull by lacing or welding thin horizontal bars to frames; or to some of the stringer bars (Fig 166). To give rigidity thin vertical bars are sometimes added, then two layers of the inner hull mesh are wired along one side of the bulkhead and back along the other side. Two layers of deck mesh are also turned downwards to form tapered fillets.

Such bulkheads interrupt plastering, so less structural ones are added later to short stubs of bar left protruding from the main hull armature. Where plywood bulkheads are intended, corner battens are easy to fix with epoxy resin, clamped with struts or woodscrews driven into standard plastic plugs (see also below).

Engine Bearers

Floors, knees and engine bearers are usually of similar construction to bulkheads, and can be added after the

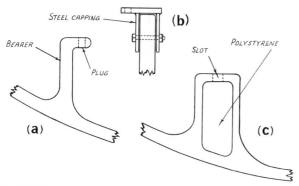

Fig 167 Two types of ferrocement engine bearer

main plastering. Floors especially need good integration with the hull.

Bearers may consist of vertical webs braced with intercostals and half-floors. Horizontal flanges on top, as in Fig 167a, are convenient to receive engine mounting bolts. Alternatively, ferro bearers may be of individual box formation (167b), filled with polystyrene foam to prevent leakage through the basket when pargeting from the outside. Rectangular nut plates lowered through slots in the top (after scraping away sufficient foam) are equipped with studs of requisite length to secure the engine and allow for shimming.

Use of Resins

Most ferro boats make good use of metal, plastics and wood. Special epoxy resins painted onto a roughened and cured ferro surface improve the bond greatly when a new ferro part is added. Creamy, filled epoxy resin will bond teak to a ferro deck. Epoxy and glass mat brackets and fillets are useful for attaching minor bulkheads and joinerwork, much as described in the chapters on fibreglass. Polyester resin is not generally a suitable adhesive. The common glass mat used with polyester is not compatible with most epoxy resins: consult the makers.

Through-bolts need coating and sealing with epoxy putty to prevent leaks and movement. For galvanized bolts this also reduces the likelihood of rust stains appearing in the future. Note, however, that resin-set bolts may have to be drilled out if removal is ever necessary, and cannot be taken out for inspection.

Epoxy putty is also ideal for filling defects in a ferro hull surface. Epoxy priming paint ensures the best adhesion inside and out. An eggshell or matt final finish is often preferred to a gloss, helping to hide surface defects and waviness.

Tanks

Built-in ferro fuel tanks are not good practice. If used, they should be carefully painted inside with two coats of tar epoxy to stop seepage and chemical attack. Water tanks are best unlined: unlike fibreglass, ferro does not affect the taste of water. Similarly, sewage holding tanks need no lining.

Tanks should have bolt-on removable lids, or large access panels with neoprene seals. To simplify construction, internal baffles can be integral with the lids. This makes them very heavy, so include nut inserts to take lifting eyes.

Developments

Most ferrocement boats are highly successful. As the material continues to strengthen for some ten years and then retains its strength indefinitely, ferro has few limitations for suitably designed one-off yachts.

Developments continue, particularly in connection with higher strength mixes, with a view to reducing skin thickness and weight. Polymer concrete utilizes resins in conjunction with (or in place of) Portland cement. It has immense strength, but at present its cost is high. Fibre reinforced concrete has great promise. It contains vast numbers of short, thin, random strands of stainless steel, carbon, Kevlar, glass or other materials. Getting the strands evenly distributed is a problem, but such materials are in general use for making thin prefabricated panels, particularly for cladding buildings.

However, the established rich mix of sand and Portland cement remains well proven, and a great deal is known about its mechanical and long-term behaviour. Trade associations do research and can offer advice. Some of the building industry 'wonder products' are not suited to amateurs, or to marine use, and have not been around very long.

Chapter 17
Metal Boats

Details of some different types of craft suitable for building in steel or aluminium are given in Chapter 1. Numerous stock cruising designs are available from such sources as Tucker Designs, Van de Stadt and Bruce Roberts. Plans for dinghies, launches and racing power and sailing craft are more difficult to get. To be complete, this chapter covers intricate processes which some designers have thoughtfully eliminated, to benefit not only amateurs but also the many companies without a history of boat building who have been attracted to metal yacht production.

Equipment The type of design makes a big difference to the range of tools required. The keen metal worker will probably possess the basic ones, but a full range (see below) can speed up work tremendously. For a big craft the heavy weights encountered demand such equipment as a chain hoist, crowbars, tubular rollers, a small ratchet winch and plate lifting dogs.

For some designs, bending skin sheets into place is simplified by welding standard plates into long lengths, perhaps up to 20 ft (6 m). It pays to weld temporary eyes to the backs of certain plates, as safety during lifting operations is paramount. A plate can make an effective guillotine if dropped! Eye and ear protectors are essential for some tasks; so are safety shoes with steel toe-caps. Welding requires protective goggles and/or face shields, leather aprons and gauntlets at least, and good ventilation.

Steel or alloy

Amateurs accustomed to metalwork should meet few difficulties when building a steel boat, provided they are prepared to become qualified in electric arc welding and gas cutting. Unsophisticated stick welding is quite suitable for mild steel work but very slow. You might be faced with half a mile of seam, which could take 500 manhours.

For light alloy welding you must use the superior and faster gas-shielded equipment. Suitable sets are not ruinously expensive nowadays. Small boats can be built entirely by riveting (Photo 66) and by using epoxy adhesives. However, underwater riveting is considered unsafe

Photo 66 Riveted light alloy construction

for boats normally moored afloat.

Common mild steel as used for oil barrels and fence stakes is the cheapest material suitable for metal boat building, and is ideal provided really effective anti-corrosion measures are adopted—preferably during as well as after building, and encompassing all fastenings and metal equipment. So-called *shipbuilding steel* is slightly tougher, with a carbon content up to 0.25%. Some yacht designs specify Type 40B in Britain and Type A283 in America. Corrosion-resistant steels are considerably more expensive than mild. The cheapest is Cor-ten, but this needs oxygen for stability, making it far from ideal on the bottom of a boat. Stainless steel is normally too costly, not easy for the amateur to weld and has other problems. Cupro-nickel (Monel) comes into a similar category.

Light alloy Although much dearer than steel, alloy scores markedly with regard to weight, for the same strength. This makes it particularly attractive for high-speed powerboats, light displacement sailboats and for the superstructure of almost any craft with much tophamper. Unlike steel, alloy does not complicate compass errors. Painting is mainly decorative. It should be everlasting, but if dissimilar metals come near it disastrous galvanic action can occur. Thorough painting and insulation of dissimilar metals helps to minimize such damage. Alloy is fine for integral fuel and water tanks, provided the design eliminates vibrational fatigue at the joints. It has poor fire resistance in comparison with steel.

Marine alloy is available in a big range of specifications and hardnesses. If adequate details of this are omitted from the plans, one of the big producers of such metals should be consulted. In Britain, N5 or N8 (5056 in America) is suitable for both plating and framing. Rivets are generally to N5, while tubes are to H30 (6061 in America). Letter S denotes sheet (plate); E stands for extruded sections; R for rivets. Thus you may encounter NS5, NE5, or NR5. Further letters after these denote the hardness grade: M, as manufactured; H, full hard; $\frac{1}{2}$H, half hard; and $\frac{1}{4}$H, quarter hard—generally best for amateur boat work.

Round-Bilge or Chine

Without the equipment for bending, rolling, heating, punching, shearing, edge planing, stamping and pressing possessed by a shipyard, perfect round-bilge construction takes a lot of time. However, it *can* be done with quite primitive tools, and is immensely interesting and satisfying work.

Various expediences are used to eliminate the need for shaping round-bilge plating. One method particularly suitable for alloy powerboats is to weld up the entire plating for each side flat on the floor, joining them together along the keel at the correct deadrise angles, then winching across the gunwales, pulling the sides up to the required shape and deck outline and fastening them there before fitting internal framing.

Mild steel is a wonderfully malleable and ductile material. Bending and straightening numerous times and hammering while hot or cold does not damage it. Magnets hold it readily for marking and welding. Gas cutting works well for most thicknesses, and parts can be *bumped-up* (thickened) by forging.

Alloy is soft enough to be cut with a suitable power saw, though a proper tooth lubricant is advisable. A plasma cutter is better. Boring and punching holes is easy. Apply heat carefully for bending and annealing in case the metal melts, which it can do with very little warning.

Plate bending for chine construction is simple in any metal. With the exception of certain for'ard areas of bluff-bowed designs, clamping to the frames or jig before welding or riveting will suffice. However, a conic section

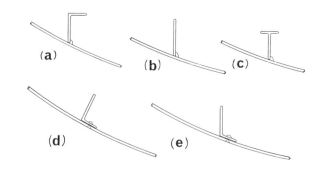

Fig 168 Metal angle and web frames

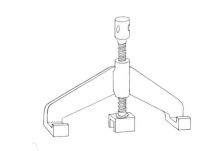

Fig 169 Hand bender for heavy metal sections

design is best to ensure attractive appearance and simplicity of plate bending (see Chapter 1). Double chine plating always bends more easily than single chine.

Frames

Standard angle arranged as in Fig 168a makes effective framing for both chine and round-bilge hulls when the skin plating is welded on. For a 60 ft (18 m) power cruiser the frames might be 2 in (50 mm) × 1$\frac{1}{2}$ in (40 mm) × $\frac{3}{16}$ in (4 mm) at about 18 in (460 mm) intervals. On a 30 ft (9 m) sailboat they might be 1$\frac{1}{2}$ in (40 mm) × 1 in (25 mm) × $\frac{1}{8}$ in (3 mm), all 14 in (350 mm) apart. Note that the open side of all angle frames should face towards amidships, to allow maximum space for welding and surface treatment. Consequently, the two frames nearest the point of maximum beam have their flanges aiming towards each other.

Webs Equal angle (Photo 67) is more readily available than the unequal type shown in Fig 168a, but as frames need most strength athwartships, wide flanges merely add unnecessary weight. For light displacement boats,

Photo 67 Steel angle frames

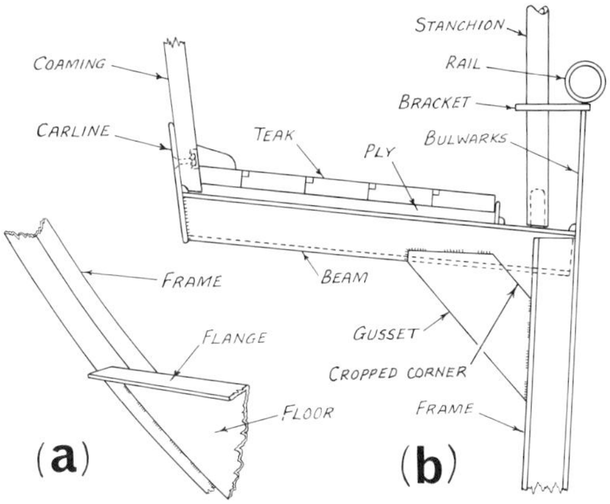

Fig 170 Metal floors, gussets and side-decks

Labels in figure: COAMING, CARLINE, STANCHION, RAIL, BRACKET, TEAK, PLY, BULWARKS, FRAME, BEAM, FLANGE, GUSSET, CROPPED CORNER, FLOOR, FRAME (a) (b)

web frames (168b) cut from flat strip or plate are sometimes specified (Photo 68).

Bending Unequal T-section (168c) looks neat for round-bilge hulls. Being symmetrical, cold-shaping without distortion is possible either on a rolling machine, with a simple hydraulic press, or with a jim crow: see Fig 169. If you order 1 × 2 in T-section, the flange will be 1 in and the web 2 in. Be careful not to order 2 × 1 in!

T-section has drawbacks: it will not lie flat on a pattern or scrieve board to enable its shapes to be checked readily, and it has no flat athwartships face to simplify the attachment of floors, gussets or bulkheads. Fixing some bulkheads, tank ends and tank baffles to their frames before setting up is often a good idea.

In alloy construction where all plating is riveted, angle or T-section cant frames must be set as in Fig 168d, with floor plates preferably butt-welded to the inboard frame edges.

Stringers Bevelled angle frames (168e) are troublesome to make, so riveted plating is often attached entirely to T-section or angle stringers which are welded or riveted to 168a type frames. Some welded designs use stringers of flat bar set edgewise to the plating with some transverse frames eliminated. This ensures beautifully fair hull plat-

ing. Intermittent welds (see below) allow any lurking moisture to drain off the stringers.

Speedy bending When shaping frames for big steel craft in well equipped yards, the metal is heated. The pattern is used to set pegs into a massive horizontal plate perforated with holes. Fine adjustments are made by dropping collars of various thicknesses over some of the pins. A red-hot frame is pushed against the pegs, then allowed to cool. To bend thin frames a perforated strip of springy steel is first wired to the pegs. This helps to avoid unfairness or dents.

Floor Plates

Nearly all steel craft have flat sheet floors (Fig 170a) welded or riveted to the heels of the frames. When T-section frames are used the flange is often burnt off in way of the floors. The top edge of a wide floor must be flanged to provide rigidity, as seen in 170a and Photo 68. A sheet metal folding machine will flange 3 mm steel at a stroke. Having cut out all his floor plates, an amateur can easily take these to an engineering shop to get the flanges folded.

Steel floors are generally about $\frac{1}{8}$ in (3 mm) thick for 30 ft (9 m) boats and about $\frac{3}{16}$ in (4 mm) for 50 ft (15 m). In light alloy they would be about 1 mm thicker. All floors except those at watertight bulkheads require limber holes

Photo 68 Flat bar frames

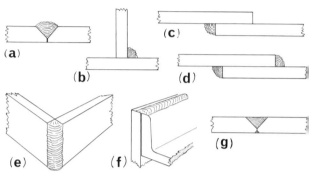

Fig 171 The most common types of welding runs

for drainage. The spaces between floors may finally be occupied by built-in tanks or ballast sealed in with concrete, so take special care to set the limber holes at the correct height.

Beams and Carlines

One of the attractions of using metal for boat building is the simplicity, rigidity and watertightness of the decking.

A beam of angle section is usually fitted to each frame head with a plate gusset (Fig 170b). The flanges of the beams normally aim in the reverse direction to those of the frames, giving all beams a solid appearance when viewed from amidships and enabling each beam and frame to meet back-to-back with the gusset sandwiched between. Appearance matters little when a boat is to have sprayed foam insulation covered by flush headlining and ceilings. Get deck beams factory rolled if they are all to the same camber. Side-deck beams are too short to roll, so cut them from longer lengths previously rolled. In some designs with parabolic deck camber the half-beams need no curvature.

Many owners like to have hardwood coachroof coamings (170b) bolted to flat-strip metal carlines. The cabin top decking is then all wood.

To fit standard teak cladding (see Chapter 13) over marine plywood, hire a nail gun to fire steel-piercing nails through both plywood and deck plating. Flush headlining will conceal the points eventually.

The difficulties of setting covering boards in way of bulwark stanchions are eliminated by terminating the deck planking in flexible bedding against a continuous vertical strip welded to the deck as in 170b. This drawing also shows typical details of gunwale and bulwarks.

Deck Plating

Curvature is applied to deck plating by just clamping it to the beams before welding. Having covered the foredeck as far aft as a single plate width will allow, fit the next centreline panel, butt-weld it to the previous plate and tack-weld to the beams, allowing the clamps to be removed. Then butt-weld a plate to one side of the centreline panel and clamp down the outer edge. Although athwartships butt joints weld nicely on top of a beam, it rarely pays to cut a sheet to achieve this. Some designs specify strip-on-edge carlines under all fore-and-aft butts: such backing plates assist good welding, especially with marine alloy.

Beam tops do not always meet perfectly with the deck plating. When proud, try to pull the beam down with a tackle or rigging screw and strop, attached to a temporary eyebolt or tang welded under the beam. When too low, a bead of weld along the top edge (or jacking between keel and beam) may suffice.

For riveted decking the beam flanges are placed uppermost. Butt-welding panels together is still advisable owing to the difficulty of housing riveted butt straps into the beams, and joggling them where the athwartships joints meet the fore-and-aft ones.

Welding

Riveting adds weight, is time-consuming, cannot be done singlehanded and rarely looks good. On the other hand, stick welding uses a vast number of costly coated rods. Gas-shielded systems need no flux or rods; they are very much quicker, but need a sheltered workplace.

Chamfers The majority of welds used in boat building are either butt welds (Fig 171a) or fillet welds (171b,c,d). Open corner welds (171e) and edge welds (171f) have similarities to both types. For maximum strength on thicknesses over 2 mm, butt edges should be chamfered as in 171a before welding. Fillet welds on steel need no preparation, especially with a bead both sides to counteract secret rusting.

A portable fast-disk grinder will quickly chamfer thin steel plate. A miniature one with a 4 in (100 mm) disk is adequate for most amateur work. For thick steel a gas torch sliding along a guide is quicker. Special electric arc rods are made for cutting chamfers.

Thin stuff If you ever need to weld sheet as thin as 1.5 mm, use gas, with the sheets held 1 mm apart. Pulse-arc equipment will tackle it, but ordinary 16-gauge sticks (even on low amperage) may burn holes through. Without pre-heating, distortion is difficult to avoid when welding any plate thinner than 3 mm.

Avoid welding thin plate to thick wherever possible. When thin plate is butt-welded to thick, a *notch* or stress point is created. Avoid this by tapering down the thick plate until its edge matches the thickness of the thin plate.

Seal welds Although it takes a great deal of time and can create weaknesses, butt welds on topsides are generally made invisible by grinding down flush as in Fig 171g. In the best work, thin seal weld runs (171g again) are set in small chamfers on the reverse side and done before starting outside. Double bead lap-welding (171d) must be used with steel to avoid the internal corrosion which is

inevitable when the 171c lap joint is used. Much the same applies to certain fillet and edge welds as seen in 171b and 171f.

Contamination Unprepared alloy needs chemical degreasing before welding. With some processes back-chipping is necessary before completing a second or third pass. The bristles of all wire brushes used on light alloy must be made of stainless steel.

Distortion

Plate distortion due to the heat of welding can be minimized by good technique, proper clamping, preheating, plus moderate amperage and thin rods when using stick equipment. Corrections are often possible by hammering. With its lower melting point, marine alloy is less prone to distortion than steel, but more liable to burn through without warning. Avoid continuous runs of weld. Dodge about with step-back or wandering sequences, gradually filling up between, thus preheating the metal while avoiding elaborate clamping.

Preparation To align plates with a consistent gap prior to welding, drill small holes at wide intervals through the butt line to receive temporary bolts with washers under head and nut. Alternatively, tack-weld plate offcuts across as required. To lessen distortion, tack-weld all plating seams (preferably on the inside) before you start any continuous welding. Start fore-and-aft seams from amidships, and any verticals from the middle. Weld to the frames last of all.

Skip-welds Continuous fillet welding where frames meet skin plating is not normally necessary. To avoid wavy topsides, use skip-welds varying from about 1 in (25 mm) long at 3 in (75 mm) spacings for frames $\frac{1}{8}$ in (3 mm) thick to about 3 in (75 mm) long at 9 in (230 mm) intervals for $\frac{3}{8}$ in (9 mm) frames. Pull plating up to frames with struts, or by using tack-welded lugs plus wedges. An alloy hull shrinks all over when welded!

Prefabrication

Amateurs find overhead welding with arc or gas far more difficult than either downhand or vertical welding. Practice makes perfect. Overhead work is essential along deck beams and for bottom plating butts which cannot be tackled from inside. In other places it may be eliminated by prefabricating large components and fitting them to the hull afterwards.

Quite large metal boats are erected inside several huge steel hoops mounted on rollers. This enables everything to be rotated effortlessly to any angle for efficient fabrication. For the amateur, building upside down as in Photo 68 is often best.

Guidance One can get valuable advice from the makers of welding rods, and gas equipment concerning rod sizes and materials, coatings and fluxes, amperage, gas nozzle sizes and gas pressure—also about general welding techniques. Welding courses are run by major suppliers and technical colleges.

Take care Always work under the eye of an expert until you become equally proficient. Remember to wear correct welder's clothing at the appropriate times, especially with regard to head, hands and eye protection. Store coated rods in a warm, dry place.

Riveting

You will not easily find stock designs for riveted boats, but most designers would produce suitable specifications and detail sketches on request, provided weight is not critical. Competent riveting does have the advantage of reducing distortion.

Plating laps usually have two rows of staggered rivets as in Photo 66. A single line will suffice along frames. To prevent creep, secure a seam by inserting a tiny bolt through every eighth rivet hole. Drive a rivet midway between each of these, then gradually fill in the gaps.

Countersunk rivet heads should be driven a little proud, then ground down flush. Snap or round heads as in Photo 66 are stronger and quicker. You need a snap dolly of correct size and shape to prevent snap heads from looking battered after riveting. If appearance is important both sides (particularly with light alloy) use a second snap dolly instead of a ball-pein hammer on the rivet tails.

Having ascertained the exact rivet length from trials, make up a bench-mounted shear with a depth gauge jig, unless they should happen to come exactly the right length.

Steel rivets over $\frac{3}{8}$ in (9 mm) in diameter are best closed when red hot. This not only speeds the operation, but the contraction on cooling ensures extra tight joints. Small annealed steel rivets close easily by hand hammering. Light alloy rivets are never heated, but they work-harden so close them with a minimum number of blows.

Pop rivets are driven blind with a special plier or scissor tool. Although not very pretty, there is no quicker clamp-up fastening. Ideal for boxed-in sections (for attaching brackets, and on alloy booms and masts), they are not reliably waterproof. Pop rivets up to $\frac{3}{16}$ in (4 mm) diameter are available in light alloy, Monel and stainless steel. Make sure you use electrolytically compatible ones, even on a superstructure.

Hull Plating

Although welded hull plating is normally finished flush, some designs adopt double bead fore-and-aft lap joints on the bottom for additional strength. If rivets must be used, joints are lapped or butt-strapped—or joggled as in Fig 172. Plans must specify the layout of any rivets. Bore as many of the holes as you can under the bench drill. A sheet metal template giving the hole positions saves an awful lot of marking-out time. Remove all burr before offering up a plate.

Riveted lap joints in steel can rust. However, with no welding heat, thorough priming and painting of all concealed surfaces is possible, plus adequate bedding compound. Remember that, as well as the boat's bottom, watertight bulkheads need sealing. With plate under 7 mm thick, one cannot use a pneumatic hammer to caulk the seam edges as in big-ship rivet practice.

Glued Where proper cleaning, clamping and temperature can be applied, epoxy-glued light alloy joints without rivets are feasible.

Plate Shaping

Up to $\frac{3}{16}$ in (4 mm) steel or 6 mm light alloy, a power nibbler is ideal for straight or curved cutting. Circular saws, bandsaws, sabre saws and routers are normally only used on alloy. Fast cutting disks are rapid, but somewhat dangerous, noisy and costly to replace. For steel above 4 mm, gas cutting (Photo 69) is best. The thicker the plate the less it distorts. Tungsten and plasma arc cutting equipment is not often owned by the amateur. Cut edges will usually need grinding smooth.

Without shipyard machinery, edge joggling may be done by peening (hand hammering) over a jig, as in

Photo 69 Using the gas cutting torch: note that the dark welder's safety goggles are missing!

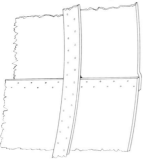

Fig 172 Butt doubler across joggled seam

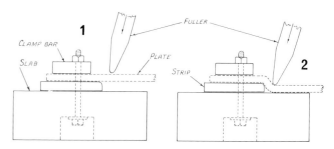

Fig 173 Simple joggling former

Fig 173. The strip is bent or cut to any slight seam curve. Using a few of the intended rivet holes, both plate and strip are through-bolted to a steel slab or screwed to a hardwood balk. The desired shape is beaten in with a fuller (Fig 174) and hammer, in two or three passes. A fuller made from an old cold chisel and struck with a club hammer suffices for steel up to $\frac{1}{8}$ in (3 mm) thick. Heating saves time, but may cause distortion.

Big plates make less wastage, but most amateurs prefer easy-to-handle sizes about 6×3 ft or 2×1 m. Random size plates as in Photo 70 are suitable for round-bilge hulls. Only on chine hulls are the longest standard sheets likely to be advantageous. Some designers will pro-

Photo 70 Random layout of hull plating

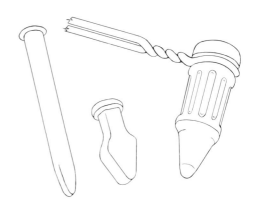

Fig 174 Common shapes of fullers

duce a shell expansion layout. This drawing shows the flattened shape of every hull plate, each dimensioned to make best use of the available sheets.

Plate Curvature

Not all round-bilge plates have difficult compound curvature. Most can be smoothly rolled with a simple hand-operated three-roll bending machine, then clamped in place across three or four frames as described below under **Try Heat**.

Tuck Plates Most keel, stem, bilge and stern tuck plates have double curvature. This fact makes many amateurs steer towards simple multi-chine designs. However, to the enthusiastic metal basher, double curvature is an attractive challenge. Read on.

Topsides Keel and stem plates are generally made first (Fig 13) for upright construction, enabling the frames to be erected. Next, plate the sheer and those flatter parts (working from amidships) which need only slight rolling and clamping before tacking to the frames. Always fit identical plating in alternating fashion to port and starboard.

One cannot hold up heavy full sheets for scribing, so templates of hardboard bent to the hull's curvature are handy. Cut the metal slightly oversize before offering up for scribing, using a felt pen on alloy, or a stick of the special hard chalk made for marking steel. Strive for accurate fits to avoid wasting time filling in great gaps with beads of weld and slivers of plate.

If a plate will not clamp home without buckling, you may need to cut a few slits with the nibbler or gas torch, running as far as 2 ft (600 mm) in from the edge towards the middle of the plate. Once faired in, such slits are easily reinstated with arc welding (Photo 71).

Try heat Apply some local heat if the desired curvature will not form by clamping alone. Tack-weld studs end-on to the inner plate surface (with nuts over bridging pieces across the frames) to facilitate clamping. Often a simple Spanish windlass or a tackle will supply the right amount of pull.

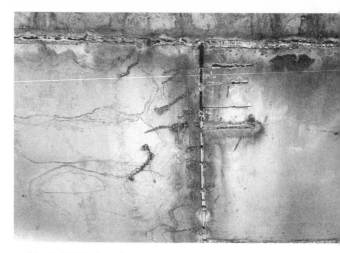

Photo 71 Truing the curvature with nicks

Raising

Having plated the simpler parts, infilling areas of pronounced double curvature can start. The process of *raising*, sometimes called *dishing*, can be done by hand peening—a noisy but fascinating job. Even the smaller boatyards use a wheeling machine for plate dishing. A plate is pulled to and fro by hand under a single castor-type roller with adjustable downward pressure. A handy amateur metalworker can make such a machine (from scrap, some steel joist, plus some turning and welding) after inspecting one at a factory or boatyard.

Make three or more curvature templates from hardboard for each plate, one at each frame and one giving the fore-and-aft shape. Chalk across the plate (or just at the edges) to locate the templates.

You can raise alloy under 4 mm thick by panel-beating with a hardwood mallet while the sheet is held on top of a domed hardwood or alloy *stake*. On steel, use a heavy ball-pein hammer while the plate is lying on a hardwood balk. Start peening at the edges and progress inwards. Rapid taps at close intervals (not quite hard enough to make dents) in straight rows will soon reach the middle. If too much curvature is building up, soften the blows. Repetition over some areas is sure to be necessary to get the shape right. Aim for slight under-bending, as a fair amount of pull is permissible on the boat. If you overdo it, either use that plate somewhere else or hold it over an upright stump of telephone pole and beat the convex side with the flat face of the hammer.

For plates thicker than 5 mm, use a fuller or power hammer. So that no parts are missed, snap chalk lines across the surface in chequer board fashion.

Setting Up

Erecting the backbone and frames for a big metal yacht hull is similar to the procedures for wood and ferrocement. However, the use of tack-welds greatly simplifies attaching struts and ribbands.

An I-girder on edge makes a fine straight base for upright construction. Clamp this down to the floor or to athwartships balks. Fix the keel plates above this by welding in short vertical poppets of tube or angle. Cut these off and grind the scars flush when the boat is finally jacked up for moving. With posts concreted into the ground, no girder is necessary.

With a rockered keel and raked stem, if you find difficulty in transferring frame positions from the floor to the inside of the keel trough, mark up an overhead centreline batten and plumb down from this.

Stemplate, sternpost and keel plates (Fig 13) do not lie comfortably flat on the ground as for a wooden backbone (Photo 7), so alignment of these parts is achieved with better accuracy on the poppets. Having positioned frames and bulkheads with clamps, magnets and light strutting, use minimal tack-welding at the keel until all have been plumbed, squared, and faired in. Several frames are sure to need a slight shift, so it must be possible to break these welds without too much effort. Once fair, permanent welding may follow.

Bracing Light steel angle is ideal for strutting frames from above, while $\frac{5}{16}$ in (8 mm) reinforcing bars tacked to frames make good bracing ribbands. For light alloy such ribbands may be wood, attached by means of tightly twisted wire ties. The pressure on frames during metal building is generally less than in wooden boat building. However, tubular chines and gunwales are best rolled to shape before installation. If bent *in situ*, heat the concave side of the curve with the oxy torch so that stress is minimized.

Detail Work

Metal construction attracts much ingenuity in the completion of details. No sharp edges must be left above decks or through the accommodation. When the method of finishing edges is not detailed on the drawings, tube or bar is generally welded on diametrically to add strength and ensure safety.

If you lack facilities for making tight bends in thick steel tube (for lining scuppers, fairleads and hawse holes), get some big, ungalvanized plumbing bends. They cover 90°, so you need two for a scupper and four for a hawse hole. Get the MM type with a male thread each end. Either cut off the threads or flush them over with filler before applying any paint.

Use plating offcuts for fabricating brackets, doublers (backup plates), under deck fittings, tabernacle, a hollow rudder with internal webs, superstructure parts, bitts, bollards etc. Much information on fabricating metal fittings and making patterns for castings is given in *Boat Repairs and Conversions*.

In alloy or steel hulls, if you must use standard bronze through-hull fittings, seacocks, cleats or winches, instead of plastic or stainless steel ones, fit nylon or Tufnol mounting pads laid in mastic for insulation. Bolts of marine grade stainless steel suit alloy and steel hulls if set through nylon bushes, washers and mastic.

It may prove troublesome, but always cut the apertures for windows or portlights through metal coamings after the latter have been bent to shape. This avoids kinks, which also commonly occur when you try to bend any metal strip which has been previously bored with even tiny holes. Similarly, the internal spigots to bring window openings flush with a lining or panelling should be welded on before cutting out the aperture.

Fitting steel or alloy webs, gussets and tank baffles is often simplified if the boxed-in internal corners are cut off at 45° some 2 in (50 mm) in from the tip, as seen in Fig 170. Such ugly gaps are usually hidden by linings and they often come in handy for housing electrical wiring.

Adding wood Although the magnetic nature of steel is a curse when it comes to compass accuracy, the same property enables one to collect every last scrap of swarf from the bilges with a magnet. This occurs because interior panelling and other fitments need holes for self-tapping screws into small brackets welded to the frames. All necessary brackets must be welded on before final painting. Alloy swarf is best removed with a powerful vacuum cleaner followed by a wad of adhesive tape held in one's fingers.

Protective Coatings

Basically, light alloy hulls need painting only for decorative and antifouling purposes. But remember that underwater paint, if kept in good condition, is a wonderful insulator against galvanic corrosion.

Traditionally, mild steel was allowed to rust before painting in order to shed the mill scale. Nowadays, steel is usually ordered ready primed. This special welding or holding primer is applied at the mill after pickling or grit-blasting. It does not interrupt welding. More primer should be put on after cutting, welding or grinding.

The current trend is not to bother with galvanizing or zinc spraying on any part of a hull. Good epoxy paint coatings are cheaper, penetrate better into crevices and between skip-welds, while reducing greatly the risk of galvanic action. Do not imagine that all epoxy paint is the same: you must get the correct type for steel. Any good maker will supply the technical data you need. Solvent-less epoxy does not fume or shrink on drying. Some will bond perfectly over a moist surface. Epoxy tar is cheaper than the enamels and comes in black and brown: by alternating these you avoid leaving holidays.

Preparation Check whether your epoxy is compatible with the holding primer used. If not, all will need grit-blasting. An alternative is to hire (with operator) one of those vicious water jets that will cut concrete—but try getting rid of every drop of water left in crevices and bilges! With grit (sand or shot) blasting, a paint covering must be applied within 30 mins for perfect results.

Some metal chine hulls need very little surface filler, but with round-bilge even professionals need filler on about 50% of the topside area. The procedure is similar to that described in Chapter 14 for foam-sandwich hulls. Epoxy filler is ideal with an epoxy paint scheme, but any marine filler will do if compatible with the type of paint you decide to use: consult the makers.

Special self-etching primers are used on slippery light alloy and zinc. They require careful degreasing first, while *gentle* grit-blasting or abrasion is even better. No metal should be painted in air cooler than 60°F (16°C) or if the relative humidity is higher than 60%. Avoid the use of metallic antifouling paints on alloy or zinc sprayed hulls, and be careful not to moor such a boat near to any craft coated with it.

Detailed painting specifications, application techniques and costings are given in *The Compleat Book of Yacht Care*. Marine paint manufacturers will supply a great deal of useful technical information, gratis.

Hollows Some care is advisable to ensure that hidden corrosion cannot occur inside large steel hollow units such as a rudder, skeg or box keel. Filling with engine oil is common practice. A single screwed plug at the top is all you need, but a pressure test before painting is worth while. After filling with oil, connect an air line and hold at 30 psi (2 bar) for 4 hours.

A different idea is called for in the case of sealed tubes as used for chines, gunwales, davits, rudder stock, stanchions and spars. To dry out any moist air trapped inside, insert an appropriate amount of silica gel in a porous sachet and leave it sealed up in there! For a pressure test, only a small screwed plug need be left. Insert a pressure gauge with cock and air pump connection. At 30 psi, shut off the air line. The gauge should remain static for 12 hours.

The old bugbear of internal condensation in metal boats need not occur on any surfaces sprayed with polyurethane foam. Adhesion is excellent and fire resistance is fair; a thickness of 2 in (50 mm) may be built up with little trouble. The big drawback is that in a fire PU gives off choking, lethal fumes containing cyanide. Mineral fibre is better in a fire but not an ideal insulator. Both these materials look ugly, so headliners and vertical panelling are essential on yachts. No insulation (except cork granule paint) is normally used under the cabin sole.

Ballast Cast iron ballast suits steel boats, though the two must never touch. Inside pigs should be cocooned individually with fibreglass and laid on pine dunnage. Concrete encapsulated ballast has been known to react with alloy, but is compatible with steel. Lead shot embedded in polyester grout may be specified for a light alloy keel trough. An epoxy fibreglass mat laid up on top of a lead or iron ballast keel makes a good inert gasket—allowed to cure before bolting on through a bed of mastic.

Corrosion Bronze, Monel or stainless steel sterngear causes few problems with steel or marine alloy hulls provided you have adequate wired anodes. Propellers of plastics and various alloys are made in certain sizes. For a fuller discussion of preventing and treating the several types of corrosion, read *Metal Corrosion in Boats* by Nigel Warren (Adlard Coles).

Appendix I Properties and Uses of Popular Boatbuilding Woods

Species	Appearance	Density lb per cu ft	Kg per cu m	Screw holding	Hand planing	Life if wet	Life if dry	Bending	Toughness	Warping	Cracking	Common uses
Afrormosia	Nut brown	50	800	Excellent	Tricky	Very long	Very long	Fair	Good	Rare	Rare	Rubbing strakes, seats, coamings
Afzelia (Doussie)	Nut brown	55	880	Excellent	Fair	Long	Long	Fair	Good	Rare	Rare	Decks, coamings, keel, rub rails
Agba	Yellow to pink	35	560	Good	Tricky	Long	Long	Good	Fair	Occasional	Occasional	Planking, coamings, laminations
Ash	Straw to white	44	704	Fair	Fair	Short	Long	Excellent	Good	Rare	Rare	Dinghy ribs, risers, gunwales, oars, joinery
Cedar, Western Red	Reddish brown	24	384	Fair	Easy	Long	Long	Fair	Poor	Rare	Occasional	Planking, canvased decks
Cedar, Yellow	Pale yellow	32	512	Fair	Fair	Moderate	Long	Good	Fair	Occasional	Occasional	Planking, stringers, oars, decks
Cypress, Southern	Straw to pink	35	560	Good	Easy	Moderate	Long	Fair	Fair	Frequent	Frequent	All longitudinals, frames
Danta	Reddish brown	45	720	Good	Fair	Moderate	Long	Good	Fair	Occasional	Frequent	Bent timbers, stem, keel
Elm, American (Canadian Rock)	Pale brown	50	800	Good	Hard	Moderate	Moderate	Excellent	Good	Rare	Rare	Bent timbers, rubbing strakes, laminations
Elm, Wych	Medium brown	43	690	Good	Easy	Long	Moderate	Fair	Good	Occasional	Rare	Keel, planking, joinery
Fir, Douglas (Oregon)	Reddish yellow	35	560	Fair	Easy	Moderate	Moderate	Good	Fair	Occasional	Occasional	Spars, joinery, bulkheads
Gum, Spotted	Brown	66	1056	Excellent	Hard	Long	Very long	Good	Very good	Rare	Rare	Bent timbers, engine bearers, backbone
Greenheart	Brown/green	70	1120	Excellent	Hard	Very long	Very long	Fair	Very good	Rare	Frequent	Keel, deadwood, rub rails
Iroko	Yellow to brown	45	720	Good	Fair	Very long	Very long	Fair	Very good	Rare	Rare	Alternative for teak, laminations
Ironbark	Nut brown	70	1120	Excellent	Tricky	Very long	Very long	Fair	Very good	Rare	Rare	Heavy planking, rudder, engine bearers
Jarrah	Dark red	60	960	Good	Hard	Long	Very long	Poor	Very good	Very rare	Occasional	Keel, deadwood, rub rails
Keruing/Yang	Dark red/brown	48	770	Good	Fair	Long	Long	Fair	Good	Occasional	Occasional	Keel, deadwood, rudder, stem
Larch/Hackmatack	Orange/brown	35	560	Fair	Sticky	Moderate	Long	Fair	Fair	Occasional	Occasional	Planking, all longitudinals
Mahogany, Honduras	Pink to brown	40	640	Fair	Tricky	Long	Long	Fair	Fair	Rare	Rare	Coamings, joinery, seats
Mahogany, Khaya (African)	Reddish brown	35	560	Good	Fair	Moderate	Long	Good	Fair	Rare	Very rare	Planking, rudder, frames, laminations
Mahogany, Philippine Luan/Meranti	Dull pink	35	560	Fair	Good	Moderate	Long	Good	Fair	Rare	Rare	Planking, coamings, joinery
Makore	Pink to dk red	40	640	Excellent	Fair	Long	Long	Fair	Very good	Rare	Rare	Joinery, coamings, laminations
Oak, American White	Straw to brown	45	720	Excellent	Fair	Long	Long	Good	Very good	Occasional	Occasional	Stem, frames, stringers, joinery
Oak, English	Straw to brown	53	850	Excellent	Tricky	Long	Long	Good	Very good	Frequent	Frequent	Framing, grown timbers, knees, dinghy ribs
Opepe	Yellow/brown	50	800	Good	Tricky	Very long	Very long	Poor	Good	Rare	Occasional	Joinery, bulkheads, keel
Pine, Parana	Straw to red	34	540	Poor	Easy	Short	Moderate	Good	Poor	Rare	Occasional	Laid deck, planking, shelves
Pine, Pitch	Red/yellow	50	800	Fair	Sticky	Long	Very long	Fair	Good	Occasional	Rare	Deck, planking, bearers
Pine, Yellow	Straw to yellow	28	448	Fair	Easy	Moderate	Long	Fair	Fair	Occasional	Occasional	All longitudinals, built spars
Sapele	Pink to brown	40	640	Good	Tricky	Moderate	Long	Good	Good	Occasional	Rare	Planking, joinery, frames
Seraya, White	Pale straw	35	560	Good	Fair	Moderate	Long	Poor	Very good	Occasional	Occasional	Keel, deadwood, engine bearers
Spruce, Sitka (Silver)	White to pink	28	450	Poor	Easy	Short	Moderate	Excellent	Poor	Rare	Occasional	Spars, oars, dinghy planking
Teak, Burma	Yellow to brown	45	720	Good	Fair	Very long	Very long	Fair	Very good	Rare	Very rare	Laid decks, coamings, planking, seats, joinery, hatches
Utile	Pink	40	640	Fair	Fair	Long	Long	Poor	Good	Occasional	Rare	Joinery, laminations, frames

Appendix 2

Table 1 Countersunk Head Copper Boat Nails and Roves
Full Range

Length in	Length mm	Thickness (Standard Wire Guage)													
5/8	16	17	16												
3/4	19	17	16	15	14										
7/8	22	17	16	15	14	13									
1	25	17	16	15	14	13	12								
1 1/4	32	17	16	15	14	13	12								
1 1/2	38		16	15	14	13	12	11	10						
1 3/4	44				14	13	12	11	10						
2	50			15	14	13	12	11	10	9					
2 1/4	57				14	13	12	11	10	9					
2 1/2	63			15	14	13	12	11	10	9	8				
3	76						12	11	10	9	8				
3 1/2	88								10	9	8	7	6		
4	100									9	8	7	6		
5	126										8	7	6	5	
6	152												6	5	4
Width across flats in		.056	.064	.072	.080	.092	.104	.116	.128	.144	.160	.176	.192	.212	.232
Width across flats mm		1.4	1.6	1.8	2.1	2.3	2.6	2.9	3.3	3.7	4.1	4.5	4.9	5.4	5.9
Rove sizes in		3/16	1/4	5/16	3/8	7/16	1/2			9/16				5/8	3/4
Rove sizes mm		5	6	8	9	11	13			14				16	19

Table 2 Number of Rose Head Copper Boat Nails per Pound
Weight

Length in	Length mm	Thickness (SWG)						
		16	14	12	10	8	6	4
3/4	18	800	609					
1	25	700	465	272				
1 1/4	32		379	222	140			
1 1/2	38		313	185	119			
1 3/4	44		272	158	103			
2	50		240	140	96			
2 1/2	63				73	49		
3	76				61	40		
3 1/2	88				53	34		
4	100				46	30	21	
5	126						17	12
6	152						14	10

For number per kilogram multiply by 2.2.

Table 3 Quantity of Copper Roves per Unit Weight

Rove Diam.	in	$\frac{3}{16}$	$\frac{1}{4}$	$\frac{5}{16}$	$\frac{3}{8}$	$\frac{7}{16}$	$\frac{1}{2}$	$\frac{9}{16}$	$\frac{5}{8}$	$\frac{3}{4}$
	mm	5	6	8	9	11	13	14	16	19
Number per lb		2940	1624	1028	775	511	328	236	209	138
Number per kg		6470	3575	2260	1710	1125	722	520	460	304

Table 4 Gripfast Silicon Bronze Ring Nails

Full Range

Length		Thickness (SWG)					
in	mm						
$\frac{1}{2}$	13	16					
$\frac{5}{8}$	16	16					
$\frac{3}{4}$	19	16	14	12			
$\frac{7}{8}$	22	16	14	12			
1	25	16	14	12	10		
$1\frac{1}{4}$	32		14	12	10	8	
$1\frac{1}{2}$	38			12	10	8	
$1\frac{3}{4}$	44			12	10	8	
2	50			12	10	8	6
$2\frac{1}{4}$	57			12	10	8	6
$2\frac{1}{2}$	63			12	10	8	6
3	76					8	6
$3\frac{1}{2}$	88						6
4	100						6
5	126						6
6	152						6
Diam.	in	.064	.080	.104	.128	.160	.192
	mm	1.6	2.1	2.6	3.3	4.1	4.9

Ring nails are normally sold in boxes of 100 or 200, not by weight

Table 1 Boring for Woodscrews

Screw Gauge	Shank diam. in	mm	Hole 1 diam. in	mm	Hole 2 diam. in	mm	Hole 3 diam. in	mm	Space 4 % screw length	Hole 2 diam. in	mm	Hole 3 diam. in	mm	Space 4 % screw length
			All woods		For hardwoods					For softwoods				
4	.108	2.8	7/32	5.6	7/64	2.7	use bradawl		5%	use bradawl		use bradawl		10%
5	.122	3.1	1/4	6.3	1/8	3.2	use bradawl		5%	use bradawl		use bradawl		10%
6	.136	3.5	9/32	7.2	9/64	3.6	use bradawl		5%	1/8	3.2	use bradawl		10%
7	.150	3.8	5/16	8.0	5/32	4.0	3/32	2.4	5%	5/32	4.0	use bradawl		10%
8	.164	4.2	11/32	8.8	11/64	4.4	3/32	2.4	5%	5/32	4.0	use bradawl		10%
10	.192	4.9	3/8	9.5	13/64	5.2	1/8	3.2	5%	3/16	4.8	use bradawl		10%
12	.220	5.6	7/16	11.0	7/32	5.6	1/8	3.2	2%	7/32	5.6	1/8	3.2	5%
14	.248	6.3	1/2	12.5	1/4	6.3	5/32	4.0	2%	1/4	6.3	5/32	4.0	5%
16	.276	7.0	9/16	14.0	9/32	7.2	3/16	4.8	2%	9/32	7.2	3/16	4.8	5%
18	.304	7.7	5/8	15.5	5/16	8.0	3/16	4.8	2%	5/16	8.0	3/16	4.8	5%
20	.332	8.4	21/32	17.0	11/32	8.8	7/32	5.6	2%	11/32	8.8	7/32	5.6	5%

Notes
To find screw gauge, measure head diameter in sixteenths of an inch, subtract 1 and multiply by 2.
To find head diameter in sixteenths of an inch from screw gauge, divide gauge by 2 and add 1.

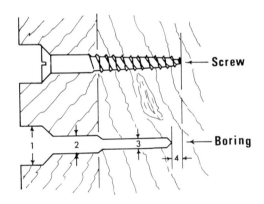

Screw — Boring
1 2 3 4

Table 2 Silicon Bronze Countersunk Head Woodscrews

Stock Sizes, GKN Make

Screw length in	mm	Screw gauge			
1	25	8			
1¼	32	8	10		
1½	38	8	10	12	
1¾	44				14
2	50		10	12	14
2½	63				14
3	76				14

Table 3 Stainless Steel Countersunk Head Woodscrews

Stock Sizes, GKN Make

Screw length in	mm	Screw gauge					
½	13	4	6				
⅝	16	4	6				
¾	19	4	6	7	8		
1	25		6		8	10	
1¼	32				8	10	12
1½	38				8	10	12
1¾	44					10	
2	50				8	10	12
2½	63					10	12
3	76						12

Appendix 4

Table 1 Fibreglass Laminates Including Woven Materials With $1\frac{1}{2}$: 1 Resin/Glass Ratio

American units			Metric units		
Material (no surfacing tissue or gel coats)	Finished thickness Nearest $\frac{1}{64}$ in	Resin weight lb per yd²	Material (no surfacing tissue or gel coats)	Finished thickness mm	Resin weight kg per m²
1 layer 9 oz/yd² cloth	$\frac{1}{32}$	0.84	1 layer 300 g/m² cloth	0.5	0.46
2 layers 9 oz/yd² cloth	$\frac{3}{64}$	1.68	2 layers 300 g/m² cloth	1.0	0.91
3 layers 9 oz/yd² cloth	$\frac{1}{16}$	2.53	3 layers 300 g/m² cloth	1.5	1.37
4 layers 9 oz/yd² cloth	$\frac{5}{64}$	3.37	4 layers 300 g/m² cloth	2.0	1.82
1 layer 24 oz/yd² woven rovings	$\frac{3}{64}$	2.25	1 layer 820 g/m² woven rovings	1.3	1.22
2 layers 24 oz/yd² woven rovings	$\frac{7}{64}$	4.50	2 layers 820 g/m² woven rovings	2.6	2.43
3 layers 24 oz/yd² woven rovings	$\frac{5}{32}$	6.75	3 layers 820 g/m² woven rovings	3.9	3.65
4 layers 24 oz/yd² woven rovings	$\frac{13}{64}$	9.00	4 layers 820 g/m² woven rovings	5.2	4.86
2 × 9 oz cloth + 1 × 24 oz WR	$\frac{3}{32}$	3.94	2 × 300 g cloth + 1 × 820 g WR	2.3	2.13
2 × 9 oz cloth + 2 × 24 oz WR	$\frac{9}{64}$	6.19	2 × 300 g cloth + 2 × 820 g WR	3.6	3.34
2 × 1½ oz/ft² chopped strand mat + 1 × 18 oz/yd² WR	$\frac{7}{64}$	5.48	2 × 450 g/m² chopped strand mat + 1 × 600 g/m² WR	2.8	2.96
2 × 1½ oz CSM + 2 × 18 oz WR	$\frac{5}{32}$	7.17	2 × 450 g CSM + 2 × 600 g WR	3.8	3.87
3 × 1½ oz CSM + 2 × 18 oz WR	$\frac{11}{64}$	9.00	3 × 450 g CSM + 2 × 600 g WR	4.2	4.88

Table 2 Fibreglass Laminates with Chopped Strand Mat and $2\frac{1}{2}$: 1 Resin/Glass Ratio

American units			Metric units		
Material (including surfacing tissue both sides)	Finished thickness Nearest $\frac{1}{64}$ in	Resin weight with 2 gel coats lb per ft²	Material (including surface tissue both sides)	Finished thickness mm	Resin weight with 2 gel coats kg per m²
1 layer 1 oz/ft² CSM	$\frac{3}{64}$	0.41	1 layer 300 g/m² CSM	1.3	2.00
1 layer 1½ oz/ft² CSM	$\frac{1}{16}$	0.48	1 layer 450 g/m² CSM	1.7	2.34
1 layer 2 oz/ft² CSM	$\frac{5}{64}$	0.58	1 layer 600 g/m² CSM	2.1	2.83
2 layers 1½ oz/ft² CSM	$\frac{1}{8}$	0.76	2 layers 450 g/m² CSM	3.0	3.70
2 layers 2 oz/ft² CSM	$\frac{5}{32}$	0.93	2 layers 600 g/m² CSM	3.8	4.54
4 layers 1½ oz/ft² CSM	$\frac{3}{16}$	1.28	4 layers 450 g/m² CSM	5.2	6.25
4 layers 2 oz/ft² CSM	$\frac{1}{4}$	1.63	4 layers 600 g/m² CSM	7.0	7.95
5 layers 2 oz/ft² CSM	$\frac{5}{16}$	1.98	5 layers 600 g/m² CSM	8.5	9.66
6 layers 2 oz/ft² CSM	$\frac{3}{8}$	2.33	6 layers 600 g/m² CSM	10.0	11.37
8 layers 2 oz/ft² CSM	$\frac{1}{2}$	3.03	8 layers 600 g/m² CSM	13.0	14.79

GLOSSARY

Apron   Wide inside part of a traditional stem assembly.

Archboard   Narrow transom across a counter stern.

Armature   Steel framing and mesh in ferrocement work.

Asymmetrical Hull   Catamaran hull with starboard shape different from port shape.

Barge Yacht   Generally large, flat bottomed, sailboat.

Basket   Same thing as an armature.

Beam Shelf or Clamp   Internal fore-and-aft stiffener where deck meets topsides.

Bevel   An edge tilted out of square, or the tool to gauge this.

Bevel Board   An offcut with certain bevel angles scribed across it.   A universal bevel board shows every bevel needed for the boat.

Bilge-Keeler   Shoal-draft sailboat with angled fin keels sprouting from port and starboard bilges.

Binding Strake   Next-but-one topside plank below the deck.

Black Varnish   Cheap lacquer made from coal tar and naphtha.

Blister   Swelling on bottom of hull where propeller shaft emerges.

Bottom Boards   The floorboards of an open boat.

Breakwater   Spray deflector across the foredeck of a launch or sailing dinghy.

Breasthook   Horizontal knee or bracket at deck level tying topsides to stem.

Building Board   Plank on edge, often curved on top, supporting keel during building.

Burr   Another name for a rove.   A drill with a toothed ball on its tip.   Fraze or roughness on metal edge.

Butt Strap   Doubling piece behind a butt joint in wood or metal.

Cant Frames   Ribs near the bow set at right angles to the topsides.

Carlines   Fore-and-aft stiffeners at sides of deck openings.

Carriage Bolt   Has domed head with square under it, to prevent rotation in wood.

Carvel Planking   Traditional fore-and-aft hull skin with flush surface and caulked seams.

Cathedral Hull   A sea sled with catamaran-like cross section below the waterline.

Ceiling   Interior lining to the topsides.   Similar overhead covering is called headlining.

Chainplates   Metal straps dissipating rigging stresses over the topsides or bulkheads.

Check   Small crack in wood.   Also a notch or joggle where one piece of wood sits on another.

Chine   The angle where bottom meets topsides in chine boats.   Also the backing piece to this.

Clamp   Can be a tool, a stiffener below the shelf (or in place of the shelf), also a notched strip holding the ends of a rowboat's stern thwart.

Clench   A long rivet, usually of copper bar, riveted over a washer at each end.

Clinker Planking   Traditional lapstrake hull skin laid clapboard fashion without caulking.

Coach Bolt   A common misnomer for carriage bolt.

Coach Screw   Large woodscrew with square head.

Coamings   Near-vertical panels sitting on deck, especially sides of cockpit, hatch, or cabin top.

Cold-Moulded   Wooden shell formed from several thin layers glued permanently together.

Composite Hull   Galvanized steel frames and beams in an otherwise wooden boat.

Conic Sections   Curvaceous topside and bottom shapes over which plywood or metal will bend without buckling.

Constant Camber   Cold-moulded port and starboard shells formed over a single jig with no compound curvature.   Finally cut out and strutted to create a hull.

Cope   Half-round or half-oval metal strip for protecting stem, keel, or deck edges.

Cored FRP   Hull or deck with inner and outer FRP skins bonded to a core of rigid closed-cell foam or end-grain balsa wood.

Counter Stern   Extension of topsides aft, above the waterline.

Covering Board   Deck edging plank, overlapping the topsides.

Cross Spall   Batten across the top of a frame to keep it in shape.

Daggerboard   A simple drop-keel which pulls up and down.

Deadrise   The midships angle to the horizontal by

which the bottom of a boat leaves the keel.

Deadwood   Wooden filler pieces between a keel and sternpost. Also fairing pieces either end of a ballast keel.

Deck Beams   The curved athwartships supports under a deck.

Dolly   Any chunk of metal held on the head while a nail or clench bolt is riveted.

Draw-File   A verb. You clamp a flat file in the vise and rub a part along it, so filing dead flat and square.

Drift Bolt   A bar driven deeply into solid wood then riveted over a washer.

Ducks   Lead weights to hold a spline to a certain curve on the floor.

Dummy or Dumbstick   A tiny oblong of wood (usually with bevelled edges and a little handle on top) to spile shapes instead of using dividers.

Dumps   Big square bronze nails. Galvanized ones are called deck spikes.

Dunnage   Packing to keep inside ballast from shifting and from bearing on the hull skin.

Electrolytic Action   Underwater corrosion caused by stray electric currents.

Exotic Materials   Mainly refers to the aramid, carbon and hybrid cloths used in high-strength FRP layups.

Fairing In   Adjusting hull curves and bevels on framing. Also, planing deadwoods flush with a ballast keel.

Fashion Pieces   Chocks around the inside of a transom to take plank fastenings.

Fasteners   Hooks and eyes, zippers, snaps, press-studs, toggles, Velcro, turnbuttons and circlips.

Fastenings   Nails, rivets, screws, clenches, bolts and panel pins.

Faying Surfaces   Where two pieces of wood or metal meet. Not necessarily a glued joint.

Ferrocement   Densely packed fine steel mesh embedded in rich cement mortar.

Flare   Outward curving topsides, especially towards the bow.

Flattie   Any flat-bottomed boat with a stem and transom.

Floors   Wooden knees or metal webs tying frames to keel, or in between frames.

Flowcoat   Finishing polyester resin, usually pigmented, curing fully in the air.

Foam Sandwich   Popular term for cored FRP construction.

Frameless Hull   The only stiffeners run fore and aft. Can also be monocoque or stressed-skin with no stiffeners.

FRP   Fibre reinforced plastics. Can use glass or exotic materials impregnated with polyester or epoxy resin.

Futtock   Any single main component of a chine or round-bilge frame in wood or metal.

Galvanic Action   Corrosion created when adjacent dissimilar metals come into contact with salty water.

Gelcoat   Glossy, unreinforced, outermost layer of a production FRP hull.

Graving Piece   Thin wood plate sunk flush to cover a knot or damage. Commonly an elongated diamond in shape.

Grillage   Light framework of crossing webs in any material, to strengthen a light hull or to form engine beds.

Gusset   Triangular wood or metal plate to reinforce a miter or similar joint.

Hanging   A carvel plank with a downward droop towards the ends.

Hard-Chine   Hull with one chine per side. Also called single-chine.

Hawsehole   Smooth circular fairlead at stemhead or in bulwark.

Hawsepipe   Tube for anchor cable from deck to topsides. Often mistakenly used to mean a navel pipe.

Hog   Wider than the keel, a flat piece on top forming the plank rabbets.

Hood Ends   The ends of any planks rabbeted into stem, transom, or sternpost.

Horn Timbers   Extensions from the sternpost to support a counter stern.

Intercostal   Athwartships web between engine bearers, or in a grillage of any material.

Inwale   Internal fore-and-aft member forming the gunwale of an open boat.

Jogged   An often used misnomer for joggled.

Joggled   Notched over, partially or fully. In metal plate, one edge cranked to form a flush riveted joint.

Keelson   In heavy wooden construction, a balk above the keel, on top of the floors.

Kerfed   Wood which is slit with a saw to simplify bending.

King Plank   Central plank on a laid deck, or the central stiffener under a plywood deck.

Knee   Same as a gusset, but of curved or laminated wood.

Knighthead   Heavy bulwark stanchion or chock near the stem.

Knuckle   Crease like a chine in flared FRP topsides, to reduce deck weight and deflect spray.

Lag Bolt   Same thing as a coach screw.

Land   The overlap of a lapstrake plank.

Lapstrake Planking   Another term for clinker planking.

Limber Holes   Framing apertures (mainly alongside a keel) to prevent bilge water from stagnating.

Lofting   Drawing the lines of a hull full size on a floor.

Luting   Doping faying surfaces with paint or mastic.

Moulds   Temporary frames for traditional construction with bent ribs.

Moulded Dimensions   Varying width of a stem, deadwood, or frame.

Navel Pipe   Vertical or angled casting to lead chain through the deck towards the cable locker.

Offset   Measurement taken at right angles from a baseline, datum, or rabbet.

Pargeting   Pressing mortar into the armature in ferrocement work.

Paying   Exposed bead of stopping along a caulked seam.

Pinch Rods   Overlapping battens, clamped together, for gauging the exact length of curved or hidden parts.

Plug   Male mockup or jig. Also a pellet of wood to conceal a countersunk screw.

Poppets   Blocks raising a keel during building or repairs.

Pultrusion   Making long FRP rails or rods by pulling through a die.

PU   Abbreviation for polyurethane, mainly as foam.

PVA   Polyvinyl acetate. Used as white wood glue.

PVAL   Polyvinyl alcohol. A release agent for FRP.

Ram Plank   The keel plank of a pram dinghy with no backbone.

Rabbet   A two-sided cut to house the edge of another piece.

Rebate   A misnomer for rabbet.

Ribband   Fore-and-aft batten to steady frames when erected.

Rift or Quarter Sawn   Board with end-grain lying like the teeth of a comb.

Risers   Fore-and-aft battens supporting rowboat thwarts.

Rove or Roove   Cupped washer set under riveted end of a clenched copper nail.

Scantlings   Mainly in wooden boats, the sizes of the major components.

Scrieve Board   All the frame shapes indelibly scribed on one panel.

Seam Batten Carvel   Thin planking where each seam is backed by a narrow strip.

Shaft Log   Wood or metal internal blister supporting propeller shaft gland and bearing.

Sharpie   Any Vee-bottomed hard-chine sailing dinghy.

Sheer Strake   The uppermost clinker or carvel plank.

Shutter Strake   The last plank to be fitted.

Sided Dimension   The regular thickness of a board or framing part where the width is variable.

Sills or Logs   The foundation balks of a big drop-keel trunk.

Sister Piece   Usually of wood, a doubler to add strength at a joint or defect.

Slash Sawn   Board with end-grain lying sandwich fashion. Also a misnomer for through-and-through log sawing.

Snaped or Nibbed   Notched in. Mainly at the tapered ends of deck planks to avoid having to caulk weak wedges.

Snying   A carvel plank with an upward sweep towards the ends.

Sole   The flooring in any cockpit or cabin.

Soling   Hollowing a carvel plank to meet the frames snugly.

Spiling   Marking the fit into a rabbet or curve by drawing a line parallel to the final shape.

Spiling Block   Same thing as a dummy or dumbstick.

Squats   Bilge struts under a boat when ashore.

Stealer   A short infill piece where the end of a carvel plank becomes excessively wide.

Sterngear   All equipment associated with a propeller shaft.

Stitch-and-Glue   Plywood skins at chine and keel pulled together with copper wire and bonded with fibreglass.

Stop water   A pine peg through a scarf or seam to prevent seepage.

Stringer   Fore-and-aft stiffener inside frames Direct on the skin in frameless construction.

Strip-Planked   Instead of carvel, almost-square strips pinned together with edge-nails and usually glued.

Surmarks   Edge marks on patterns or frames to show positions of waterlines, sheer-line, or plank seams.

Tabernacle   A deck bracket with pivot bolt, allowing a mast to be hinged down flat.

Tabling   Steps in the faying surfaces of heavy timbers, to prevent sliding.

Through-and-Through   Sawing up a log so that each board is the full width.

Thunder Shake   A crack at right angles to the grain, mainly found in tropical hardwoods.

Timber   Any rib in a round-bilge hull; usually a steam bent one.

Transom   Rarely dead upright, the flat (or sometimes rounded) panel across a boat's stern.

Trenail   Wooden nail secured with a wedge at each end.

Trepanning   Boring a big hole with a single peripheral cut.

Turnbutton   Swivelling toggle to keep a door shut, or to hold bottom boards down.   Often wrongly called a turnbuckle.

Turned Nail   One way to clench a copper nail, by dressing the point back into the wood.

Washboards   Drop-boards in grooves to keep spray out of a companion hatch.   Often wrongly called weatherboards.

WEST   Popular name for the Wood Epoxy Saturation Technique invented by the Gougeon Brothers.

NOTE: In addition to the above glossary, many of the unfamiliar words used in this book can be found in any good home dictionary.   The most important ones are as follows:

Sheer, taffrail, ovolo, spline, dovetail, stem, cutwater, oar loom, partners, stocks, bulkhead, tenon, stanchion, tumblehome, trammels, bulwark, scupper, turnbuckle, caulking, forefoot, gudgeons and pintles, sternpost, Spanish windlass, garboard, camber.

Recommended Reading

Woodworker's Bible   A Martensson   Nautical Books
Boatbuilding One-Off in Fiberglass   A Vaitses   International Marine Publishing Company
Boatbuilding in Steel   G C Klingel   International Marine Publishing Company
Building Small Boats, Surf Craft and Canoes in Fibreglass   J Toghill & J Flett   Nautical Books
Clinker Boat Building   J Leather   Adlard Coles
Cold-Moulded and Strip-Planked Wood Boat Building   I Nicholson   Stanford Maritime
Ferro-Cement Design, Techniques and Application   B Bingham   Cornell Maritime
Fine Yacht Finishes – For Wood and Fibreglass Boats   P & M Butler   Stanford Maritime
Gougeon Brothers on Boat Construction   Gougeon Brothers   Western Marine
Lofting   A Vaitses   International Marine Publishing Company
Small Steel Craft   I Nicolson   Adlard Coles
West System Manual   Gougeon Brothers   Gougeon Brothers Inc
Boatowner's Mechanical and Electrical Manual   N Calder   Nautical Books
Metal Corrosion in Boats   N Warren   Adlard Coles
Steel Boatbuilding Vols 1 & 2   T E Colvin   International Marine Publishing Company
53 Boats You Can Build   R Henderson   International Marine Publishing Company
Build the New Instant Boats   H Payson   Stanford Maritime
Ferro-Cement Boat Construction   J R Whitener   Cornell Maritime
Lapstrake Boatbuilding Vols 1 & 2   W J Simmons   International Marine Publishing Company
Boat Building Techniques Illustrated   R Birmingham   Adlard Coles

Index